MEN AND WOMEN OF
PLANTAGENET ENGLAND

KNIGHT AND LADY OF THE LATE FOURTEENTH CENTURY

Fr.   From a manuscript in the British Museum

MEN AND WOMEN OF PLANTAGENET ENGLAND

BY

DOROTHY MARGARET STUART

AUTHOR OF
"THE BOY THROUGH THE AGES" "HISTORICAL SONGS AND BALLADS"
"HORACE WALPOLE" "CHRISTINA ROSSETTI" ("ENGLISH
MEN OF LETTERS" SERIES) ETC.

NEW YORK
HARCOURT, BRACE AND COMPANY
1932

Printed in Great Britain by Neill & Co. Ltd   Edinburgh

FOREWORD

THE Plantagenets ruled longer than any dynasty in England's history has yet contrived to do, and the Plantagenet period is closely packed with incident. Ordinary text-books can give, therefore, only the cold and meagre outlines, leaving the great pageant that began with Henry II and ended with Richard III hinted at rather than described. Magna Carta, the Crusades, the Black Death, the Peasants' Revolt, the French and Scottish wars, the beginnings of English literature, the first stirrings of the Reformation, these and many other movements and events have been recorded many times, with varying degrees of picturesqueness and vivacity. But what of the people who formed the living fabric of Plantagenet England? What of the knights and the squires, the craftsmen, merchants, and field-labourers, the doctors, lawyers, and priests, the monks, pilgrims, and nuns, the poets and the players? Books concerned with broad outlines and fundamental facts can give the student or the general reader only the most indistinct idea of these men and women. Masses of most fascinating materials exist from which a picture of Plantagenet England can be reconstructed, but they are scattered, complicated, often difficult of access. The essential point, the detail which gives a sudden sense of contact with the past, may be buried in some ponderous antiquarian tome or embedded in some dusty old inventory; it may lurk in a churchwarden's entry or lie half obliterated upon a monumental brass.

How, then, can the student or the general reader who is attracted by the colour, comedy, and human interest of the Middle Ages, but repelled by grey and arid summaries, step back into the dominions of the Plantagenet kings and get into

5

touch with some of their subjects and citizens? This book represents an attempt to answer that question.

Thanks to the poems of Langland and Chaucer and the illuminations of the Luttrell Psalter the reigns of Edward III and Richard II seem less remote than do the reigns of, let us say, Edward II or Richard III. Full advantage has here been taken of the riches stored in such works as these, but light has also been thrown whenever possible upon the thirteenth and the fifteenth centuries, so crowded with romantic and memorable figures, so full of significance in things artistic and intellectual. Individuals as well as types are made to emerge from the shadows, and certain characters usually treated as 'supers' are given speaking *rôles*. The present book is based in part upon two earlier volumes, *Chivalry and Social Life in the Middle Ages* and *Men and Women of the Middle Ages*, but it contains a great deal of fresh material, derived from new sources and extended researches, and has been carefully revised in the light of recent historical discoveries and critical reconsiderations.

In order to keep the historical perspective true it has been found desirable to glance back occasionally to Anglo-Saxon and to Norman England or forward to the England of the Tudors, but attention is focused throughout upon the period during which the descendants of the fair-featured Geoffrey Plantagenet and his masterful wife, the Empress Matilda, occupied the English throne.

D. M. S.

CONTENTS

CHAPTER   PAGE

I. THE KNIGHT AND THE SQUIRE   11

II. ARMS, ARMOUR, AND COSTUME   33

III. THE CHIVALRIC IDEA   53

IV. THE TILLERS OF THE SOIL   73

V. THE CRAFTSMEN   92

VI. MERCHANTS AND MERCHANDISE   111

VII. TRADE GUILDS AND COMPANIES   131

VIII. MEN OF DIVERS CALLINGS   145

IX. CHURCHES, PRELATES, AND PRIESTS   162

X. MONKS, FRIARS, AND NUNS   184

XI. THE MIRACLE PLAYS   205

XII. PILGRIMS, PILGRIMAGES, AND FESTIVALS   220

XIII. THE POETS: I. THE TELLERS OF TALES   230

XIV. THE POETS: II. THE SINGERS OF SONGS   246

XV. WOMANKIND   259

INDEX   281

FULL-PAGE ILLUSTRATIONS

PAGE

KNIGHT AND LADY OF THE LATE FOURTEENTH CEN-
TURY   *Frontispiece*

A MANOR HOUSE OF THE THIRTEENTH CENTURY   16

EQUESTRIAN ARMOUR OF THE FIFTEENTH CENTURY   42

EARL RIVERS PRESENTING TO EDWARD IV THE FIRST BOOK
PRINTED BY CAXTON IN ENGLAND   64

ST GEORGE   70

EFFIGY OF ELEANOR OF CASTILE   98

ALABASTER ALTAR-PIECE OF THE FIFTEENTH CENTURY   104

CROSBY HALL   116

ABBOT'S KITCHEN, GLASTONBURY   190

FRANCISCANS IN CHOIR   194

THE ADORATION OF THE SHEPHERDS   218

THE WYF OF BATHE   222

TOMB OF JOHN GOWER IN SOUTHWARK CATHEDRAL   236

JASON IN QUEST OF THE GOLDEN FLEECE   246

THE VIRGIN AND CHILD   254

LADY MARGARET BEAUFORT   276

9

MEN AND WOMEN OF PLANTAGENET ENGLAND

CHAPTER I

THE KNIGHT AND THE SQUIRE

THE bargain struck between Stephen of Blois and Henry of Anjou in a Berkshire meadow one winter day in 1153 gave to England the first of her thirteen Plantagenet kings and ushered in a period of three hundred and thirty-two years, a period packed with memorable events and pervaded by picturesque figures both high and low. The thirteen kings were a mixed lot, weak and strong alternating with almost pendulum-like regularity, but there was none of them, not even the graceless John, the foolish Edward II, the fantastic Richard II, wholly devoid of some quality, good or bad, which appeals to the imagination. Two of them were Crusaders; three of them were very great military commanders and leaders of men. From their Angevin ancestors, the first bearers of the broomflower badge, they inherited their almost invariably handsome features and their recurrent tendency to lapse into folly; from their Norman stock they drew their physical vigour; and such of them as governed well may have derived their instinct for kingship from the same source.

The centuries during which the crown of England was worn by Plantagenet kings saw the signing of the Great Charter, the building of many English cathedrals in their existing form, the rise of Parliament, the foundation of Oxford and Cambridge, Winchester and Eton, the coming of the friars, the Hundred Years War, the Scottish War of Independence, the Black Death, the rise of Lollardy, the decay of the feudal system, the introduction of printing, the Wars of the Roses. No other sequence of three hundred years between the coming of the Romans and the outbreak of the World War has been more rich and varied in character and in colour, or more clearly marked by the broad lines of national evolution.

It may be that a greater number of famous Englishmen has been born since the Tudors came than before their coming; it is certain that England's commercial and imperial expansion did not begin until nearly a century after the Plantagenet succession had ended with Richard III on Bosworth Field. But there was assuredly no dearth of romantic and illustrious figures in the span of years which covered the lives of churchmen like Becket, Hubert Walter, Grosseteste, Roger Bacon, Wykeham, and Wyclif, statesmen like Hubert de Burgh and Simon de Montfort, warriors like Edward I, Edward III, William Pembroke, the Black Prince, John, Duke of Bedford, Harry Hotspur, Talbot, Earl of Shrewsbury, Henry V, poets like Gower, Chaucer, Langland, and the myriad nameless singers of ballads and little songs.

Behind all these men, half obliterated by the gleam of scarlet and purple, the glint of gold and steel, stretches the infinite multitude of people who formed the living substance of Plantagenet England, the tillers of the fields, the craftsmen, the masons who helped to build the castles and cathedrals, the archers and foot-soldiers who fought in the French and Scottish wars, the merchants, the knights, and the squires, the monks and the nuns, the minstrels and mummers, the pilgrims, pedlars, and vagabonds.

To wander among the bypaths of Plantagenet England, to meet the people, enter their homes, follow them to field and forest, sit at table and have speech with them, drink with ploughmen, ride a-hunting with princes, go forth to battle with horsemen and footmen, fight in the lists, jog along the pilgrims' track, is a pursuit as fascinating as any in the world; but many a cheerful traveller has turned back discouraged because he knew not how the road ran nor what company he would meet upon the way. He will do well at starting to remember that between the twelfth and fifteenth centuries three great ideas exercised a powerful influence over the daily lives of men. They were chivalry, monasticism, and the trade guild. We shall consider each in turn, and we shall see that each represented a sort of brotherhood in which fighting men, thinking men, and buying-and-selling men instinctively bound themselves together.

What was a knight? How did he become one? What were the privileges and responsibilities of the knightly caste? Here, as so often happens, the history and the inner meaning are summed up in a word. 'Knight' in English comes from the Old German *Knecht*, a servant or vassal. The knight was often the servitor of some great lord, baron, or prince; always he was —in theory at least—the servitor of his king. *Chevalier* in French, *cavaliere* in Italian, *caballero* in Spanish, all mean the same thing—a *horseman*. A knight always went into battle on horseback. In a medieval army the knights represented the cavalry, but that branch of the military forces was composed of officers only. It was not until a much later date that men-at-arms were mounted.

The knight, in whatever country of Europe he happened to dwell, was a member of a great fraternity, extending throughout Christendom, sharing certain simple but very definite principles, codes, and customs. Every one understood the significance of the heraldic shield and the golden spurs. No one who was not himself either a knight or a priest could confer the honour of knighthood upon anyone else. The ceremony, however, might be performed in three different ways:

1. By the giving of the *accolade*, the touch of the sword on the shoulder, on the field of battle. In the Plantagenet period a knight thus honoured was called a 'knight banneret,' because upon that glorious occasion the points attached to his pennon were rent off, "and thus the small flag was reduced to the *square*

form of the banner by which henceforth he was to be distinguished." [1]

2. By a purely ecclesiastical ceremony, for which the proper form was set forth in the service books of the Roman Church.

3. By a ceremony of which the greater part was performed by priests and in some sacred edifice, though the giving of the accolade and the buckling on of the golden spurs characteristic of knighthood were assigned to some illustrious layman.

It was when the second method was chosen that the young candidate for knighthood kept vigil over his armour before the high altar, and, on the morrow, took a symbolical (and actual) bath—usually in a wooden tub covered by a sort of tent—wherein all his sins were supposed to be washed away.

We have seen—and William the Conqueror saw—that every knight is in theory the servant and the defender of the throne. The first and greatest of our Norman kings, scenting danger in the growing power of the barons, encouraged his liegemen to seek knightly honours. The idea of knighthood was well established by the time of the Conquest, but its origins are remote and obscure. Some scholars descry in the ancient Roman equestrian order (*equestris ordo*) the germ of the Christian chivalric idea; others quote Tacitus to prove that the Germanic tribes had some such system; others, again, detect Saracenic influence, and it was certainly from their Moslem enemies that the Frankish warriors of Charlemagne learnt to fight on horseback. Charlemagne and his twelve paladins were, indeed, the prototypes of Arthur and his twelve knights, and of all the orders of knighthood later called into being.

The first order of knighthood founded in Christendom was that of the Star, instituted by Robert the Pious of France in 1022. (We cannot count the Order of the Ampulla, said to have been created by Clovis I some five hundred years earlier, as the

---

[1] Boutell, *English Heraldry*.

membership was restricted to four persons, and their principal duty was to carry the *ampulla*, the flask of consecrated oil, at the coronations of the French kings in Rheims Cathedral.) The Knights of the Star were thirty in number, and the collar of the order was composed of threefold golden chains studded alternately with red and white enamelled roses, and completed with a pendant in the form of a golden star.

As the chivalric idea took a stronger and stronger hold upon the imagination of kings and princes orders of knighthood multiplied all over Europe. But it must be remembered that *every* knight was not necessarily a member of some such order. The founders, and their successors, the heads, of these orders chose a limited number of gently born warriors, almost always knights already, whom they honoured by election. The 'common or garden' knight was a singularly lucky person if he were elected.

The importance of chivalry to the world in general and the principles for which it stood are thus summed up in a curious thirteenth-century French poem (translated by "F. S. E."):

> If the world knew no Chivalry
> Small worth would then its lordship be;
> For Holy Church it aye defends
> And ready help to justice lends
> 'Gainst men whose deeds this world do stain:
> Ne'er can I from its praise refrain. . . .
> Were not the wicked kept in awe
> Good men should stint of life and law.

Thus, in theory always and in practice often, the duties of a knight were to defend Holy Church, to protect the helpless, to punish evildoers, and to be ready to die in defence of his knightly honour and in fulfilment of his knightly vows.

The poem alluded to above contains a very curious and interesting account of the actual ceremony of making a knight, and of how, after purification in the bath, the candidate was wrapped first in a robe of snow-white linen, symbolizing the stainlessness of the life he must now lead, and then in a crimson mantle, symbolizing the blood he must be willing to shed in a righteous cause; finally he is given hose of black, to remind him of

La mort et la terre où girrez,
D'où venistes, et où irez.

(Of death and of thy mother earth,
Where thou must go, whence thou hadst
birth.)

The sharpness of the gilded rowel spurs is here said to symbolize the alacrity with which a knight should gallop into the

ARMING A KNIGHT
From a manuscript of the thirteenth century

fray; the double edge of the sword signifies the double virtues of justice and loyalty.

Setting aside the knight-errant, the valiant wanderer in search of adventure, whom we shall meet again later on, and considering the knight as a unit in the nation during peace-time, we shall find closely associated with the chivalric idea the *manorial system*.

Roughly speaking, the manor was the estate of a knight, the manor-house (often known as 'the Hall') was his home, and he was lord over the lives and fortunes of the people, the *villeins*,

16

A MANOR HOUSE OF THE THIRTEENTH CENTURY

Reconstructed at Southchurch, Essex

dwelling on his lands. The word comes from the Latin verb *manere*, to remain, and signified originally a dwelling-place; hence also 'mansion' and 'manse.' In each such estate, under the feudal system, the total area was divided into the *demesne*, the holding of the lord, the arable and meadow-lands in which the villeins had a share, and woods and rough pasture common to all. The tenants owed certain duties to their lord, the work

HALL OF A FOURTEENTH-CENTURY MANOR-HOUSE

of their hands in peace-time, the services of certain of their numbers in his retinue in time of war.

Each of these manors maintained a family of gentle birth and of knightly rank. The head of the family was almost invariably a knight, and any one of his sons might hope to win the golden spurs in due course. Thus the great body of the knightly order consisted of country gentlemen—'country squires,' as they came to be called at a much later date. Their sons and their younger brothers were the raw stuff of which knights were made. Such of them as did not follow the career of arms usually entered the Church. In the later Middle Ages men

B

of good birth began to enter the legal profession, which at first was almost inextricably involved with the ecclesiastical. The cadets of impoverished knightly houses were sometimes glad to betake themselves to commerce—as witness Richard Whittington—but the ranks of the merchants were chiefly recruited from the class immediately below that to which the knights and their kinsfolk belonged.

CHAUCER'S SQUIÉR
From the Ellesmere MS.

How was a knight trained? For obviously he could not learn the duties of his calling by instinct or by imitation only! There were three well-defined stages in the career of the typical gentleman of high birth in the Middle Ages. He began as a page. At the age of twelve or thirteen his father placed him in the household of some important nobleman, the owner not of one manor, but of many, and there, with two or three other boys of the same age and rank, he learned courtesy, table-manners, the legends of Troy and Camelot, of Hector, Arthur, and Bevis of Hampton, the arts of riding and jousting, the use of sword, battleaxe, and lance, and enough of the elements of heraldry to understand the coats of arms of other families as well as of his own.

At the age of sixteen or seventeen the page became an *esquire* (literally, a shield-bearer), and was especially attached to the service of one particular knight.[1] The duties of an esquire, or a squire, as he soon came to be called, were much more arduous than those of a page. Not only had he to carry the shield and take charge of the spare horses of his knight; he had also to

_____

[1] All the great noblemen of the medieval period were knights as well, but the principle of hereditary knighthood was not introduced until James I and VI invented *baronets* in 1611.

buckle on his master's spurs, close the rivets in his armour, and, if so desired, comb *and curl* the knightly hair. That he often curled his own is made clear from Chaucer's famous and delightful description of the "Yong Squiér," whose locks were "crulle" (*i.e.*, curled) as if they had been "leyd in presse." We shall meet this Squiér again when we come to consider chivalry in literature and in art, but what interests us at the moment is the list of his accomplishments:

> Wel koude he sitte on hors and fairė rẏde;
> He koudė songės make, and wel endyte,
> Juste [1] and eek daunce, and weel purtreye [2]
> and write. . . .
> Curteis he was, lowely and servysáble,
> And carf [3] biforn his fader at the table.

Thus we see that, in addition to riding and jousting, the perfect squire had to have some knowledge of drawing and music, prosody and carving, dancing and penmanship! Carving was not the least difficult of his tasks, for in addition to ordinary game and poultry he had to tackle such birds as heron, peacock, bustard, and crane.

Chaucer has left us a picture of the ideal knight as well as of the ideal squire, and the picture is indeed a charming one:

> A knyght ther was and that a worthy man
> That fro the tymė that he first bigan
> To riden out he lovėd chivalry,
> Trouthe and honóur, fredom and curteisie.

This knight had fought in far and strange lands, in Russia, Egypt, Spain, and Anatolia. His fustian tunic was stained with the rust of his coat of mail, for in his haste to set forth on the Canterbury pilgrimage on his return from one of his warlike wanderings he had not paused to provide himself with newer and finer array; from which we may learn that simple and fervent piety was another knightly virtue. Yet this battered and scarred warrior was gentle as a woman, modest and mannerly in discourse, just and benign to all men.

[1] joust.   [2] draw.   [3] carved.

He never yet no vileynye ne sayde
In al his lyf unto no maner wight.
He was a verray parfit, gentil knyght.

The knight-errant, or knight wandering about in quest of adventure, was a familiar figure in medieval legend, and examples of this type were occasionally to be met with in real life. Whether in fact or in fancy, he was usually a youthful warrior, newly dubbed, who went out into the perilous world attended by a trusty follower to whom was given the courtesy title of 'squire,' though *he* was no candidate for knightly honours and probably belonged to the yeoman class. At one time it seemed as if the ranks of knighthood might be thrown open to men of non-gentle birth, as witness the ballad of

the squire of low degree
That loved the King's daughter of Hungarie,

but the movement was short-lived and spasmodic. The yeomen were small landholders, not technically 'gentlemen'—that is, not entitled to armorial bearings—but forming a solid stratum between the gentry and 'the rest.' Every son of a yeoman was himself a yeoman, whether he personally held land or not. In the fifteenth century, according to Medley's *English Constitutional History*, the yeomen represented "the small freeholders of the feudal manor." The son of such a freeholder would, if he had a taste for adventure, be only too eager to follow the son of the lord of the manor in his quest of danger, glory, and —sometimes—gain. Glory was the chief objective of the knight-errant, but he did not disdain more solid rewards, and these might come to him in several different ways: by gifts, or grants of land, from kings or princes whom he had served well in battle, by the ransoms of noble captives, or by the dowry of a fair bride won by his prowess in the lists or on the field.

The world into which the knight-errant and his follower thus boldly plunged differed in many respects from the world of to-day. Supposing them to be Englishmen, they would find themselves journeying through a country of dense forests and

20

pathless marshes, bleak heaths and grim hills, broken here and there by strips of cultivated land, where manors stood, by villages, large or small, each with its church and its mill, and, less frequently, by fair-sized towns encircled with strong walls.

Thanks to the energy of the Romans, England in the Middle Ages was covered with a network of roads; but as these fell into disrepair there arose no second race of great engineers and road-builders to make them sound and solid again. The badness of the non-Roman roads was almost proverbial. In theory,

A STATE CARRIAGE OF THE FOURTEENTH CENTURY

the landholders were responsible for their upkeep, and the tenants were bound to give their labour for that purpose; but theories are seldom translated quite successfully into practice, and the badness of many medieval roads was such that wheeled vehicles constantly became bogged in them, and the usual and much safer method of travel was on foot, on horseback, or by horse-litter. And it must be remembered that the most important of these highways were the channels along which poured a tremendous stream of wayfarers, merchants, pilgrims, pedlars, messengers, strolling minstrels, mendicant friars, poor scholars wending to and from the universities, and bands of thieves and footpads.

Along such a road, and in company with such a motley horde of fellow-travellers, the knight-errant would set forth. His accomplishments, even if they were less numerous and elegant than those of Chaucer's Squiér, would include, as we have seen, a thorough mastery of horsemanship, of the use of the sword, battleaxe, and lance, and a knowledge of the legends of chivalric

romance, and of the etiquette and the code of conduct observed by gentlemen of his class all over Christendom. Unless he were intended for the honourable calling of a herald, a medieval gentleman would not necessarily familiarize himself with all the ancient and complicated lore of heraldry, but he would certainly be familiar with its elementary principles and interested in their application. Not only had he a family coat of arms of his own, which he might hope to augment by some deed of outstanding valour;

A FRENCH HERALD OF THE FIFTEENTH CENTURY

he would be able, thanks to his knowledge of the herald's craft, to identify by their armorial bearings many of the knights and nobles whom he would afterward encounter on his travels, in camp, at Court, or even on the field of battle. The veriest 'prentice-page could have told you at once what were the *tinctures* of heraldry. These were two metals, five colours, and eight furs. The colours were (and are) known as *azure* (blue), *gules* (red), *sable* (black), *vert* (green), *purpure* (purple). In an *uncoloured* representation of a shield or other armorial

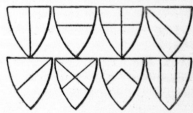

PRIMARY DIVISIONS OF THE HERALDIC SHIELD

device these colours are represented as follows: azure, by horizontal lines; gules, by perpendicular lines; sable, by a chequerwork of horizontal and perpendicular lines; vert, by lines sloping diagonally from left to right; purpure, by lines sloping diagonally from right to left. The two heraldic metals *or* (gold) and *argent* (silver) are represented in the first instance by a closely spotted and in the second by a blank surface. The eight heraldic furs include three varieties of ermine and two of vair, and their representation is a complicated matter, involving much placing of white, black, and gold spots on gold, white, and black backgrounds, and the tracing of a perfect cross-word puzzle of argent and azure.

Our page—and therefore, of course, our squire and knight— would also know how a shield is divided; that when a line is drawn *down* the centre it is *parted per pale*; that when one is drawn *across* the centre it is *parted per fesse*; that when the downward and transverse lines meet in the centre it is *parted per cross* or *quarterly*; that a dividing line running from left to right is a *bend*, and from right to left a *bend sinister*; while a shield in which two bends *meet*, forming a St Andrew's cross, is *parted per saltire*, that one divided by a pyramidal line with its apex in the centre of the field is *parted per chevron*, and that one divided into three sections by two vertical lines is *parted per tierce*. A simple law in English heraldry lays down that metal must not be placed upon metal, nor colour upon colour. So if our knight-errant encountered a knight upon whose shield a golden device appeared against a silver background, or a red one against a background of blue, he would conclude at once, and probably with good reason, that the stranger was no Englishman. There was—and, since heraldry is not yet a dead art, we may alter the tense and say there is—an astonishing variety in the objects depicted on knightly shields: animals, real and fabulous, birds, flowers, trees, feathers, swords, daggers, wheatsheaves, stars, ships, keys, and salamanders jostle each other there.

Some ancient devices are really puns upon the names of those who bore them. Islip, Abbot of Westminster, for example, bore as his personal device a representation of a man falling from a tree and (presumably) exclaiming "I slip!" and also a human *eye* beside a *slip*, or small cutting, from a tree. The

Shelleys bear three golden whelk-shells on their shield, and the Applegarths three crimson apples. Both the device and the motto on a shield may crystallize some far-off, romantic episode in the history of the family bearing them. Such are the device —an oak-tree half sawn asunder—and the motto—"Through" —of the ducal family of Hamilton. To find their origin we must go back to the stormy days of Robert the Bruce. A certain English knight, Sir Gilbert Hamilton, being then at Court, was tactless enough to express openly his admiration for the Bruce, whose name was odious in English ears. John le Despencer there-upon struck the tactless fellow, who promptly challenged him to single combat. They met on the morrow, and Hamilton, having slain his foe outright, fled northward, with the English in hot pursuit, and with no other attendant than his faithful squire. Near the Border the fugitives encountered some woodcutters, whom they persuaded to allow them to help in the felling of a great oak-tree, so that their pursuers should not recognize them. They were busy with their arduous and unfamiliar task when their foes came upon the scene. Hamilton's squire, greatly alarmed, started, and looked anxiously round, but the knight, continuing to ply the saw stoutly, steadied him with the one word *Through!* and the English horsemen galloped unsuspectingly past.

HAMILTON CREST
AND MOTTO

The Arthurian romances throw floods of light upon the romantic idea of knight-errantry. We read there how divers gallant warriors, Sir Epinogris, Sir Dinadan, Sir Tristram, Sir Kay, rode through forests, challenged and fought other knights as bold as they, defended or attacked towers and bridges, and obtained hospitality in castles by defeating the owners thereof in (more or less) friendly combat. Many castles were, appar-ently, provided with tilting-grounds in anticipation of such episodes. Thus we read that

Sir Percival passed the water, and when he came unto the castle-gate he said to the porter, "Go thou unto the good knight within the castle, and tell him that here is come a knight-errant to joust with him." "Sir," said the porter, "ride ye within the castle, and there shall ye find a common place for jousting, that lords and ladies may behold you."

These heroes of romance seem to have been fortunate in

KNIGHTS ENTERING THE LISTS

that they never lacked either adversaries or rewards. Sometimes the adversaries were decidedly alarming—giants and ogres; sometimes the rewards were of dazzling splendour—well-dowered princesses for brides, or whole provinces over which to reign. But in real life—which was more prosaic and colourless than romance even in the Middle Ages—the knight-errant usually had to make sure beforehand that a joust or tournament was to be held on some particular date, at some particular place, and to enrol himself as a competitor almost as unheroically as does a competitor in a golf or tennis tournament to-day.

25

These formal combats were a recognized feature in medieval life, and were a source of great interest and amusement to all who were permitted to witness them, from the fair ladies sitting under a canopy on a raised stand to the humble archers and yeomen huddled together by the ropes or palings which enclosed the lists. Sometimes pageantry played a great part, and there was little or no real danger to the combatants. Such was the

SINGLE COMBAT
Early fourteenth century

case at a tournament held in Windsor Park in the sixth year of Edward I, when the helmets of the knights were of gilt or silvered leather, their shields of wood, and their weapons also of parchment, painted to represent steel, silver, and gold, and stiffened with whalebone. At other times there was great peril to life and limb. Generally speaking, the earlier in date the tournament occurred, the more violent and bloody it was likely to be. As the Middle Ages waned and the Renaissance dawned jousts, tilts, and tourneys became more and more artificial, and less and less strenuous, until finally the custom fell into disuse and died a natural death. Readers of *Ivanhoe* will remember the tournament of Ashby-de-la-Zouche, in which the Disinherited Knight and Le Noir Fainéant gave such a good account of themselves, and how Sir Walter Scott drily remarks that

> although only four knights . . . had died upon the field, yet upwards of thirty were desperately wounded, four or five of whom never recovered. Several more were disabled for life; and those who escaped best carried the marks of the conflict to the grave with them. Hence it is always mentioned in the old records as the Gentle and Joyous Passage of Arms of Ashby.

When only two combatants contended it was called *jousting*. If only a friendly trial of skill were contemplated the lances had blunt tips, and the swords sharp *edges* only, not the keen, thrusting points likely to cause a fatal injury. This was the *jouste à plaisance*. If the combatants were allowed to use sharp weapons, and to put forth all their force and skill against one another, this was the *jouste à l'oultrance*, or *à outrance* (the former is the archaic form). When many combatants fought on each side the name 'tournament' was employed.

A knowledge of the rules and traditions of heraldry was especially useful to the young knight who aspired to take part in a tournament, and one of the heaviest sources of incidental expense to him was the 'tipping' of the heralds. These officials loomed large when knightly pride and valour found their

A KING-AT-ARMS ABOUT TO PROCLAIM
A TOURNAMENT

expression in the lists. The holder of the tournament, the *challenger* as he was called, never dreamt of drawing up the conditions without the assistance of a properly qualified herald. It was a herald of inferior rank, a *poursuivant*, whom he sent forth to proclaim the date and place of the tournament and the prizes offered: a herald gave the signal for the commencement of each 'round' (as we should now say) in the actual combats, crying, "*Laissez les aller, laissez les aller, les bons chevaliers!*" and at the conclusion of the proceedings their cries of "*Largesse, largesse!*" were answered by showers of gold coins from the noble spectators and the valiant warriors present. It sometimes happened that several young knights would band themselves together to protect a certain tree, or shield, or fountain, or image against all comers, offering rich prizes to any who should worst them in fight.

Very great personages had heralds attached permanently to their households, and reigning monarchs had a whole retinue of kings-at-arms, heralds, and *poursuivants*, as the King of England has to this day. Edward III had two principal kings-at-arms, Norroy and Surroy, with authority one north of the Trent, the other south of it. It was Henry V who created the office of Garter King-at-Arms and decreed that the holder should take precedence of all other English heralds—as he still does; and it was the last of the Plantagenets, that much-maligned 'wicked uncle,' Richard III, who banded these heralds together in a collegiate body and granted them a house in Poultney Lane, upon Thames-side.

Henry V's own Garter King-at-Arms, William Bruges, had a country house at Kentish Town, where he entertained the Emperor Sigismund when that perturbed potentate came to England in 1416 on a diplomatic mission. The last will and testament of William Bruges still exists, and from it we know that he possessed many beautiful things: covered cups of silver gilt, candlesticks of silver, boxes of ivory. We know, too, that in the private chapel of his house he had painted stone images of Our Lady and of St George, candlesticks, both great and small, of that brass alloy called 'latten,' a large stone carving of the Holy Trinity, and sets of vestments of russet velvet, black satin, and cloth-of-gold.

William's will is dated 1449, when Richard Duke of York's

star was in the ascendant, four years before the birth of a son to Henry VI and Margaret of Anjou barred the Yorkist succession to the throne, thus rendering inevitable the Wars of the Roses. Henry V had little leisure and his son had little inclination for tilts and tourneys, so it seems probable that an important part of their chief herald's duties was allowed to lapse during their reigns—that is, directing the procedure of knightly contests in the lists. When a knight rode into the lists a trumpet or horn sounded, and then one of the heralds in attendance declared what were his armorial insignia—which was called 'blazoning his arms.' It was the heralds, too, who kept the score, counted the strokes, advised the judge if any knotty points arose, and ran to separate the combatants when the judge gave the signal.

Warriors fought either on horseback or on foot, and the choice of weapons usually lay with the challenger, who often offered alternatives, according to the wishes of those who took up his challenge. The two-handed sword, six feet in length, was a favourite weapon; so was the lance, so was the battleaxe. We shall return to the subject of weapons and armour in a later chapter. Here we are concerned rather with the procedure at the tournament, and it is of interest that if the holder of the tournament happened to be very much in love with some fair lady he often wore her sleeve or her handkerchief in his helmet as a 'favour.' At the conclusion of a long-drawn-out and numerously attended assembly of knights, such as that described in *Ivanhoe*, the victor was invited to choose from among the ladies present her whom he deemed the most worthy to be called the Queen of Love and Beauty, and from her hands he received his prize.

At a later period the perils of contests on horseback were considerably lessened by the introduction of the *toile*. This was first of all simply a piece of rope stretched rather tightly down the centre of the lists, about three and a half feet from the ground: over this a long tapestry would often be hung. Later still the toile was a wooden screen covered with arras-cloth, and quite a solid affair. The knights approached each other from the two ends, keeping the toile between them and meeting and passing each other in the centre. Thus were prevented those 'head-on' encounters in which man and beast had formerly suffered so severely. Glancing blows were now struck, instead

THE TOILE

of deadly thrusts; 'misses' became more frequent; and it was seldom indeed after the introduction of the toile that an accident occurred such as that in which Henri II of France lost his life, when a splinter from a spear entered his eye. This was in 1559, when the glories of the chivalric tradition were growing dim and faint. Not many decades later they belonged to the realm of things that have been, but are no more.

One of the most impressive ceremonies ever witnessed in the Middle Ages was the formal and public degradation of a knight who had been adjudged guilty of some grave breach of knightly honour and virtue, such as treason, murder, or witchcraft. This

30

ceremony was usually—though not always—followed by the execution of the degraded knight. It was preceded by a trial in which the judges were twenty or thirty irreproachable knights and squires, and the part of prosecuting counsel was taken by a king-at-arms or a herald. A scaffold was erected opposite the raised stand where the judges sat, and there, on a rough post, was hung the shield of the erring knight, upside down and smeared with black paint. Then the heralds brought him forth, dressed in complete armour and wearing all his decorations, with the collar of his knightly order. On either side of the scaffold sat twelve surpliced priests, who, as the ceremony proceeded, sang the office known as the Vigils of the Dead. At the end of each of the psalms they paused, and during the pause the heralds stripped one piece or another of the poor wretch's armour from him, beginning with the helmet. The reversed shield was broken into three pieces, and a bowl of dirty water was emptied over the head of him who once bore it with pride. Then, tied to a hurdle and covered with a pall, the miserable creature, no longer a knight, was dragged into a church, where the priests chanted over him the psalms for the dead, and whence he was usually delivered into the hands of the Provost Marshal for instant execution.

A knight who believed himself to have been wronged by another knight could always—and not infrequently did— challenge him to a judicial combat in the lists. Or some claim or cause might be decided in the same way, as was the fate of Rebecca in *Ivanhoe*. One of the most celebrated public duels of this kind was fought as late as 1547, between two French nobles, Chastaigneraie and de Jarnac, who, after being close friends, had quarrelled over the love of a fair lady.

Nor were knights alone permitted to settle their claims and quarrels in this vigorous and romantic fashion. Priests, ladies, and persons of either gender under twenty-one years of age might nominate a champion to represent them in the lists. Wealthy abbeys which found themselves rather frequently involved in lawsuits, either with rival religious houses or with powerful laymen, often kept a champion, as one might keep a watch-dog, in case of need. In medieval England these hired fighting-men were known as *puggyls* (Latin, *pugil*, a boxer), and a certain Bishop of Salisbury was so well pleased with the services of the abbey puggyl that he caused a small image of the man to be introduced upon his own monumental brass.

Though men continued to be dubbed knights—and are so to this day in certain countries—and though jousts and tourneys were held well into Tudor times, the ancient chivalric idea was dying before the fifteenth century was half spent, and had died by the time that it ended. Many of the well-born families had been ruined through pledging their estates in order to raise funds for the Crusades; the younger sons of many such families were turning to commerce for a means of livelihood. On the other hand, wealthy traders might now hope to receive the accolade. With the break-up of the feudal system and the introduction of professional warriors serving frankly for hire and salary came the closing phrases of 'an auld sang.'

CHAPTER II

ARMS, ARMOUR, AND COSTUME

MAN'S first weapon was probably the branch of a tree, or a heavy, angular lump of rock—something, that is to say, with which he could smite, or something which he could hurl. Then followed the chipped flints, roughly attached to wooden hefts, and so used as axes, arrows, and spears. Among the ancient Greeks the spear was the principal weapon. They had swords, and we read in the *Iliad* of the purple scabbard of Ajax, but whether these swords were used for thrusting or cutting we do not know. In the Bible we read of both swords and spears; bows and arrows were as early an invention as either—probably a good deal earlier than the sword —and the ancient Egyptians were mighty archers. It must be remembered that the sword was originally a *thrusting* weapon, not a *cutting* one—*i.e.*, the point, and not the edge, did the work. As centuries passed men learned to sharpen one edge, then both, and so the ANGLO- swordsman slashed at his foe instead of stabbing him. SAXON Then, curiously enough, the more advanced peoples, SWORD notably the Romans, returned to the idea of the *thrust*, and it was their barbarian opponents who used the *edge* of the blade. Tacitus tells us how the Roman legions with their sword-points had the advantage over the Britons with their clumsy, blunt-tipped weapons. The sword was the chief arm both of the Norsemen and of the Saxons. In the latter instance the very name of the people was derived from the word which in their language signified a sword—*sachs*. To their skill with the sword

c

these Norsemen, after they had settled in the Seine valley, added skill with the bow and with the spear. It was the Franks and the Normans who learned from their Saracenic adversaries to fight on horseback, and it was the prowess of his cavalry which gave William the Conqueror so great an advantage over the infantry of Harold at Hastings.

Very early in the history of warfare mankind invented body-armour. Helmets, breastplates, shields, and greaves appear in the most ancient art, and are mentioned in the most ancient literature. These were usually of bronze in classical times—'brass' in Biblical language must be understood to mean bronze —but by the period of the Norman Conquest steel and iron were in general use. The body-armour of a Norman fighting-man consisted of a tunic and breeches of thick padded and quilted stuff. Very often this stuff was closely sewn with small iron rings, or with overlapping scales of iron or horn. Later came chain-mail, consisting entirely of interlaced rings, and worn over the quilted garments or, at a later date, over a tight-fitting suit of leather.

Armour covered with scales was called *mascled* armour (Latin, *macula*, the mesh of a net); armour covered with rings, or con-sisting of rings, was known as a *cotte de mailles*, a coat of mail, the word *maille* having, curiously enough, the same derivation as *mascle*, though it is used to indicate a different type of defen-sive covering. Plate armour, as we shall see, was not intro-duced until the end of the thirteenth century.

The Saxon shield was circular, and of no great size. The Norman shield was kite-shaped, slightly concave, and some-times nearly as long as the body of him who bore it. As years passed the shield tended to grow broader and shorter, until it achieved the form with which we are most familiar—the form suggested by the phrase 'shield-shaped.' It was from the devices painted on their shields, by which the warriors might be distinguished in battle, that the whole art (or science) of heraldry developed. First of all a certain pattern or picture

34

would be recognized as belonging to one particular baron or knight; then his brothers, sons, and grandsons would adopt it; and thence it would come to be the peculiar sign of the *family*, the coat of arms, or armorial bearings, by which they and their descendants should always be known.[1]

The weapons used by the knights during the Norman and early Plantagenet period were the sword and the spear or lance.

NORMAN HORSEMEN AT HASTINGS
Part of the Bayeux Tapestry

The battleaxe and the mace, though not unknown, came into favour somewhat later. Except in hunting, the bow was seldom used by the upper classes, but it was the chief weapon of the foot-soldiers until the introduction of muskets and other fire-arms. There were two types of bow, the long-bow and the crossbow, and it was with the former that the archers of England won imperishable renown. The long-bow was *very* long, usually about six feet, and each arrow measured about a yard. The sharp tips, or 'barbs,' of the arrows were feathered with goose-quills, and the 'fletcher,' or arrow-maker, had to take

[1] See Chapter I.

great pains to make the shaft straight, as a crooked, bent, or warped shaft might put the archer 'out' in his aim. The yew-tree supplied the tough and yet supple wood of which the bow itself was made, and the bowstring, which the archer never forgot to grease well, was of strong gut. The arrows were carried in a quiver, either girt about the body and swinging on the left hip, or slung across the back so that the arrows were drawn forward over the shoulder. The crossbow was a much more complicated affair, and, though it could not be made to discharge its 'bolts' (as crossbow arrows were called) as rapidly or as accurately as an expert archer could send the shafts from his long-bow, it needed less strength and less dexterity, and became widely popular in the second half of the Middle Ages. Italian archers were especially skilful in its use. This bow was usually of steel, and the string had to be rewound with the aid of a little winch between each 'shot.'

The mail tunic of the Norman and Plantagenet warrior was called a hauberk, and was, as we have seen, originally worn without any outer trappings, over a quilted undergarment, padded with tow, vegetable fibre, or shreds of cloth. Toward the end of the twelfth century it became the fashion to wear a surcoat of linen or silk *over* the hauberk. King John is thus represented on his Great Seal.

The Norman helmet was conical, and it left the face bare with the exception of the nose, which was protected by an odd-looking guard called a nasal. Then followed the flat-topped, cylindrical *heaume*, which covered the whole skull, and was pierced with oblong slits to enable the wearer to breathe and to see—though he can have done neither with ease! Richard Cœur de Lion wears such a *heaume* in his second Great Seal. Another type of helmet in vogue during the second half of the thirteenth century was round-topped, and had a movable *ventaille*, or perforated guard. Then came the great sugarloaf-shaped helmet, which had to be attached by a chain to the girdle, or laced to the shoulders of the wearer. This helmet was worn *over* the *coif de mailles*, or chain-mail hood, and the weight of the two together must have been overwhelming! The *coif de mailles* may be studied closely in the Temple Church, where the effigies of several of the Knights Templars are thus 'bonneted.' Next came the *basinet*, which, as its name suggests, had the form of a basin. Sometimes the basinet had a movable visor, sometimes it left the face bare, without even a nasal to protect the warrior's nose. Instead of wearing a *coif de mailles* under the basinet, our warrior now attached to his helmet a sort of flap or screen of chain-mail, called a *camail*, which effectively protected his neck and throat from the foeman's blade. These knights must have possessed remarkably well-developed neck-muscles, for they sometimes wore the *heaume* over the basinet! As the thirteenth century waned the basinet grew larger and heavier, and it was then

BASINET WITH CAMAIL
AND VENTAILLE
About A.D. 1360

no longer possible that the two should be worn together. Gradually the custom established itself that the *heaume* should be the head-covering of the warrior in tournaments and jousts, while the basinet, strengthened by a visor and a camail, was worn in battle. In its simpler form the basinet was adopted by archers and pikemen as well as by knights and nobles, and this is true also of a later type of helmet, the *salade*, which came into favour early in the fifteenth century. But by that time chain-mail had given place to plate armour, the most striking change in the history of the armourer's craft.

The beginnings of this change may be discerned in the second half of the thirteenth century, when knee-caps and elbow-caps of solid steel were added to the *cotte de mailles*. Then came two queer little wing-shaped shields, called *ailettes*, attached at right angles upon the shoulders, partly to ward off a slashing cut from a sword, and partly, it would appear, for ornament pure and simple. It is thought that both the knee- and elbow-guards and the *ailettes* may have been of *cuir bouilli* first of all, and that the *real* change which led to the development of plate armour occurred when steel was substituted for this 'boiled leather.'

In the year 1285, in the reign of Edward I, a law was made that "every man should have in his house harness wherewith to keep the peace," each according to the value of his goods and lands. Thus, a man who possessed land to the value of £15 and goods to that of forty marks, was compelled to keep by him a hauberk of iron, a sword, and a dagger, while a poor fellow whose total belongings were worth less than forty shillings must have bows, arrows, knives, and *greisarmes*, or broad blades fixed to long wooden shafts. One cannot help doubting whether this accumulation of weapons really led to the peace being kept any better than it would have been if the greater part of the population had been then—as now—unarmed. On the other hand, when a sudden and rapid levy of raw troops became necessary, to repel an invasion or to reinforce a depleted army abroad, it was very convenient for the king to be able to count upon having men ready armed, and with a rough knowledge of the manner in which their weapons should be used.

Among the knightly weapons of the thirteenth and fourteenth centuries were the *estoc*, or long, narrow sword for thrusting, the *falchion*, a curved cutting blade (*cf.* Shakespeare, *King Lear*: "I have seen the day, with my good biting falchion I would have made them skip"), the *anelace*, a double-edged dagger, the *baslard*, a short sword of the dagger type, much worn by civilians, and the *misericorde*, or 'dagger of mercy,' which had a fine point, and was intended to penetrate the joints of the armour and put a fallen adversary out of pain. The lance never went out of fashion, the longer kind being used in tournaments only, and the shorter, the lance-gay (Arabic, *zagaye*, a pike or javelin), being rather a weapon of actual warfare, and used, when desired, as a javelin. Sometimes the long tournament lances were made with hollow shafts, so that they should break

38

more easily. The phrase 'to set one's lance in rest' is a decidedly
picturesque one, but a writer of historical romance who introduced it in the description of a combat prior to the year 1360
would be guilty of error, as the 'rest' did not come into use until
that date. It consisted of an iron support, hooked and hinged
and screwed to the right side of the breastplate, and
it relieved the hand of the combatant of part of the
weight of the lance, at the same time transferring part
of the shock of the blow to the breastplate from his
arm. In the Wallace Collection there is a fine suit of
fifteenth-century armour with the rest still in position.

The whole evolution of arms and armour, from
the earliest times to the present, is represented by a
series of pendulum swings between the idea of defence
and the idea of attack. Each new weapon was, in turn,
met and counteracted by a new protective invention; ESTOC
and then yet another new weapon was devised, and In the Musée
de Cluny
so the alternations continued, and continue still.

Chain-mail strengthened with a certain amount of plate metal,
and aided by *cuir bouilli* and thickly quilted material, proved an
effective defence against swords, arrows, and lances for some
years; but as the swordsmiths, the fletchers, and the makers of
lance-heads grew more cunning it became necessary for warriors
who held their lives and limbs dear to bethink them of some new
protective covering. This necessity led to the introduction of
the *cyclatoun*, or *cyclas*, a sleeveless tunic, longer behind than in
front, and laced up the two sides. The favourite material was
silk, and the favourite colour green, though linen was also used,
and the knight seems to have had freedom of choice in the matter
of colour. The ample folds of the *cyclatoun* deprived a sword-
stroke of much of its force, and the cautious wearer was further
shielded by *three* other garments, the *gambeson*, the *hauberk*,
and the *haqueton*. The *gambeson* was a padded garment, either
with or without sleeves, fitting closely round the neck; the
hauberk, at this period made of a kind of mail in which the rings

39

are arranged in bands, as if threaded upon strips of cord or leather, had loose sleeves, slit up to allow freedom of movement. Under the hauberk was the *haqueton*, another stuffed garment, and under that a thin shirt of wool. Thus muffled

and swaddled, even the most slender and willowy warriors must have presented a somewhat podgy appearance; but without these intervening layers of padding the weight and the chafing of their armour would soon have become intolerable. The interesting brass effigy of Sir John de Creke, in Westley Waterless Church, Cambridgeshire, enables us to trace the development of plate from chain armour step by step. The good knight, who gave up the ghost somewhere about the year 1325, has arm defences of plate, *demi-brassarts*, reaching from the shoulder to the elbow, and *vambraces*, or armour for the forearm, between the elbow and the wrist; *demi-jambarts*, or leg-shields covering the front part of the lower leg only, protect his shins after the fashion of cricket-pads,

BRASS OF SIR JOHN DE CREKE

and his knees are encased in *genouillières*, either of steel or of *cuir bouilli*. The *sollerets*, metal sheaths for the feet, consisting of overlapping plates, had not yet been introduced when Sir John de Creke prepared for the fray, but he *has* steel defences upon his very highly arched insteps. His hands, clasped in prayer, are half hidden by his shield, so that we cannot tell whether he is wearing gauntlets or not. It seems probable that gauntlets of *cuir bouilli* preceded those of overlapping steel, as in the earliest representations of the gloved hands of warriors no rivets are to be seen. About this period the rowel began to replace the more barbarous prick-spur.

Let us take a forward stride of twenty or thirty years, and find how the warriors were armed who fought at Crécy and Poitiers. The *cyclatoun* has vanished now, though the *camail* remains. Arms and legs are encased in plate armour, but thigh-pieces, or *cuissarts*, have not yet appeared. Toward the middle of the fourteenth century armourers began to experiment with the so-called 'splinted' armour, consisting of separate strips of over-lapping steel skilfully riveted together upon a leather founda-tion. The disadvantage of this type of armour was that the sword or lance of the adversary might slip upward between the 'splints.' As the period was one of transi-tion, the body-armour of the knights of Edward III was of great variety, some of the more conservative clinging to fashions that were passing away, while others, of a more enterprising turn of mind, eagerly tested each new invention of the armourer. The basinets, too, show infinite variations of form in this interesting century. Though the *camail* had not been discarded, a *gorget*, or collar, of solid steel sometimes took its place. Some basinets had no visors, but movable brims; some visors were of very quaint shapes, peaked and hollowed and oddly curved. The *ailettes* vanished about the

CRESTED HEAUME OF
THE BLACK PRINCE
In Canterbury Cathedral

time when the *cyclatoun* came in, and the place of the *cycla-toun* was taken by a sleeveless, tight-fitting tunic, lacing up the back, and often embroidered with the armorial bearings of the wearer. This tunic was called a *jupon*: it will be remembered that Chaucer's knight wore a simple one of fustian. Over the conical-topped basinet the fourteenth-century warrior sometimes wore a sort of hat, surmounted by his crest moulded in *cuir bouilli*. In Canterbury Cathedral may be seen the *heaume*, crest, shield, and gauntlets of the Black Prince. At a slightly earlier date crests in the shape of fans or cocks' combs had made their appearance on knightly helmets, and toward the middle of the fourteenth century the *panache*, or tuft of feathers, came into fashion. Sometimes a flowing veil, called a *contoise*, was attached by a staple to the top

41

of the *heaume*. The feathers were usually those of the ostrich, though proud masses of peacock-plumes were not infrequently seen.   In the succeeding century these *panaches* became more and more fashionable—and more and more elaborate.   It will be remembered that in his play of *Henry V* Shakespeare makes the English king, contrasting the gorgeousness of the French forces before Agincourt with the battered and dilapidated condition of his own army, say:

> There's not a piece of feather in our host—
> Good argument, I hope, we will not fly.

The breastplate originally protected the front of the body only, but as the fourteenth century advanced it became customary to add back- and shoulder-pieces, thus lending it rather the character of a cuirass.   The *jupon* fitted closely over this breastplate, and many of the warriors would appear, from their effigies in brass and marble, to have admired and cultivated the waspwaist.

The transition from chain-mail to plate armour was not complete until the first decade of the fifteenth century, when the surcoat was discarded.   When the skirt of mail vanished it was replaced by *tauces*, or bands of steel overlapping in an upward direction.   Spikes sprouted from knee-caps, and even from the knuckles of the jointed steel gauntlets.   A knight who had lost his battleaxe, lance, and sword would still have a sporting chance of defending himself with his fists.

The steel foot-gear of the knight waxed narrow or broad as civilian fashions changed.   In the reigns of Edward III and Richard II shoes with exaggeratedly long peaks were introduced from Poland—whence their name of 'Pologne' or 'Cracowe' shoes—and then no warrior who had the slightest regard for his appearance would have dreamed of wearing sollerets of any other form.   When he fought on horseback the tapering steel peaks looked quite graceful, bending downward over the stirrups, but in a combat on foot they would have hampered

EQUESTRIAN ARMOUR OF THE FIFTEENTH CENTURY
Wallace Collection   42

him severely, and for this reason they were usually detachable. In the battle of Poitiers those knights who had lost their horses proceeded to shed not only the peaks of their sollerets, but their gilded rowel-spurs as well. This probably explains in some degree why the battle fought at Courtrai in 1302 should have been called "the Battle of the Spurs." Of the four thousand spurs left on the field of battle many must have been torn off by warriors un-horsed in the shock and stress of the fray.

The sword of the Edward III period was double-edged, a little over a yard in length, and worn attached to the left side of the richly jewelled sword-belt, while the *misericorde* hung by a small chain on the right. The great two-handed sword, a formidable weapon between five and six feet in length, was intended for use in foot-combats only, and even a stalwart knight needed all his strength to wield it effectively. Cautious warriors were wont to carry one of these hefty blades buckled to their saddles, for use if they should be dis-armed of their lighter weapons and unhorsed in the *mêlée*.

BRASS OF SIR JOHN LEVEN-THORPE

Two other medieval weapons of considerable importance were the mace and the battleaxe. The mace was used at the battle of Hastings, and did not fall into disuse until the Tudor period. The heads were of divers fashions, oval, circular, oblong, studded with sharp knobs or spikes, or set round with perpendicular iron blades. One type, used by ordinary foot-soldiers as well as by mounted warriors, was pleasantly called the 'Morning Star.' Another, which terminated in a chain to which was fixed a spiked globe of metal, bore the grim title of the 'Holy Water Sprinkler.' Prelates and priests who loved war better than peace found in the mace a singularly useful weapon, since the scriptural injunctions against shedding blood and smiting with the sword could not, in their view, possibly apply to a tool used principally for cracking skulls!

Until the fifteenth century the axe was regarded rather as the weapon of the ordinary man-at-arms than as one meet for knightly hands to wield, but by the reign of Edward IV it had become the favourite for knightly combats on foot in the lists. Richard Beauchamp, Earl of Warwick, fought with such a

weapon against Sir Pandolph Malacat at Verona, and gave his adversary such a shrewd thrust upon the left shoulder that the fight was stopped and the Englishman adjudged the winner. It will be seen from the very interesting contemporary drawing here reproduced that these axes had hammer-heads and thrusting points: some

THE DUEL AT VERONA BETWEEN THE EARL OF
WARWICK AND SIR PANDOLPH MALACAT

others had a cutting blade on one side and a sort of hook, called a *bec de faucon*, on the other. The helmet of Lord Warwick is surmounted by his family crest, the famous Bear and Ragged Staff, and he wears, not the now obsolete *jupon*, but a square-cut, short-sleeved tunic modelled on those worn by heralds and adorned with his armorial bearings. From the helmet of Sir Pandolph rises one solitary but decidedly magnificent ostrich-feather. Here the transition from chain-mail to plate armour is complete, and the warriors are, in Shakespeare's phrase, "locked up in steel."

In the Wallace Collection is to be seen a complete suit of fifteenth-century armour for man and horse, and nobody looking upon it would be inclined to dispute with the expert who declared not long since that such a suit is "the most perfect work of craftsmanship that exists." Encased in this finely wrought and cunningly planned defensive harness, the warrior would not be greatly perturbed by blows from swords, thrusts from lances, or hits from arrows. Perhaps we are more conscious of the beauty of his armour than he was himself, and certainly in our eyes its beauty is very great.

There is no superfluous ornamentation, no unnecessary complication of line and curve, no sacrificing of purpose to effect; yet the whole thing is exquisitely graceful, harmonious, lucid, and vigorous. The grace is never feeble, the vigour is never crude. There lies the mysterious and delightful secret of fifteenth-century art. If we compare, let us say, Sir John Leventhorpe [1] with Sir Robert Staunton we shall see at a glance the principal developments, variations, and modifications which occurred in the third, fourth, and fifth decades of the century. Sir John wears a basinet, he has roundels covering the gussets of his laminated shoulder-guards; his *tauces* consist of seven layers of steel, the seventh and lowest being hinged and indented to allow

BRASS OF SIR ROBERT STAUNTON

free movement of the legs. Now let us look at Sir Robert, who died just twenty-five years later. The first point of difference that strikes us is the helmet. Gone is the basinet, and in its stead we see a new type of head-covering, the *salade*, usually forged in one piece, and not attached in any way to the body-armour. The *salade* was shallow, fitted more or less loosely to the skull, and had a shelving projection behind to guard the neck. The earlier type had no visor, but, being pierced with two eyeholes, could be pulled forward at will to defend the upper part of the wearer's face. Sir Robert *has* a visor, but not a very elaborate

[1] See page 43.

one. His shoulder-guards are heavier than Sir John's, and his elbow-guards, or *coudières*, are enormous. His *tauces* consist of only five bands, and attached to the fifth are two steel flaps protecting the upper thigh. While Sir John's gauntlets are of comparatively modest dimensions, Sir Robert's are of surprising size.

Surprising also are the size and thickness of the armour worn by combatants in the lists as the age of chivalry waned. In a

museum case, or high above a carven tomb, we sometimes see a helmet so huge and so heavy that we wonder how its wearer can have fared in battle. But he did not wear it in battle. These are tilting-*heaumes*, designed to protect the head from the lance of a knightly adversary, and for that reason made of ponderous metal and attached securely to the backplate and breastplate of the warrior.

TILTING-HEAUME
Late fifteenth century

By this time the shield had practically fallen into disuse as far as actual warfare was concerned, and the shoulder- and elbow-armour on the left side was therefore reinforced. In tournaments and jousts, however, the shield was still borne, though not so frequently used, as it was necessary that the heralds should be able to recognize and record the arms (that is to say, the armorial bearings) of the knightly competitors. These armorial bearings also appeared upon the voluminous housings of their steeds.

The exact date at which horse armour came into general use is a little uncertain, but housings were employed by both the Anglo-Saxons and the Normans, and often included a covering for the horse's head. It would seem that some sort of horse armour, probably consisting of face-guards and breast-pieces of *cuir bouilli* or padded material, was known in the army of Edward I, but that not until the third and fourth decades of the fifteenth century did the elaborate and often beautiful suits of equine armour come into being. Then were seen the spiked

46

chamfron, sometimes surmounted by a tuft of plumes, the *crinet* of chain-mail following the line of the mane, the saddle with its high cantle and bow, the *peytral* to protect the breast, and the crupper-pieces guarding the quarters and the flanks. Exactly what the sentiments of the horse himself may have been it is rather difficult to imagine.

This mass of metal, wood, *cuir bouilli*, quilting, and leather which made him look so gorgeous and saved him from so many hard knocks must also have added greatly to the arduousness of his duties when his master went forth in full panoply of war.

'PURFLED' ARMOUR OF THE SIXTEENTH CENTURY

As the Middle Ages waned craftsmen, and armourers among them, began to lose that purity of line, that severe grace of curve, that characterized their work in the best period. The art of dama-scening, or inlaying steel with gold, was introduced from the East by way of Spain, and while it added to the beauty of the surface of a suit of armour, it could not fail to have a regrettable effect upon the form, since the intricate designs demanded flat spaces, uninterrupted by any curves or irregularities, and it was impossible to provide these spaces without some sacrifice of the general plan. The art of the armourer surely touched its lowest point of degradation in those early sixteenth-century suits whereon the steel is so wrought as to imitate the puffings, and slashings, and purflings, then fashionable in civilian attire!

47

The introduction of *portable* firearms, as distinct from un-wieldy and cumbersome cannon, slings, and culverins, modified and altered the ideas of armourers profoundly. At first it seemed as if body-armour must disappear altogether. Gorgets and visors *did* disappear, but the breastplate or cuirass and the leg- and arm-pieces lingered on until the beginning of the eighteenth century. Between the time of Marlborough and that of Wellington even these lingering relics vanished, one might have thought for ever. On the eve of the Great War troops, such as the French *Cuirassiers* and the English Life Guards, wearing body-armour of burnished steel were regarded as picturesque but somewhat fantastic survivals of other days. But it was soon discovered that there was no better defence against shrapnel and flying shell-splinters than a metal head-protector closely resembling the *salade* of the fifteenth century —and thus was brought into existence that familiar object the 'tin hat' of the modern foot-soldier.

The differences between the garments of a thirteenth-century and a fifteenth-century Englishman were not so great that either would stare at the other in amazement if they could be planted face-to-face. Both of them would probably utter ejaculations of mixed horror and mirth if they were confronted by an Elizabethan gallant, a Georgian beau, or a Regency buck. When Henry of Anjou, son of the Empress Matilda and grandson of Henry Beauclerc, mounted the throne of England the simple style of dress favoured by the Normans still prevailed, as it did for some time afterward. A gentleman would wear a long, straight garment, with a surcoat over it in winter, and perhaps a mantle clasped on the shoulder with a jewelled or enamelled brooch. A 'chapelaine' or hood, fitting over the shoulders and provided with an oval opening for the face, was worn by all classes, and on the top of this hats and caps of various forms might be perched. The peaked shoes, often held by an ankle-strap, were of gaily dyed leather. His lady walked abroad in a graceful, flowing gown with tight sleeves buttoned to the wrist,

48

over which in cold weather she draped an ample cloak lined with fur, rabbit, squirrel, miniver, or vair. A white linen wimple, covering her head, met usually under the chin, and was occasionally surmounted by a stiff linen cap with a pleated brim.

Rich silken stuffs from the East were known already in Anglo-Saxon times, but it was Eleanor of Aquitaine, Queen of Henry II, who introduced them into England in such quantities that all proud ladies and powerful prelates soon appeared in dresses and vestments of many-coloured fabrics interwoven of silk and gold-thread and embroidered with designs borrowed from China, Persia, and Greece.

John, the worst of the Plantagenets, shares with Edward II and Richard II the dubious honour of having been the most gorgeous in his personal attire. The backs of his gloves and the clasps of his shoes sparkled with rubies and emeralds, and his clothes—for which he seems very seldom to have paid—

LADY WITH WIMPLE AND
FUR-LINED CLOAK
Late thirteenth century

were of the most delicate linen and the most sumptuous silk. His son Henry III and his grandson Edward I were men of simpler tastes, but the ladies of England hastened to follow the example of Eleanor of Provence when she introduced a new style of gown scalloped or pinked at the edge and so exaggeratedly long that the wearer had to hold it up in one hand, or in both, if she did not wish to trip over it and tumble on her nose. The hair was gathered into a network of gold beneath a flowing veil, or else concealed by a wimple beneath which a gorget of silk or linen was folded tightly round the cheeks and chin.

Then came Edward II, feeble, fantastic son of a great and

D

warlike father, and with him came the close-fitting *côte-hardie*, which got shorter and tighter as time passed, to the alarm of old-fashioned critics, accustomed to the ampler garments of the previous reign. Edward delighted to dress his Queen, himself, and his favourite courtiers in white velvet, flame-coloured silk,

SIR JOHN HARSYCK AND
HIS WIFE
From a brass of 1384

gold tissue, and other dazzling stuffs. On one occasion we find him ordering six pairs of boots with silken tassels and silver tags from a cordwainer in Fleet Street. Nor was his wife, the vindictive and relentless Isabella of France, the sort of woman to use her influence against these luxurious habits. Their son, Edward III, doughty man-at-arms though he might be, inherited something of his unfortunate father's taste for pomp and pageantry, and throughout his reign colours became gayer and forms more fanciful in the raiment of men and women both. The clothing of the Canterbury pilgrims was certainly vivid in hue and diverse in cut, and

if the Luttrell Psalter is to be believed even the villeins toiling in the fields wore hoods and tunics coloured like the violet and the rose.

As the fourteenth century waned fashions became more and more extreme. The courtiers of Richard II, with their incredibly long peaked shoes and their flapping scalloped sleeves, were the butt of mocking rhymesters and the theme of troubled moralists. Under Philippa of Hainault ladies had adopted the *côte-hardie*, and had taken to braiding their hair inside two cylinders of golden network, one lying closely against either cheek. Her granddaughter-in-law, Anne of Bohemia, seems to have introduced the horned or peaked headdress which

50

reached such prodigious dimensions in the fifteenth century and drew forth so many angry rebukes from monkish satirists.

In the days of Henry IV and Henry V a curious form of feminine headgear was in vogue, somewhat resembling the canopy of a throne: strangling high collars were worn by both sexes, and men sported baldrics hung with bells. The last three Plantagenets ruled over an England peopled by lords and ladies who must have looked liked tropical flowers — or even like the brilliant, broad-winged insects flitting among them. The long robes and little sleeveless over-jackets of the ladies were graceful enough, but of the three kinds of head-tire in vogue it is difficult to say which was the most absurd. There was the horned

ROBERT SKERNE AND HIS WIFE
From a brass of 1437

and peaked affair; there was the 'hennin,' a sort of dunce's cap of velvet or stiffened silk from which floated a veil; and there was the butterfly arrangement, a jewelled coif half hidden by two huge, wire-supported wings of thinnest linen. Meanwhile gentlemen wore padded tunics of rich, large-patterned brocade, with very short, closely pleated skirts, or furred robes caught tightly round the hips with a belt of goldsmith's work. Their headgear was almost as varied as that of their ladies, and might consist of a hat something like the modern bowler, though with a higher crown and a narrower brim, a tall, brimless cap, or a sort of toque bunched up at one side with an enamelled clasp and adorned with a very long tail called a 'liripipe.' A

51

rhymester in the reign of Henry VI thus apostrophized the
Englishmen of his day:

> Ye prowd galonttes hertlesse,
> With your highe cappis witlesse
> And your schort gownys thriftlesse,
> Have brought this londe in gret hevynesse!
>
> With youre longe peked schone,
> Therefor your thrift is almost don;
> And with youre long here into your eyen,
> Have brought this lond to gret pyne!

It was certainly not the fault of Henry of Windsor if his
subjects dressed foppishly, for he himself wore the plainest of
grey fustian and the broadest of unfashionable shoes.

CHAPTER III
THE CHIVALRIC IDEA

IT may well be that the roots of the chivalric idea strike deep into the soil of ancient Rome; it may well be that the code and the customs of the Saracenic warrior-chieftains lent colour to its earlier phases; but it is also beyond doubt that in its fullest development it was a Christian idea, intimately associated with Christian practices and principles. Every knight was, *ipso facto*, a defender of the Church as well as of the throne; every knight, in theory if not in fact and deed, was the foe of all 'paynims,' eager to defend the holy places of his faith from heathen usurpation, and, in a sense, "God's soldier."

This affinity between Christianity and chivalry is obvious and insistent in medieval painting and sculpture; but in literature the lesser and younger element achieves a distinct existence, and can be considered by itself. At a very early date bards and wandering minstrels began to sing of the valiant deeds, the *hauts faits et gestes*, of the knights of the very solid Charlemagne and the somewhat hazy Arthur. The subject was pleasant and interesting to all their hearers, of whatsoever condition and degree; nor were they slow to add brighter colours, making what was ordinary marvellous, and what was already remarkable strange beyond belief.

First in point of time, and by no means last in point of value, is the *Chanson de Roland*, the great French epic telling of the valiant deeds and pitiful death of Charlemagne's nephew, *Roland le preux*, Roland the brave. Some critics assert that in its second and final form the existing *Chanson* was probably copied in England, and may have been the composition of an Anglo-Norman

53

scribe. However this may be, it had far less influence in England than on the Continent, and on this side of the Channel left only faint traces in the figurative speech of the people. In medieval England you would have been perfectly well understood if you called a man a Ganelon, for Ganelon was a notorious traitor, the villain of the *Chanson de Roland*; and in modern England 'to give a Roland for an Oliver' is a common enough expression, though it is improbable that every one who uses it is aware that he is alluding to two of Charlemagne's most doughty paladins.

KING ARTHUR
From the tomb of Maximilian I in the Franciscan church at Innsbruck

The real hero, the great central and dominating figure of English chivalric romance, is King Arthur.

Whether any living and breathing man, any king or leader with an actual historic existence, lies beyond the mist that enfolds Arthur, must remain a subject for debate among the learned and the wise. In the twelfth, thirteenth, and fourteenth centuries popular belief in his reality was fervent and profound; but by the end of the fifteenth, when Caxton printed Malory's *Morte d'Arthur*, "divers men" had already begun to "hold opinion that there was no such Arthur, and that all such books as be made of him be but feigned and fables." In *The Last Age of Roman Britain* Mr Edward Foord advances the interesting theory that the real man, whose form has thus been made indistinct by many golden veils of legend, was a Romano-British general, Artorius by name, to whom was entrusted the defence of Britain against the invasions of the barbarous Picts, Angles, and Saxons.

However this may be, the fact remains that the *legendary* Arthur is one of the great figures of romance. Nor was his renown confined to the island over a large part of which he is reputed to have reigned. Throughout Christendom he was numbered among the Nine Worthies, his companions being Joshua, David, Judas Maccabæus, Hector, Alexander, Julius Cæsar, Charlemagne, and Godefroy de Bouillon. *Le roi Artus* and his *chevaliers de la table ronde* were only one degree less familiar to Continental scribes and bards and chroniclers than were Charlemagne and his paladins. The plot and narrative of Malory's *Morte d'Arthur* are, in great part, derived from French originals, but these, in turn, may have been carried across the Channel by Norman minstrels who had learned them from Welsh bards during the Norman occupation of Wales. The close racial and linguistic kinship between the Welsh and the people of Brittany at the time when the Arthurian stories were as yet in a fluid state makes it very difficult even for scholars and experts to determine whether the real beginnings of the whole cycle are to be discovered in Breton or in Welsh soil. There was a constant flux and reflux of ideas, myths, epics, and ballads between the two peoples, and the imagination of each was coloured by that of the other. The earliest allusion to Arthur as an *historical character* would seem to bear out Mr Foord's theory. It occurs in the *Historia Brittonum*, an eighth- or ninth-century compilation attributed to one Nennius, where he is represented not as a king, but as a sort of supreme general, the equivalent of the Roman *dux bellorum*, the leader of the battle. From the eleventh century onward the Arthurian legend rolled along, gaining in weight and mass at every revolution, like some gigantic snowball, until the searching rays of the Renaissance fell upon its swollen bulk, and it began to dwindle. Milton, none the less, hesitated between Arthur and Adam as the hero of his mighty epic. And it was to the "legend of the Table Round" that Tennyson turned when he too was minded to woo Calliope, the muse of epic poetry.

At a very early date, certainly before the dawn of the twelfth century, the belief had grown up among the people of England, especially Western or Celtic England, that Arthur was not dead, that he would some day return. One of the most ancient of surviving Welsh poems says that "There is a grave for Mark, a grave for Guythur, a grave for Gwgawn of the Ruddy Sword; a mystery is the grave of Arthur." The four warriors here mentioned were British chieftains, valiant in battle against the barbarians who poured into Britain after the withdrawal of the Roman legions. And of the four, only Arthur had no known or remembered sepulchre. Here is the fountain-head of the legend of his immortality.[1] However, the Arthur of Welsh myth and legend does not greatly resemble the Arthur of chivalric romance. In the Celtic half-light he is seen dimly, a great king endowed with magical powers, and attended by a band of devoted warriors only a little less marvellously gifted than he. It was not until the Normans had overrun Western England, and Norman minstrels had carried the songs of Charlemagne and his paladins from castle to castle up and down the land, that the hero of Celtic mythology girt himself with a knightly sword, buckled golden spurs upon his heels, and rode forth to the joust and the tourney, as the characters in a chivalric romance never failed to do.

We encounter this later and infinitely more picturesque Arthur in the Latin chronicle of Geoffrey of Monmouth, Bishop of St Asaph. Geoffrey posed as a serious historian, and claimed to derive much of his information from an ancient book lent to him by his friend Walter, Archdeacon of Oxford;[2] but the truth would appear to be that this early twelfth-century (1100–54) churchman was one of the first, and not the least great, of English story-tellers. From him poets and dramatists of later centuries borrowed many stories which their works have made familiar to us all—the stories of King Lear and his three daughters, of King Cymbeline, of Merlin the Wizard, and, above all, the stories of Arthur. He was indeed a marvellous

---

[1] *Cf.* the similar legends relating to Frederick Barbarossa and Holger Dansk.

[2] There is evidence, however, that prior to the year 1151 a certain Walter Espec, Archdeacon of Oxford, *did* possess "a book about the British Kings."

person, the Arthur of Geoffrey's *Chronicon*. Crowned at the early age of fifteen, he began by defeating a combined army of Saxons, Picts, and Scots, and conquering Scotland. Then he proceeded to subjugate Iceland and Ireland, Norway, Dacia, and Gaul. He placed Normandy under the rule of "Bedwyr, his Butler," and Anjou under that of "Kay, his Seneschal." Having slain two giants, one of whom wore a mantle furred with the beards of kings whom he himself had slain, this doughty monarch next inflicted a crushing defeat upon the Romans. Athirst for fresh victories, he entrusted the care of his kingdom and of his queen, the fair Guanhumara, to his nephew Sir Mordred, and set off across the Alps with the intention of subduing Rome itself. Before he had reached the Italian side of the great mountain-barrier, however, word was brought to him that Mordred had seized both the crown and the queen for his own. Arthur, not unnaturally, made haste to retrace his steps, and in a desperate battle "by the river Camel, in the country of the west," he and his warriors defeated Mordred and his men. The guilty queen fled to a convent and became a nun. Gawain and many another valiant man lay dead on the field. Arthur was sore wounded, and like to die, but "he was borne thence unto the Island of Avalon for the healing of his wounds."

Here we have the canvas upon which later poets and chroniclers embroidered a rich and elaborate design in golden threads and silks of many colours. They were not slow in setting about their task. What did it matter though Brother William, a carping monk of Newborough, accused Geoffrey of having "lied saucily and shamelessly"? The stories in the *Chronicon* spread over England with incredible rapidity. Copyists were kept busy for years transcribing them. They passed into the everyday thoughts and words of the highest and the most humble. In 1155 a Norman clerk, Wace by name, dedicated to Queen Eleanor, wife of Henry II, a translation of Geoffrey of Monmouth's work into the Norman-French then spoken at Court. Wace was something more than a mere mechanical translator.

He added some new material, probably derived from Breton or Norman sources unknown to the Bishop of St Asaph; and it is in *his* pages that we hear first of the famous Round Table. Wace called his poem *Brut*, after the mythical founder of the kingdom of Britain, but its atmosphere is purely Norman. It is otherwise with the *Brut* of Layamon, parish priest of Arley Regis, by the banks of the Severn, who set out to translate Wace into the English tongue as it was then spoken by the mass of the English people, and who incidentally made of Arthur an intensely English hero, and of the legends an intensely English epic. According to Layamon, Arthur one day encountered in Cornwall "a man from beyond the sea," who offered to make for him a table of great beauty, at which sixteen hundred men "and more" might sit. This offer the king accepted, and thus was brought into being the famous Round Table, by which the quarrels of Arthur's knights were settled, as every one was seated at the head of the board. Although such a large number of persons could seat themselves at it, the table had the magic property of shrinking to such a small size that Arthur could carry it everywhere with him. Truly, a wonderful table!

As the Arthurian legends multiply, in French and in English, in verse and in prose, the central figure tends to lose his definitely English character, and to acquire a more international interest. He is anybody's Arthur; he is everybody's Arthur; his capital and his Court might be anywhere—or nowhere—in Christendom. Also certain of his knights, notably his nephew, the gallant Gawain, soon begin to force their way into the foreground of the picture, thus causing Arthur's own image to recede and to become less vivid in colour, less clear-cut in form.

Before the twelfth century closed the Arthurian cycle had been yet further extended and enriched by other than English hands. Chrétien de Troyes, a French Court poet, wove a series of poems round Arthur and his knights, and these in turn were translated and adapted by German bards such as Wolfram von Eschenbach and Hartmann von Aue. At this period, and for

58

the following hundred years, it seemed as if the chivalric idea were summed up in Arthur, though it found expression, both artistically and poetically, in many different ways.

At the beginning of the fourteenth century France paid back some of her borrowings, and English translations were made of French metrical romances telling of the wizard Merlin and the mysterious passing of Arthur; one hundred and fifty years later follows a prose translation of much greater merit. And all the time the Arthurian cycle is growing more and more elaborate and unwieldy, and knights (not Arthurian knights *only*) are performing more and more impossible feats, and enduring wilder and wilder adventures. Marie de France, a French poetess at the Court of our King Henry III, set down many such tales, not directly Arthurian, and mostly of Breton origin.

As we have seen, Arthur's nephew, Sir Gawain, early won the goodwill both of the chroniclers and of them who loved their chronicles. He is the hero of several independent romances, of which the best known is that of *Sir Gawayne and the Grene Knight*, a tale of faerie, where the central figure contends with a fierce green-clad opponent of gigantic proportions, and incidentally exhibits all the chivalric virtues, courage, courtesy, fidelity to the pledged word, clemency in triumph, cheerfulness in defeat.

Scholars and historians agree, for the most part, that the original Arthurian root was *Celtic*. But upon this Celtic root and stem were grafted other tales, of non-Celtic colour. Such is the story of the gallant but false knight, Sir Lancelot of the Lake, who loved Arthur's queen, the fair and faithless Guinevere; such is the story of Sir Perceval (Wagner's *Parsifal*) and his quest of the Holy Grail, the cup from which, according to the legend, Christ drank with His disciples at the Last Supper. These were among the narratives chosen and used by Tennyson when, in 1859, he began to write the twelve *Idylls of the King*, once regarded as his highest achievement. It is curious to observe how Tennyson, like his far-off medieval forerunners, could not avoid making Arthur a somewhat stiff and unconvincing figure. Indeed, W. H. Mallock, in setting forth in *The New Republic* the ingredients necessary for such a concoction as that of the Laureate, actually begins, "Take one blameless prig."

In the rich flowering-season of chivalric romance many rhymed tales were current in England which were only remotely

THE FOUR SONS OF AYMON
From a manuscript of the thirteenth century in the
National Library, Paris

connected with Arthur's Court at Camelot, or not obviously connected with it at all. Such were *Sir Bevis of Hampton*, *Sir Cleges*, *Sir Isumbras*, *Amis and Amiloun*, and *Sir Ipomedon*. After the first Tudor king was seated on the throne of England Caxton, realizing that the popularity of these old knightly narratives had not yet sunk low, "set in imprint" the story of *The Four Sons of Aymon*, long familiar in France. Some nameless Kentishman of the early fourteenth century translated into English from a French original the story of Merlin and Arthur, but there the wizard looms far larger than the king over whose destinies he exerted such a mysterious influence. Here it is to Uther, the father of Arthur, that the credit of instituting the Round Table is given, and the curious information is added that however many knights joined the band and sat at the board it was never *full* until they were born that should "fulfill the mervaile of the Greal." According to some critics, the rhymed romance of *Richard Cœur de Lion*, which belongs to the same period, is the work of the same hand. Here it is Richard I who is the perfect knight, and here we see how the return of summer brought with it the return of what we may call the Tournament Season.

> Merry it is in time of May
> When fowlès sing in their lay; ...
> Ladies strew their bowers
> With red roses and lilly-flowers; ...
> The damiseles lead dance;
> Knights play with shield and lance;
> In jousts and tournaments they ride.

We have noted that by the time that another Kentishman, William Caxton, printed Malory's *Morte d'Arthur* faith in the historical reality of all these knightly heroes was much less fervent and far-reaching than it had formerly been. But before the fourteenth century closed another and an even more famous Englishman had both exalted and derided the chivalric idea in verse. This was Geoffrey Chaucer.

We have already seen, in the chapter on the Knight and the Squire, how Chaucer drew a vivid and memorable portrait of each type in the Prologue to *The Canterbury Tales*, and how the knight was valiant, gentle, pure of heart, and the squire gay, gallant, and accomplished. Not only had the knight fought in far and strange lands; he had jousted in the lists to such good purpose that thrice he had slain his adversary outright. There was nothing of the glitter and glow of chivalry about his outward looks. His horse, we are told, was good, but he "was nat gay"; his gypoun was of simple fustian, stained with the rust of his hauberk. Such must have been the appearance of many of those knights in actual, everyday life, who upon their monumental brasses look so amazingly slim, and elegant, and neat. His curly-haired son, the musical and romantically minded Squiér, was a much more decorative figure in the procession of pilgrims, with his long-sleeved short-cut gown, embroidered

> as it were a meede
> Al ful of freshė flowrės whyte and reede.

In the whole pageant of English literature these are assuredly the chivalric figures that stand out most clearly. And the chivalric idea pervades Chaucer's poetry, sometimes giving very quaint forms and colours to pre-chivalric scenes and characters. The background of the tale told by the knight himself is the Athens of Theseus, but the morals and manners of the Greek 'knights' would have done credit to them of the Round Table, and when the two young heroes, Palamon and Arcite, are found half dead on the battlefield the heralds know by their coats of arms that they are of the blood royal of Thebes![1] Theseus makes the disguised Arcite his "chief squiér"; in order to decide which of the two is to wed the fair Emelye, he suggests that each of them should bring a hundred knights

> Armėd for listės up at allė rightes

and let the victor in the general *mêlée* have the princess as his prize. When the knights duly assembled some wore hauberks, some breastplates, some favoured "a light gypoun." Every detail of their battle-harness is of Chaucer's own time.

This transplantation of chivalric images to classical soil is even more remarkable in Chaucer's most considerable sustained narrative-poem, *Troilus and Criseyde*, the scene of which is laid in Troy during the siege. The hero and all his friends, in speech, costume, mind, and body, might well be knights and squires in the train of Lionel of Clarence or John of Gaunt. Here—and elsewhere—the poet treats the chivalric ideal with

---

[1] There were, of course, 'heralds' in Greek classical drama, but their functions were not akin to those of the medieval heralds, and their *rôle* was rather that of messengers.

respect. But he was too essentially sane, his sense of humour was too keen, for its absurdities to pass unmarked and unrecorded by his eyes and his pen. In *The Canterbury Tales* there occurs one of the earliest and most amusing of the many parodies of the exaggerated and incredible chivalric stories then current. Chaucer himself, being called upon by the Host to "sey now somewhat, syn oother folk han sayd," protests that he knows no tale to tell unless it be a "rym" which he had learned long before. And he then proceeds to babble in six-lined stanzas "of a knyght was fair and gent," whose name was Sir Thopas. We hear first of his bodily perfections:

> Sire Thopas wax a doghty swayn;
> Whit was his face as payndemayn,[1]
>   His lippès rede as rose;
> His rode [2] is like scarlet in grayn,
> And I yow telle in good certayn
>   He hadde a semely nose.

His virtues, his valour, his skill in archery, hawking, and wrestling are next described in the same mock heroic vein. Inevitably this paragon must ride "thrugh a fair forest," fall in love with the Elf-queene, and meet a giant; but here there is an abrupt break with tradition, for instead of worsting the fearsome creature in single combat the knight, after bragging of what he will do "tomorwe" when he is more adequately equipped for fighting, is pelted with stones by the giant and "drow abak ful faste." Unfortunately it was a case of "never shall sun that morrow see," for although Chaucer gives an elaborate description of his hero's preparations for the encounter, and urges his hearers, in the authentic strolling-minstrel fashion, to listen to his tale, we are not allowed to learn the sequel, for the patience of the pilgrims gave out before the thirtieth stanza was done, and the Host told the narrator in blunt terms,

> "Thou doost nought ellès but despendest tyme;
> Sire, at o [3] word, thou shalt no lenger ryme."

---

[1] fine bread.   [2] rosiness, ruddiness.   [3] one.

Such, if they had but known it, was the doom pronounced upon all these old rhymers by the new spirit that was then astir in Europe. Yet the old idea died hard. When Caxton set up his printing-press at the Sign of the Red Pale, under the shadow of Westminster Abbey, one of the earliest of its productions was Malory's *Morte d'Arthur*. Caxton was a conservative to the very bones. He chose, as he himself tells us, to "set in imprint" this translation "out of certain books of French," in order that noble men might "see and learn the noble acts of chivalry, the gentle and virtuous deeds that some knights used in those days, by which they came to honour." And he tells them that the book treats of "prowess, hardiness, humanity, love, courtesy, and very gentleness, with many wonderful histories and adventures." So, indeed, it does. But the adventures are *so* many, and *so* wonderful, that "the sense faints picturing them." There are five hundred and seven chapters in the *Morte d'Arthur*, and there is hardly one of them without its marvellous incident, while not a few contain several such incidents within their narrow limits. The tales are often tedious, the figures are often stiff and unconvincing; but the *Morte d'Arthur* remains one of the great masterpieces of English prose. It is of very unequal texture, threadbare and moth-eaten stretches of canvas alternating with patches of Tyrian silk and cloth-of-gold. It is the easiest thing in the world to parody, and the most difficult to imitate. Arthur, though not the "blameless prig" of Tennyson's *Idylls*, is, perhaps, the least impressive of the characters. But Lancelot, Gareth, Galahad, Tristram, and Gawain, though they are alive only by fits and starts, spring sometimes into an intense and passionate reality.

Between June 1483 and August 1485—the exact date is uncertain—Caxton printed the *Book of the Order of Chivalry*, an English translation from French and Latin translations of a book written in the last decades of the thirteenth century by a Majorcan mystic, Ramón Lull (or Lully). To Ramón's work the earlier translators had made many additions, and his English

64

EARL RIVERS PRESENTING TO EDWARD IV THE FIRST BOOK
PRINTED BY CAXTON IN ENGLAND

W. F. Mansell photo

sponsor made many more. It would appear that even the 'imprinting' of the five hundred and seven chapters of the *Morte d'Arthur* had not fully aroused the "knyghtes of England" to a sense of their duties and responsibilities. So Caxton returns to the attack. He provides them with a manual of chivalric lore, he urges the King (it was by that time Richard III) to institute periodical jousts, he urges the 'knyghtes' themselves to emulate the memorable deeds of their forerunners; but at the same time he accuses them of sloth, of indolence, of taking too many baths (an unexpected reproach in an age which we have been taught to regard as exceedingly unhygienic in its personal habits), and of playing too many games at dice.

In Lambeth Palace there is an illuminated manuscript showing Edward IV in the act of receiving from the hands of a kneeling knight a very large book with a gilt clasp. The knight was the King's brother-in-law, Antony Woodville, Earl Rivers,[1] the book was *The Dictes and Sayings of the Philosophers*, the first ever printed in England, and the respectful figure in the furred robe to the left of the picture is that of Caxton himself. There was good reason why Rivers should present the printer to the King, for not only was he Caxton's patron, but it was he who had translated the book, an improving French treatise with which he had whiled away the time during a pilgrimage to Compostella.

However keenly Caxton may have been conscious of the shortcomings of "the knyghtes of England," he must surely have felt that in Rivers the very spirit of chivalry lived again. The brother of the beautiful Queen Elizabeth Woodville had something in him of Chaucer's knight and something, too, of Chaucer's squire. Though a doughty antagonist in the lists, he was no mere tournament warrior, but had fought in several pitched battles, always with conspicuous valour. He had

---

[1] For some years Antony Woodville was known as Lord Scales, a title which he enjoyed by virtue of his marriage with the daughter and sole heiress of Thomas, Lord Scales; he succeeded his father as Earl Rivers in 1469.

journeyed to far lands; he had skill in the craft of the verse-maker; and in a coarse and pleasure-loving age, during an active and busy life, he had the patience to sit down and translate books of philosophy and poetry "for to be enprinted and so multiplied to goo abroad among the peple."

Rivers had been a Lancastrian in his youth, and had fought for the red rose at the battle of Towton, but when it became clear that the victory of Henry VI would mean that England would lie at the mercy of the Earl of Warwick he changed sides, and remained a faithful Yorkist to the end. The marriage of his sister Elizabeth with Edward of York brought him honours and dignities which he certainly did not seek and probably did not desire: he was made a Knight of the Garter and given the lordship of the Isle of Wight. In 1467 he jousted with Antony, the famous Bastard of Burgundy, in the lists at Smithfield, before the King, as the result of a challenge as picturesque as any described by Malory, and with trappings and ceremonies as gorgeous and as complicated as any in the chronicles of knighthood. A splendid figure he must have looked, emerging in "complete steel" from a pavilion of blue satin, and mounting a horse housed with white cloth-of-gold bearing a St George's cross of crimson velvet and "bordird with a frenge of golde half foote long." Nor was his antagonist less magnificent, for *his* steed was housed with crimson velvet adorned with gold and silver bells. The King having forbidden the use of "speres right jepardous and perilous," the two warriors fought on foot with axe and dagger, giving and receiving "many thik strokes" till Edward, perhaps fearing the political and diplomatic results of any serious damage to the visitor's person, shouted "*Whoo!*" and cast down his *bâton* as a signal that the duel should cease. The previous day they had fought on horseback, but rather inconclusively, as by an extraordinary mischance the Bastard's horse stunned itself by an impact between its head and the high pommel of the challenger's saddle.

A year later Rivers was in Burgundy, taking part in the

Tournament of the Golden Tree held at Bruges in honour of the nuptials of Margaret of York, the King's young sister, with Charles the Bold. There he and the Bastard met once more, but not in the lists, as they had sworn that neither of them should again "dele with othyr in armys." When for a brief space the star of the Lancastrians was in the ascendant Rivers followed Edward of York into exile and, returning to England, fought for him at the battle of Barnet, but he did not take part in the battle of Tewkesbury, for we find him foremost among those who defended London against the Bastard of Fauconberg.[1]

During all this time, when he was acknowledged to be one of the most gallant and comely knights of Edward's Court, Rivers had held deep in his heart a sense of the mutability of earthly fortune and the vanity of worldly greatness and worldly delights. He dreamed of going on a Crusade, and for that purpose betook himself to Portugal, but the day for crusading was over, and he had to be content with pilgrimages to Compostella, Rome, and Bari. As we have seen, it was during the voyage to Compostella that he first read the edifying little book which he afterward translated for Caxton. It was lent to him by his Gascon esquire, Louis de Bretaillez, who had taken part in the jousts at Smithfield six years before. Honours continued to shower upon his head; he was made governor to his young nephew, Edward, Prince of Wales, and Chief Butler of England. When Edward IV died Rivers was with the Prince at Ludlow, and thither came Richard, Duke of Gloucester, accompanied by a group of nobles who shared his not unnatural dislike and distrust of the Woodville family. The character of Richard remains something of an enigma, and his apologists, Horace Walpole and Sir Clements Markham among them, rightly point out that all evidence in his favour was destroyed by his successor, with the result that he is condemned unheard. It may be that this cryptic prince with the keen, restless face was not

[1] See Chapter VI, p. 117.

responsible for the death of his two nephews; but it cannot be denied that he brought about the death of their uncle on their mother's side.

On a flimsy charge of having conspired against the life of the Duke of Gloucester Rivers was arrested and imprisoned, first in Sheriff Hutton and then in Pontefract Castle, the same grim Yorkshire fortress that had been the scene of Richard II's mysterious end. There, on June 23, 1483, he wrote his last will and testament, in which he shows an honourable anxiety that all his debts should be paid, and sets aside considerable sums of money for "werkes of mercy" and "dedes of charité." He desires that all his body-armour and horse-harness shall be sold to buy "shyrtes and smokkes" for the poor, bequeathes to the Prior of Royston his "gowne of tawney cloth of gold," to Our Lady of Walsingham his housings of "blakk cloth of gold," and five marks to Tybold, his "barbor."

After his execution, which took place without the trial by his peers to which he was entitled by English law and custom, a hair shirt was found next his skin. This instrument of self-mortification was hung up before the image of the Blessed Virgin in the Carmelite church at Doncaster, for the edification of the pious. So perished he whom Caxton calls "the noble and vertuouse Lord Anthoine, Erle Ryviers," one of the most gallant and romantic figures in the chronicles of chivalry.

Another of Caxton's noble collaborators who perished on the scaffold was John Tiptoft, Earl of Worcester. Like Rivers, he was a man of scholarly tastes; like Rivers, he went on pilgrimages to far countries, fought for the white rose on land and sea, received the Garter, and served Edward IV in more than one administrative post of honour and authority. There, however, the resemblance ends, for the gentler and more engaging qualities of Antony Woodville were conspicuously lacking in John Tiptoft.

During a somewhat prolonged sojourn in Italy Tiptoft heard John Argyropoulos lecture in Greek at Florence, and himself pronounced a Latin oration before Pius II which is said to have made his Holiness shed tears at the exceeding elegance of its Latinity. He bought innumerable books wherewith to enrich his library in England, and enjoyed the friendship of many of the most distinguished scholars of the day. One cannot help regretting that he did not devote himself entirely to the pursuit of learning, for his ruthlessness as Chancellor of Ireland has left a dark stain on his memory. Even Judge Jeffreys at Taunton Assizes two centuries later did not throw himself into the task of punishing 'rebels' more heartily than did Tiptoft when he went to Drogheda to mete out 'justice' on behalf of his King.

There followed that brief eclipse of the sun of York during which Edward IV fled to Burgundy and the Lancastrians found themselves almost unexpectedly in power again. Tiptoft, unable to get clear of the country, disguised himself as a herdsman and hid in a Huntingdonshire forest, where he was discovered, and whence he was dragged to captivity in that same tower over which he had ruled as Constable not long before. Unlike poor Rivers, he was given some semblance of a legal trial, though the verdict was a foregone conclusion. Tried at Westminster, he was beheaded on Tower Hill, meeting death with quiet fortitude, and requesting the executioner to give him three strokes of the axe in honour of the Blessed Trinity. Caxton, for whom he had translated Cicero's *De Amicitia* and Buonaccorsi's *Declaration of Nobleness*, declared that from his death all men might learn to die.

The chivalric idea faded, and grew vague and formless in early Tudor literature, though it seemed to enjoy a brief reincarnation in the person of Sir Philip Sidney. When we come to Spenser and his *Faerie Queene* we cannot but realize that the "gentle knight" whom we there see "pricking o'er the plain," and who is "Ycladd in mightie armes and silver shield," is not an authentic knight, not Chaucer's knight in his youth, or Chaucer's squire in his prime, but a Tudor hero wearing fancy dress. Spenser has imitated the diction of an earlier age, and he has tried

69

valiantly to reproduce its thoughts, its colours, its point of view. The result is a magnificent poem—or fragment of a poem—but the attempt has not been successful. The body and the garments of the chivalric idea have been revived, and brought from dust and darkness into the light of day, but the *spirit* eludes the poet's hand.

That chivalry and romance were closely associated was perceived by the leaders of the romantic revival in the eighteenth century, and this fact was later seized upon and exploited by Sir Walter Scott, notably in *The Talisman* and *Ivanhoe*. There is much to be learned from the latter novel about the outward trappings of chivalry, and even about its "inward and spiritual grace," though the details—such as the premature introduction of plate armour—are not all severely accurate. The knights whom we meet later, those in Tennyson's *Idylls*, in Keats's *La Belle Dame sans Merci*, in Maurice Hewlett's *Richard Yea and Nay*, to mention only a few at random, belong to the same type and class as Spenser's knight, and, despite many merits, are obviously not "the thing itself." We have seen that Chaucer made merry at the expense of the chivalric idea in "Sir Thopas." Many other satirists did the same. Cervantes, though it was the obsolete outer trappings of chivalry that he derided in *Don Quixote* and not the chivalric ideal itself, did as much as any man to sweep away the last remnants of the system. Samuel Butler followed with *Hudibras*. Peacock, Barham, Thackeray, and Calverley parodied its epic and its lyric manifestations with malicious glee. Now we can look at it from afar off, and behold it as a strange, beautiful, imperfect, half-pitiful thing, once potent to rule the lives of men, and still potent at times to touch the heart and the memory.

As the Church was the sole custodian of art during the Dark Ages, and their chief nourisher and protector during the medieval period, it is natural that the idea of knighthood should be summed up and expressed by the painters, sculptors, glass-stainers, and goldsmiths in the persons of St Michael, the arch-

ST GEORGE
Carpaccio
Anderson photo

70

angel, and St George, the slayer of the fabled dragon, "the ouggely monstre," as Lydgate calls it. Individual knights were, of course, depicted in various places and in various ways—in Purbeck marble, alabaster, or brass upon their tombs, in illuminated miniatures in their prayer-books, in quaint, vivid little pictures illustrating the lives of valiant warriors, legendary and real. But the idea, in the abstract, was most often symbolized by one—or both—of these two saints.

The favourite manner of depicting St Michael was either struggling with, or trampling upon, Satan. Occasionally he is seen weighing the good and bad souls upon a gigantic pair of scales at the Day of Judgment. Always he wears the knightly armour and wields the knightly weapons of the age in which the painter or sculptor happened to live. Artists of the Primitive Flemish school were very

ST MICHAEL
From a fresco of the fourteenth century at Pisa

fond of encasing him in beautiful plate armour; but Raphael, under the influence of the classical revival, dressed him as an ancient Roman, with embossed cuirass and flowing military cloak. St Martin, who really *was* a Roman soldier, provided medieval painters with another opportunity of making an effective picture of a warrior in battle-harness; nor did they hesitate to depict the heroes of antiquity, Hector, Æneas, and Jason, in chain-mail or well-wrought steel, with golden spurs upon their sollerets, vambraces on their arms, and basinets or *salades* upon their heads.

The favourite embodiment of the knightly ideal, however, was St George. Raphael twice painted him riding a plump white horse, once driving his spear with glorious energy into the scaly dragon sprawling on the ground, and once flourishing his falchion over a grim beast which rears up and clutches at his right foot. Donatello, the great Florentine sculptor of the fifteenth century, showed him dismounted, a slight, boyish figure, with his two hands resting on his shield, of which the base touches the ground between his feet. Dürer, the German painter and engraver, imagined him as a fierce-looking fellow in elaborate armour, mounted on a heavy and shaggy steed, and wearing a queer wide hat; Carpaccio mounts him on a dark and fiery Arab charger, and sends him spurring full-tilt against a monstrous dragon.

CHAPTER IV

THE TILLERS OF THE SOIL

Of earth thou shalt with sweat and swink
Win that thou shalt eat and drink.

SO wrote a North Countryman in the thirteenth century,
relating the story of Genesis and the doom pronounced
upon the father of mankind. The verb 'to swink,' which has
somehow dropped out of the English language, was once one
of the most expressive in it. No other verb—'toil,' 'work,'
'labour,' none—conveys the same sense of arduous and monotonous activity. Nineteenth-century writers, Robert Louis
Stevenson and William Morris among them, felt its picturesqueness so strongly that they even tried to make a living word of it
again. But it has passed away as irrevocably as that medieval
England where so many poor folk were fain to turn it into
action.   It is no shame for to swinken

they were kindly assured by the author of the old epic of
Havelok. This seems fortunate, as "to swinken" was then the
lot of the greater part of the population of this realm. The
town-dwellers, the craftsmen, the merchants and their men,
formed a very small minority. And, indeed, the craftsman,
be he never so laborious, could hardly be said to 'swink.'
The true swinker was the villein, the bondsman working in the
fields, and winning a hazardous harvest from an unbountiful
soil.

Straight across the centre of the medieval page in English
history runs a bitter black line; above it and below it the forms
and colours of the chronicle are not the same. Let us take the
portion above the line as representing the twelfth and thirteenth

73

centuries and the first half of the fourteenth, and the portion below as representing the second half of the fourteenth, the whole of the fifteenth, and the first decades of the sixteenth. You will then see that the sombre line marks the middle of the divided century, and begins somewhere in the late 1340's. It was in 1348 that the terrible pestilence known as the Black Death first appeared in the land. Whence it came is uncertain; probably from the bleak steppes of Tartary by way of the gilded carracks of Genoa. Not for ten years did the plague abate; and even then there were fresh outbreaks in 1361 and 1368. When finally the wave had spent itself England was a changed country, and many of her most ancient and characteristic habits and customs had passed away. In fourteen months between one-third and one-half of the total population perished. Fields went out of cultivation, sheep and oxen roamed at will among the unreaped corn, mill-sails stood still, church-bells were silent, apples and cherries hung disregarded on the trees. We shall see later what were the effects of this visitation upon the daily life of the English people, and how its two chief results were the setting free of the serfs and the development of the wool trade. For the moment we will pause to look at this same people as they were before the Black Death.

In Anglo-Saxon times the thrall or bondsman was a mere domestic animal, as much the property of his master as any hound or hog, and bound, like the former, to wear a collar about his neck, if not, like the latter, a ring through his nose! With the coming of William and his hard, practical, constructive Normans came the feudal system. This system became strangely complicated, and was at no time very simple or absolutely uniform; but nothing could be simpler than the root *idea*. In theory, *all* land belonged to the king. His tenants, those who held the estates (Latin *tenere*, to hold), were his liegemen, owing him and swearing to him homage, fealty, and service. Thus did the proud and puissant Dukes of Burgundy hold their dukedom of the French Crown. These superior landholders could, and did, grant smaller holdings to men of lower rank and narrower fortune, and also to people born on their estates. These last, though their position was decidedly better than that of the Anglo-Saxon thrall, were still apt to be reckoned with the rest of the livestock in the sum-total of their lord's possessions. These were the serfs or villeins, not to be confounded with the freeholders of land granted under manorial law. The freeholder had to kneel before his lord, place his hand between his hands, and swear fealty to him, but in England this oath was so worded as to except the man's duty to the king, while in France he simply pledged his faith to his lord, without any reservations or exceptions in favour of the sovereign. The villein, though he belonged, in a sense, to his lord, was no slave. As long as he performed the services required of him by tradition and by law he was secure in the possession of his cottage and his strip of land, and could hand on both to his son, just as he had, most probably, received them from his own father. Under Magna Carta his tools might not be confiscated by way of fine. Nor was he invariably a miserable wretch shivering in a dismal hut. Comfort as we understand it was, certainly, beyond his reach, and perhaps beyond his ken; but if he were a sturdy, industrious fellow, and if his lord was humane and his lord's bailiff honest, he could, and often did, lead a tolerably pleasant and cheerful life.

Each manor, whether its owner were a great noble, a great monastery, or a simple knight, was a sort of kingdom in little, every dweller within its boundaries being subject to the lord of the manor, as he, in his turn, was subject to the king. The free-born holders paid rent, in labour and in kind; the villein owed his lord a certain proportion both of his toil and of his time. As Roman law, which is unrelenting toward all slaves, permeated English law more and more, the *legal* status of the villein did not tend to improve. But theory is one thing and practice another, and his *actual* position had begun to alter for the better even before the Black Death made these odds all even. He was born into villeinage, poor fellow, and might not —unless his lord gave him leave to wend on a pilgrimage—stray from the place of his birth. He could not be sold, like a slave, but he and his children might be transferred *with* an estate from one owner to another, by inheritance, grant, gift, or purchase. The free-born tenant, if a dispute arose between him and his lord, or if he were accused of any misdemeanour, had the right of appeal to the king's courts of justice; the villein was, and remained, at the mercy of the local manorial court.

For three days a week the villein had to work upon the lord's demesne, and in the spring he had to plough four acres of that land; in the spring and winter seasons he must supply two oxen for his lord's plough-team on three out of six working days, and in summer on one out of six. Gradually there grew up the custom whereby a villein might, upon payment of a certain sum, be excused from these rather burdensome duties. This was called *commutation of service*, and it is obvious that the more general it became the better did the status of the villeins become. This yearly toll—really equivalent to rent—might be paid partly in money and partly in kind. Two shillings and a penny half-penny, with a hen and sixteen eggs, was a typical toll.

The lot of the tiller of the soil in medieval England would certainly have been far more tolerable if he had been a little more resourceful and enterprising in his daily work. He was desperately conservative and slow, distrustful of new ideas if any reached him, and most unlikely to have any of his own. Each manor contained land of three kinds: arable, pasture, and waste or common. But the yield of the cultivated land was very poor, often only six bushels from an acre in return for two. The principle of the rotation of crops was not unknown. It was realized that when the same crop has been grown continuously upon a certain piece of land for a certain period the soil becomes exhausted and the grain poorer; and also that by alternating deep-rooted with shallow-rooted crops better results are obtained in both kinds; so each year a third of the area was left

76

fallow, while two-thirds were cultivated. Wheat, barley, and oats were the crops chiefly grown, though hemp and rye were occasionally seen, and gallant attempts were made to cultivate vines. Parsley, leeks, cabbages, and onions lent variety to the hard fare of the poorer folk. The common land might consist of open moor, bare down, or dense woods. If there were woods the numerous pigs of the community were turned out to forage for themselves there, and when the acorns lay thick on the ground there must have been joy among the grunting herds.

FEEDING PIGS

The aspect of the country was very different from what it is now, and decidedly less attractive. Few hedges divided the fields from the highroad and from each other. The various holdings were marked off by baulks of un-ploughed turf, and, as they were usually strips instead of squares, the surface of the land must have had a queer striped appearance. The homes of the villeins were little better than huts, the walls made of wattle and daub. This was a very simple method of construction, practised by the ancient Egyptians. A wall of this type consisted of a row of upright stakes connected by twisted withes and then covered with rough plaster. Just as in prehistoric times the potter was wont to ornament his clay pots with rows of scratches or thumbnail imprints, the medieval plasterer liked to make a crude pattern of herring-bone lines or intersecting angles upon the pale grey mud before it hardened and dried. The roofs of these cabins would be either of thatch or of interwoven boughs, and on the floors of bare earth straw was thickly strewn. Since straw served as bedding for both man and beast, it was a very useful thing; hence the medieval habit of cutting the grain very high up on the stalk when reaping. In the smaller houses chimneys were unknown, and the smoke of the winter wood-fires escaped as best it might through a hole in the roof. The family pig was frequently a fellow-denizen, and the hens whose owners were too poor or too lazy to build a coop or a run for them were suffered to join the group indoors.

The two great poets of medieval England, the plump and cheery Chaucer and the gaunt and saturnine Langland, have both left vivid pictures of the interior of such a house as this. The date of each picture is subsequent to the Black Death, so we are free to imagine what the same scene would have looked like twenty or thirty years before. On the one hand conditions were rather better for the villein after the pestilence; on the other dearth and hardship then oppressed the land. If we strike a balance between these two factors we shall probably come to the conclusion that the hut of 1345 and that of 1375 (or 1385) resembled each other pretty closely.

Chaucer's nine-and-twenty pilgrims are jogging on their way to Canterbury, beguiling the journey with the telling of tales. The Knight, the Miller, the Man of Law, the Prioress, and several others have already been called upon by the jovial, stalwart Host to take their turn in amusing the rest; the Monk, despite his gay and bluff outward mien, has damped the general cheerfulness with "sad stories of the deaths of kings," and has been interrupted by the Knight, who declares roundly that

> Swich talkyng is nat worth a boterflye;

and now the Host, "with rude speche and boold," turns to the Nun's Priest and says:

> Com neer, thou preest, com hyder, thou sir John.
> Telle us swich thyng as may our hertès glade.[1]

Obligingly the Nun's Priest agrees, and proceeds to tell the old fable, told long before by Marie de France, of the proud, bright-plumed cock Chauntecleer, and the dainty little hen Pertelote. But first he—or rather Chaucer—devotes twenty-

---

[1] gladden.

six lines to the "poure widwė" to whom both the cock and the hen belonged, and her manner of life in her

narwė cotage
Beside a greve,[1] stondynge in a dale.

It was, he tells us, "a ful symple lyf," for her possessions were few, "litel was her catel and her rente." Most of her wealth consisted of livestock:

Thre largė sowės hadde she, and namo;
Three keen[2] and eke a sheep that hightė Malle.
Ful sooty was hir boure and eek hire halle
In which she eet ful many a sklendre meel;

.   .   .   .   .   .

No wyn ne drank she, neither whit ne reed;
Hir bord was servėd moost with whit and blak—
Milk and brown breed—in which she foond no lak;
Seynd[3] bacoun, and somtyme an ey[4] or tweye.

The Nun's Priest speaks in a kindly, compassionate tone of the "widwė," faring frugally under her smoke-encrusted roof in her "narwė cotage"; yet her lot was pleasant and enviable in comparison with that of the poor folk to whom Langland—himself a peasant's son—introduces us. Here again it is the woman rather than the man who wins the pity of the poet:

Reuthe is to rede othere in ryme shewe
The wo of these women that wonyeth in cotes.

(Pitiful it is to tell or to show forth in rhyme
The woes of these women that dwell in cots.)

And here again a great part of his attention is devoted to the important and frequently distressful question of eating and drinking. A farthing's worth of mussels were a feast to these poor folk, and a farthing's worth of cockles "these were almės, to helpe." The children cry for food, the parents themselves feel the sharp pinch of hunger. In the long, bitter nights of winter the mother must rise and rock the cradle; she must spin and comb and card wool, patch and wash and mend, and peel

[1] grove.   [2] cows.   [3] singed.   [4] egg.

rushes for rushlights. Elsewhere, however, the same hand traces a less disheartening picture. We are introduced to a ploughman, Piers Plowman, the allegorical Piers, type and exemplar of patience, industry, and poverty. Piers is hospitably inclined; he laments that he has "no peny" wherewith to buy pullets or geese; he can offer his visitor only two green cheeses —probably made from ewes' milk—a little curds and cream, an oat-cake, "and two loves of benes and bran" intended for his children; to these he adds baked apples and ripe cherries. It all sounds rather pleasant, though a little suggestive of the menus recommended by modern food-reformers preoccupied with Vitamins A and B. But Piers himself would fain have given his visitor finer fare. If only it had been "Lammas tyme" the harvest would have been 'in,' and everything would have been different!

Harvest was the great event of the year. University students were released from their books in order that they might lend a hand in the fields; hence the length of the 'Long Vac' in summer to this day. At harvest and haymaking time the labourers often received small gifts in kind. Thus at North Curry, in Somerset, each reaper might claim a sheaf bound with a band "long enough to go twice round the reeve's head"; the man who made hurdles had thirty cut saplings, and the hayward could take as much hay as he was able to raise to his 'medkniche,' or mid-knee. Communal farming was practised in England until the middle of the fourteenth century, and did not pass wholly out of use for some time afterward. Under this system all the lands, both the lord's lands (the demesne) and the tenants' holdings, were cultivated *together*. The holding of the free tenant averaged about thirty acres; that of the villein might be little more than a plot, or might extend to five or ten acres, or more. Each holding was divided into separate strips, sometimes at a considerable distance from each other, so that poor and rich land should be fairly shared out. Whenever the corn was cut and gathered into barns all the cattle of the village

80

were let loose to graze upon the stubble. Meanwhile the grain was threshed and winnowed, and taken in sacks to the manorial mill to be ground. All grain was not, however, the raw material of the miller, the baker, and the cook; a certain proportion was set aside for the production of ale and beer, and found its way into the manorial brew-house. Hops were not used by brewers in this country till 1524, and the villein, poor though he might be, could quaff a rare malt liquor when he halted in his toil.

THRESHING
Luttrell Psalter

The comfort which he found in this quaffing is cheerily expressed in a song of the fifteenth century, a song sung first by some sturdy Englishman whose name is forgotten now:

Bryng us yn good ale, and bryng us yn good ale,
For our blyssyd Lady sake, bryng us yn good ale;
Bryng us in no browne bred, for that is made of bran,
Nor bryng us yn no whyt bred, for therein is no game:
But bryng us yn good ale!

And no doubt they did.

Eight years before the Black Death appeared in England a certain Lincolnshire knight, Sir Geoffrey Luttrell by name, had a beautiful psalter, or book of Psalms, in Latin, written and illuminated for his own oratory. It is a masterpiece in its queer way, this hefty volume known as the Luttrell Psalter. In the centre of each of the three hundred and nine pages the text of

F

the Psalms is written in large black-letter characters, very easy
to read, even by the flickering light of tapers in a dim chapel
after dusk.   The upper margin and the sides of each are populated by the most weird and amazing grotesques, demons, imps,
and monsters, except where a capital letter occurs at the beginning of a Psalm, and is overlaid with delicate gold-leaf, still bright,
and made to frame some little scene or figure from sacred legend
or story.   The rather broad space at the foot of the page gave
the illuminator his great opportunity, and he seized it with

PLOUGHING
Luttrell Psalter

enthusiasm.   In the first part of the psalter these lower margins
are occupied chiefly by episodes from the lives of the saints or
imaginary portraits of the saints themselves; but it seems as
though the second half of the book were the work of a different
illuminator, a whimsically minded fellow with a love for realism,
whose monsters are even more fearsome than those that go
before, and whose marginal pictures, instead of representing
saints and angels, give glimpses of English rural life as it was
lived in East Anglia before the Black Death.

There we see the husbandmen ploughing, harrowing, sowing
seed, breaking clods, reaping, gathering in the harvest; and we
see their wives lending a hand in the lighter tasks, weeding, and
feeding the hens, and spinning, and even helping the clod-
breaker in what looks a rather heavy job.   The forms and
fashions of their tools and implements are so simple that we
can well believe they had altered little, if at all, since Roman
times.   As for the clothes worn by the men and women, we may
safely accept the evidence of the Luttrell Psalter in the matter of

what a modern tailor's advertisement would call 'cut and style'; as regards colour, there is a certain amount of doubt in the minds of some students. Did the illuminator deck his peasants in gay hues simply to make them look prettier upon the vellum page? Or did these hard-working and—it must be added—hard-favoured folk really wear stockings of scarlet, tunics of pale purple, hoods of rose-colour lined with green? Were the handles of their whips actually painted green and blue? Or did all these pleasing tints exist only in the eye, and upon the palette, of the painter, and should we be wiser to imagine Hob and Wat in tunics of dingy homespun, and Gillian and Joan in gowns of homely grey? The evidence of John Gower suggests that in the fourteenth century English country-folk *did* imitate the brilliantly hued attire of their 'betters.' One thing at least is certain: the rough linen aprons of Gillian and Joan were ornamented with a strip of stitchery along the waistline. These aprons had no bibs, and seem to have been worn in front or behind according to the fancy of the wearer or the needs of the moment. Wives of craftsmen also wore aprons, but these were "whit as mornė milk" and elaborately pleated.

The garments of Hob and Wat are designed to give the greatest possible amount of warmth combined with the greatest possible freedom of movement. The woollen tunics are girt easily about the waist by leather girdles studded with metal-rimmed strap-holes; the woollen hoods protect the shoulders and chest as well as the head, and the ploughman and the sower wear large brown felt hats over their hoods. Thick gloves, divided into three, one part for the thumb, and one part for each two fingers, were worn both by women and men, and were stuck through the girdle when not in use.

They were not always under the necessity of providing their own cloaks and hoods, for sums of money were often left by wealthy people to purchase these for a certain number of humble folk who should walk in their funeral procession. So numerous were these bequests that the custom must have been of very great advantage to large numbers of the poor and needy. In 1339 Joan, Lady Cobham, willed that on the day of her obsequies "twelve poor persons clothed in black gowns and hoods" should carry twelve torches. This was a very usual arrangement, the number being chosen to correspond with that of Christ's apostles, but William, Earl of Suffolk, in 1381 had forty-eight torch-bearers clad in white, and Hugh, Earl of Stafford, in 1385 had a hundred. Sometimes a small fee was given to each torch-bearer, and sometimes the cloaks were red, russet, or even green.

Though it is known that children were made to work with

HARROWING
Luttrell Psalter

their parents in the fields from an early age, there are no little girls and very few little boys in the Luttrell Psalter. Two lads, one with crisply curled hair, are helping to heave a cart-wheel out of a rut in one scene, and elsewhere a scarlet-stockinged urchin, who has left his shoes on the ground, trembles among the branches of a cherry-tree, while the irate owner threatens him with a hefty-looking stick. Oxen, not horses, were used to draw the clumsy ploughs. For harrowing, and for carting corn and hay, thickset horses with hogged manes and spiked shoes were employed. The roads being incredibly bad, the task of man and beast must often have been grievously hard, especially as, owing to the greater area then under forest, the climate was probably even rainier than it is to-day. These sturdy draught-horses were called 'capels,' and we know from Chaucer that favourite names for them were "Brok" and "Scot." There

84

are two horses dubbed "Scot" in *The Canterbury Tales*, the dapple-grey bestridden by the Reeve and the 'capel' in the Friar's story. The Friar gives us a racy and lifelike sketch of a carter and his team.

> Deepe was the wey, for which the carté stood; [1]
> The cartere smoot and cryde as he were wood,[2]
> "Hayt, Brok! hayt, Scot! what spare ye [3] for the stones!
> The feend," quod he, "yow fecchè, body and bones. . . .
> The devel have al, both hors and cart and hey!"

This sounds rather terrible; but when Brok and Scot put

CARTING
Luttrell Psalter

forth all their patient strength, and the wheels begin to turn, the mood of their driver changes suddenly.

> "Heyt! now," quod he, "ther Jhesu Crist yow blesse!
> And al his handwerk, bothè moor and lesse!
> That was wel twyght,[4] myn owene lyard [5] boy!
> I pray God save thee, and Seintè Loy! [6]
> Now is my cart out of the slow,[7] *pardee!*"

Whether the life of Hob and Wat and their families was tolerable or the reverse depended almost entirely upon the personal character of the bailiff or reeve to whom the general management of the estate was entrusted. Few lords had either the

[1] for which reason the cart was at a standstill.   [2] mad.
[3] why do you pause?   [4] pulled.   [5] grey.
[6] Eligius.   [7] slough.

leisure or the inclination to devote much of their own time and energy to such matters, though during the long reign of Henry III there was an awakening of interest in their lands on the part of the great landholders of England. The reeve must not be confounded with the *manor-reeve*, who represented the villeins at the manorial courts, nor with the steward, whose chief duty was to hold these courts on behalf of his lord. Nor must it be imagined that the manorial courts existed simply to enforce the rights and uphold the privileges of the ruling caste. The villeins had their rights also, some of them defined in law, others based upon local or general custom and tradition. So energetic were many of the villeins in defending and demanding these rights, especially after the Black Death had dislocated the whole machinery of the manorial courts, that landowners presently began to think that the more villeins they had the more troubles they endured, and to prefer sheep to men, and pasture to plough-land. This was one of the factors which led to the emancipa-tion of the serfs and the expansion of the wool trade.

What was the method of procedure in a manorial court and what were the cases decided there may be seen from an ancient French manuscript written in the thirteenth century, apparently for the guidance of English manor officials, called *La Court de Baron*. Imaginary cases are set forth in which, for example, Walter 'of the Moor' is accused of stealing perch from the pond of the lord of the manor, and a certain William, of no surname, is convicted of horse-stealing. William's trial is sufficiently interesting and characteristic to be quoted at some length. The Steward asks the Bailiff: "For what cause was this man taken?" and receives the reply: "Sir, for a mare which he took in a field . . . in other wise than he should." Then follows this dialogue between the steward and the prisoner:

STEWARD. What is thy name?
PRISONER. Sir, my name is William.
STEWARD. Now, William, answer me. How camest thou by

this mare? For thou canst not deny that she was found in thy possession and thou didst claim her as thine own.

PRISONER. Sir, I disavow this mare. Never did I see her until now!

STEWARD. Then full boldly canst thou put thyself upon the good people of this vill that thou stolest her not.

PRISONER. Nay, sir, for these men have their hearts big against me, and they hate me greatly because of the ill things which are believed of me.

STEWARD. Deemest thou, William, that any man would commend his soul to the Devil for thee, either for love or for loathing of thee? Nay, in truth, they be good folk, and law-abiding, and thou canst oust from among them all those whom thou didst suspect of desiring to see thee condemned. Do thou what is right, having God before thine eyes; yield not to the allurements of devils; confess the truth, and thou shalt find the more mercy with us.

PRISONER. Sir, in God's name have compassion upon me! I will confess the truth. My great poverty and need and the beguiling of the Devil caused me to steal this mare, and often they have made me do other things that I ought not to have done.

STEWARD. God pardon thee! At least, thou hast confessed in this court that larcenously thou didst take this mare. Now name some of thy comrades, for it cannot be that thou hadst no fellowship in thy wrongdoing.

PRISONER. Of a truth, sir, I had no companion in my wrongdoing save only the Evil One.

STEWARD. Take him away, and let him have a priest.

This was a polite, official way of saying "let him be hanged forthwith"; so poor William is led off to execution, and the court passes to the next case.

In pre-pestilence days a villein was forbidden by law to quit the place of his birth and seek service with another master, and he was liable to be seized and set in the stocks, or even cast into prison, if he defied the law. It happened occasionally, however, that his overlord released or 'manumitted' him and his heirs voluntarily from the yoke of perpetual servitude. This act of grace might be performed as a reward for services rendered, or in fulfilment of a pious vow, or out of regard for some kinsman of the villein himself. Fortunate was William of Wythington whom in 1278 Richard, Abbot of Peterborough, set free from bondage, and confirmed in the possession of certain houses and meadows held by his ancestors from the Abbey, "for the love of lord Robert of good memory, formerly Abbot . . . maternal uncle of the said William, and at the request of the virtuous Brother Hugh of Mutton, kinsman of the said Abbot Robert." William of Wythington had the good fortune to have two churchmen among his kinsfolk. To the villein who had no family connexions of any weight or influence two other ways of escape were open, one slightly irregular, the other entirely respectable. If, by cunning and audacity, he could contrive to remain for a whole year within the boundaries of a free town, a town protected by a royal charter, he automatically acquired freedom, and might even hope to blossom into a merchant or an alderman. And if he entered minor orders, received the tonsure, and became a clerk or "a priest all shaven and shorn," he ceased at the same time to be a bondsman, and to be subject to any but ecclesiastical courts of law. So many villeins chose this method of release from the trammels of birth that Parliament became alarmed, and set to work to frame laws and statutes to curb this dangerous tendency. Advancement *par clergie* was becoming altogether too common. It was repressive measures by Parliament which were largely responsible for the Peasants' Revolt in 1381, led by Wat Tyler and Jack Straw, and inflamed by that priest-demagogue and catchword-coiner John Ball. One of the objects of the Statute of Labourers, passed in 1351, was to thwart the excessive new demands of the surviving peasants by fixing wages throughout the realm. The Black Death had swept away so many thousands that those who remained very naturally sought to profit by their survival. No, said the faithful Commons, this must not be; wages *and prices* must be exactly the same as they were before the pestilence. This was very short-sighted legislation, for it strove to impose an artificial rigidity upon elements which were in a natural and not an unhealthy state of flux. In the event the statute had little influence upon national life. People were exasperated but not cowed by it. Landowners, eager to see their deserted acres under the plough again, turned a blind eye to the law, and when wandering husbandmen presented themselves gave them work upon their own terms, instead of putting them in the stocks. And the labourers themselves followed wherever Interest, called by Langland "Lady Meed," should beckon them.

Even so, there were not enough men to till the old fields. More and more land was turned into pasture. Later, when the balance between population and area had been restored, this concentration upon sheep-farming led to unemployment and distress among the people who, in earlier days, would have found plenty of work on their ancestral acres. That, however, was not until

SOWING SEEDS
Luttrell Psalter

after the Wars of the Roses. The decades after the final disappearance of the Black Death were not either unpleasant for the tillers of the soil or inglorious for England herself. High wages led to greater comfort ; Edward III's Continental wars, though they cost a good deal of money, brought indirect gain to the nation at large. The villeins, whose villein-age was now nothing more than a name, took a firmer and ever firmer hold upon their rights and advantages. Village life had never been one unbroken round of weary toil; there had always been saints' days and holidays, church-ales, wakes, and fairs. Now came the miracle plays, of which more anon, to bring new colour and vision into the eyes and the minds of men. Horizons widened. Returning pilgrims retold tales of travel that lost nothing in the telling. New words and new ideas were brought home by the archers who had fought under the Black Prince in France or under John of Gaunt in Spain. After 1406, when the Law of Apprentices was passed, a villein might, if he would, send his sons to the village school without incurring any penalty.

One result of the agricultural changes that followed the great pestilence must have been that there were more shepherds in

SHEPHERD WITH GLOVES AND PIPES
Luttrell Psalter

the land, and not so many millers. At all times the miller had a somewhat shady reputation. He was suspected of taking more than his lawful proportion of the grain delivered to him to be ground. In the Luttrell Psalter we see mills of each kind, a water-mill, with eel-traps cunningly laid in the swift blue current, and a slate-roofed windmill, with squat, tawny-coloured sails. Chaucer's miller, with his white coat and blue hood, his red hair, and his bagpipes, belonged to the least scrupulous type:

Wel koude he stelen corn and tollen thries

—that is to say, he took *thrice* the percentage or "toll" (about a twentieth part) allowed him by law.

Of medieval shepherds we shall have a charming glimpse

90

when we come to the miracle plays. Two of them, supposed to be they who "watched their flocks by night," appear in the Luttrell Psalter. One wears a blue tunic, scarlet hose cross-gartered with grey, a buff hood, and striped red-and-green gloves; the other has a buff tunic, blue hose, and a blue hat. Each has his double pipe hanging at his belt, and in a later picture you see how these pipes were played. The chief purpose of the pipe was, of course, to direct the sheepdog, who learnt to recognize and obey its various 'calls'; but in the second pastoral scene the shepherd seems to be making music simply for his own delight, while overhead, in the lapis-lazuli sky, burns an enormous star of gold.

WATER-MILL WITH EEL-TRAPS
Luttrell Psalter

CHAPTER V

THE CRAFTSMEN

OF all the handicrafts practised by the human race that of the potter is probably the most ancient. The same instinctive desire to make mud pies which moves the average infant to-day stirred the unskilful hands of his far-off ancestors when the race itself was in its infancy. Primeval man, when he had kneaded a lump of tawny clay, and made a dint or hollow in it with his fist, left it to dry and harden in the sun. After that he might turn it to various uses, but he could not hold water in it for long, since it had a disconcerting tendency to melt into its original muddiness again. Then, one day, perhaps by pure chance, he dried this earthen vessel in the ashes of his cave-fire instead of in the sunlight outside the cave, and thus made *fired* pottery, much more durable than the crumbling and dissolving stuff he had made before. The first gift of the earth to her last-born child was this wonderful substance—clay. As the long, slow centuries passed he learnt to do many things with it. Lamps, fed with bison-tallow, spindle-whorls, toys, were only a few of the things he learnt to make. He must have produced countless failures and suffered countless disappointments before the invention of the potter's wheel, which gave symmetry to his pots, and the discovery of the metallic glaze, which gave them colour.

According to the ancient Greek legend, the resourceful Talus, nephew of Dædalus, invented both the potter's wheel and the saw, and, having been summarily slain by his jealous uncle, was changed into a partridge by the compassionate gods. It was natural that the Greeks, keenly conscious of their intellectual supremacy, should attribute to their own genius two such useful inventions, but it would appear that the story, even divested of its fabulous tints, *is* a story and nothing more. The potter's wheel probably came from the East, the Far East, reaching Egypt from China by way of Scythia, and Greece and her Italian colonies by way of Egypt. The metallic glaze may have been discovered by some lucky chance. The Egyptians learnt quickly to produce gorgeous surfaces, brilliant purple, intense green, and vivid blue; the Greeks, with their austerer taste, tended to dead black and pale red, and instead of the enamelled glitter of the Egyptian ware their beautiful cups and vases had a fine, delicate, silken gloss.

SLIP-WARE JUG
British Museum

What of the medieval potter? He lived more than three thousand years after the men who wrought Tutankhamen's peacock-hued statuettes, and nearly two thousand after those who fashioned the red-and-black vases given as prizes in the Panathenaic festivals at Athens; yet his handiwork would look woefully rough and crude set side by side with theirs. He worked, as they had worked, with the wheel and the kiln to help him; but he had lost almost all the skill they had won. You see the parent earth, as it were, *through* the pottery of his making. The glaze is thin and patchy, reddish brown, buff yellow, or leaf green; sometimes it runs in streaks down the sides of his pots, as if it were soup or jam that had boiled over and dried hard. When he attempts patterns they are as simple as those scratched with thorns or thumbnails by primeval man upon his clay jars. One reason for the roughness of medieval pottery may well have been the rough uses to which it was put. The day was then far distant when the secret of the Chinese porcelain-clay, the subtle and exquisite *kao-lin*, should be brought to Europe, and when the rich should eat off plates and drink from cups of transparent, luminous china. In medieval

93

times the platters upon lordly tables were often of wood or pewter, and the cups, tankards, and flagons were almost always of silver, silver-gilt, or gold. Not till the fifteenth century did the Italians perfect the highly glazed pottery known as majolica ware, and even the finest specimens of this, with their portly gods and goddesses of orange and azure, are not worthy to rank with Greek and Etruscan pottery at its best.

PITCHER WITH FACE

The potter of Plantagenet England plied his craft chiefly for the benefit of the humbler folk. He made the great high-shouldered pitchers in which villagers carried water from their well and Londoners from their conduit; he made the sturdy mugs from which his fellow-craftsmen quaffed their frothing ale, and the pots and pans and pipkins which their wives used in cooking, storing, and serving their solid if simple fare. He made cake-moulds in the form of saints' heads, and money-boxes like towers and pigeon-cotes. For pilgrims he made gourd-shaped flasks, for clerks little green inkpots. For chilly people he made small, basket-shaped braziers to hold charcoal embers and to be held between the palms. Occasionally his handiwork *did* find its way into the company of the great, as when he made drinking-troughs for the pet birds of the long-fingered ladies, or pitchers from which the pages poured water over the sticky hands of the knights after a banquet. This type of pitcher was called an *aquamanile*, and was often modelled to represent a knight on horseback. The Continental potters sometimes produced a flagon sufficiently fine to be adorned with a lid and a stem of silver-gilt; but the English potter seems to have been an unenterprising sort of fellow, who jogged on from year to year, moulding and glazing and firing his simple green

94

and brown and yellow pots, and quite contented so long as his patrons were content. Though his wares seldom appeared at the tables of the mighty, they were much in demand in their kitchens. The executors of Eleanor of Castile paid a sum of eight-and-sixpence to Juliana "la Potere," apparently a feminine plier of the craft, for three hundred pitchers. This sounds exceedingly cheap, even allowing that the value of money was then many times greater than it is now. In 1466 Sir John Howard could obtain only "xi dosen potes" for "iv*s*. v*d*."

AQUAMANILE OR PITCHER
IN FORM OF HORSEMAN
British Museum

As charcoal was used to heat the kilns, it happened rather frequently that iron-workers and clay-workers gravitated to the same spot. This was the case on the Weald of Sussex. Looking now at that lonely, undulating land, with its patches of shaggy forest and its "hamlets brown and dim-discovered spires," it is difficult to realize that here in the later Middle Ages was the Black Country of England, where iron was smelted and tools and weapons forged.

After clay, metals; after the potter, the smith.

If we pause to think how great a part was played in the everyday life of our ancestors by that stout fellow the smith we shall cease to wonder at the numerousness of those descendants of his who bear his name. In our ears the word 'blacksmith' calls up visions, if not of a spreading chestnut-tree, at least of a dusky smithy, lit by the wavering flames of a huge fire, with two powerful figures beside an anvil sullenly red, and two or three patient, drowsy horses tethered hard by. But to shoe horses was one only of the many jobs which the medieval smith had to tackle, and before him the divine smith of the Scandinavians, Wayland, and before *him* Vulcan, the divine smith of the Greeks.

The armourer, he who made the breastplates and helmets and leg- and arm-pieces of the medieval knight, was himself a sort of glorified smith. Yet the everyday smith, to whom the carter turned for his axle-pin, the fisherman for his hooks, the cobbler for his awl, the cook for his spit, was the indispensable of every village, lacking whose handiwork life would soon have been at a standstill. In Anglo-Saxon times he even provided the tailor with his needles! It was not until 1370 that highly polished and sharply pointed needles were introduced from Damascus into Nuremberg; and not until the reign of Henry VIII were the needle-makers of London granted a royal charter, with three crowned needles as their coat-of-arms. To judge from the banner of the pin- and needle-makers of Douai in the fourteenth century, the French craftsmen then made thimbles as well. The pin-makers of England must have been rather more enterprising than their fellows, the 'needlers,' for as early as 1483 the industry had become sufficiently important for a law to be passed forbidding the importation of foreign-made pins.

ARMS OF PIN- AND
NEEDLE-MAKERS
OF DOUAI

Naturally, the shoeing of horses was a very important branch of the smith's many activities, so much so that the farrier, who specialized in this job, was permitted by law to work on Sunday should any stranger passing through the town require his horses shod. There were innumerable other tasks, however, to which the worker in iron had to be ready to turn his hand. If he fashioned buckles, keys, or chains only, he ceased to be a 'smith' strictly so called, and ranged himself with one of the group-divisions of his trade or 'mystery.' His was never at any time a monotonous life, for he had to make all sorts of useful, interesting, and even beautiful things: it might be a clip for a rushlight, a box to hold a miser's hoard or a king's alms, a hook for a butcher to hang a joint of beef upon, or a traceried *grille* for the tomb of some fair dame with folded marble hands. He too it was who made the iron tops for poor men's rabbit-skin pouches, and the iron spikes that tipped the ploughman's ox-goad and the pilgrim's staff. There is in the British Museum a fourteenth-century manuscript which gives us a vivid glimpse of a smithy. The painter is anxious that we should be in no doubt as to the nature of the smiths' task and of their various

BLACKSMITHS AT WORK
From a manuscript in the British Museum

accessories. Over the anvil he has written *ferrarii duo demulcent ferrum*, "the two smiths smooth out the iron"; and, with equal care and attention to detail, he labels the fire *igs* (*ignis*) and the hammer *malleu* (*malleus*). The smith on the left of the picture is a fearful fellow, and he seems to be bringing down his hammer with a vindictive thump on the red-hot iron, while his 'mate' watches him with a queer mixture of amusement and disapproval.

The fume of the fire and the din of the hammer rendered the smith unpopular with his neighbours, who, however greatly they needed his handiwork, objected none the less violently to the smoke and the noise. This useful but troublesome person worked chiefly, if not exclusively, in iron. There were other metal-workers whose materials were finer and whose tasks were less arduous and less prosaic. There were bell-yetters, who cast church-bells, founders, responsible for the effigies on many noble tombs, pewterers, silversmiths, and—most magnificent of all—the workers in good red gold. These last made their

IRON ALMS BOX
Early fifteenth century

appearance very early in the history of the human race. Cretan chieftains, Egyptian Pharaohs, Babylonian high-priests, Celtic warriors, all adorned their brows and their wrists with circlets and bracelets of gold. In the Rome of Numa Pompilius, when as yet neither weavers nor bakers were, the goldsmith took his recognized place with the potter and the carpenter among the craftsmen of the infant city-state. In the London of the Norman and Plantagenet kings goldsmiths played a proud and worthy part. To them came princes and queens, bishops and abbots, knights and ladies. At one moment the job in hand might be a royal sceptre, at another an altar candlestick; to-day a golden tankard for a stalwart fist, to-morrow a delicately wrought ring for a long, fair finger. From the twelfth to the fourteenth century the family of Fitz-Otho were the royal goldsmiths. At the close of the fourteenth, however, William Faringdon was even more renowned for his skill than the Fitz-Otho of the time, for he it was whom the monks of Beverley chose to fashion a gorgeous new shrine, set about with images and fretted with fine tracery, for the relics of their patron saint.

The medieval English word for a bell-founder was bell-yetter, but in medieval Latin he was called an *ollarius*, or pot-

EFFIGY OF ELEANOR OF CASTILE
From a cast in the National Portrait Gallery   98

POEMS

maker, apparently because he also made domestic utensils—skillets, pans, bowls, and saucepans—of metal. The making of bells was an elaborate process, and is illustrated in a magnificent window in York Minster—a window in memory of a bell-founder of the city, Richard Tunnoc by name. The medieval bell was an object of affection as well as of veneration. When it was hung in its tower it was christened with almost as much ceremony as if it had been a baby. Sometimes it received the name of the donor, sometimes that of some appropriate archangel or saint. Gabriel was the godfather of many bells, most of which bore the inscription **Missa De Cœlis Habeo Nomen Gabrielis.** When the godfather was a mere mortal his name was apt to cling to the bell in a shortened and familiar form, and so we have Great Tom of Oxford, called after Cardinal Wolsey, and Bell Harry at Canterbury, the gift of Henry VIII.

RUNNING BELL-METAL
INTO A MOULD
From the Tunnoc window,
York Minster

In ancient contracts and indentures the men who cast the metal effigies for tombs are usually described as 'coppersmiths,' but the metal they employed was more commonly bronze or 'latten.' Alabaster, Caen stone, and Purbeck marble were greatly admired and extensively used, but the difficulty, danger, and expense of transporting large masses of heavy stone over long distances made resourceful craftsmen cast about for some simpler and yet not less effective and durable material. The earliest surviving example of a gilt-bronze effigy is that of Eleanor of Castile in Westminster Abbey. That much-loved and much-mourned Queen is there represented as a sort of conventional angelic type, and it is improbable that Master William Torel, who wrought her monument, attempted to make a faithful portrait of her. The coppersmiths to whom was entrusted the task of producing the gorgeous sepulture of Richard II and Anne of Bohemia were Nicholas Broker and Godfrey Prest, and they received £400 for their handiwork, which included the life-sized figures of the King and Queen, twelve images of saints and angels, a number of enamelled escutcheons, two lions for the King's feet and an eagle and a leopard for the Queen's. The process employed was the 'waste wax' process, by which a layer of wax was first modelled over a core of rough timber, and then skilfully replaced by molten metal. Henry V was, for a time, much more splendid than his father's victim, the hapless Richard, for *his* wooden image was encased not in latten, but in silver. Now, however, only the battered, headless, oaken core remains, while Richard and Anne, though their interlocked hands have been destroyed, lie stately and impressive upon their goodly tomb hard by.

Monks often acted as architects and sometimes as masons in the building of the great English cathedrals. The monks of Gloucester "with lively zeal" helped to complete the vaulting with which their flat Norman roof was replaced after the offerings of pilgrims at the tomb of Edward II had made their Abbey rich enough to undertake rebuilding operations on a large scale, and it is recorded of St Hugh, the saintly and witty Bishop of Lincoln, that he carried hod-loads of hewn stone and of mortar during the building of the glorious Angel Choir of his cathedral. In this structure, as an ancient chronicler says,

the art equals the precious materials; for the vault may be compared to a bird stretching out her broad wings to fly; planted on its firm columns, it soars to the clouds. On the other hand the work is supported by precious columns of swarthy stone . . . of this are formed those slender columns which stand round the great piers even as a bevy of maidens stand marshalled for a dance.[1]

The "swarthy stone" was a variety of dark fresh-water limestone thickly dappled with the fossil shells of the *Paludina*

[1] Translated by G. G. Coulton in *Social Life in Britain from the Conquest to the Reformation*.

carinifera family, and called, from its place of origin on the Dorsetshire coast, 'Purbeck marble.' Before it could be worked with the chisel it required patient smoothing with sand and vinegar, but it took a beautiful high polish and was much in favour among architects and builders at the time when the great English cathedrals were in process of construction.

As the 'masons' marks' roughly scratched upon countless walls and pillars attest, the services of professional masons were often enlisted to supplement volunteer labour. Inspired by the presence and example of a man like St Hugh of Lincoln, a man so charming and so lovable that a bird as fierce as a swan would follow him meekly about and a community as unsentimental as the Jews of Lincoln shed tears when he died, we may imagine that the masons worked as cheerfully as the monks, each vying with his comrade as to who should toil longest and to best purpose. It was otherwise at Cambridge, during the fifteenth century, when the workmen were liable to be fined for such offences as coming late, playing, chiding, or hindering their companions at their task. We know something about the characters and personalities of these English labourers of the late Plantagenet period. One of them would never work at all unless he happened to be in a working humour; another, whose name—Robert Goodgroom—ought surely to be held in remembrance, was such a stickler for his dinner-hour that never under any circumstances would he take up his tools and begin again until the clock should "smyte."

The materials with which the masons would have to work varied according to the neighbourhood in which the church was being erected and the wealth of the foundations or endowments. Dusky speckled marble from Purbeck, fine cream-coloured limestone from Caen, in Normandy, sandstone from Northern and Western England, were shipped by sea and carted by land to many parts of the realm, but as a general rule builders took what was nearest to their hands, flint and chalk in Kent and Sussex, magnesian limestone in Yorkshire, oolitic limestone in Somersetshire, Wiltshire, and Lincolnshire. The neatness and symmetry of the wall surface would also depend upon the medium used, flint being hard and irregular, lime-stone easily cut into ashlar work and fitted together. The beginning of Plantagenet rule in England coincided with what might almost be called an epidemic of church-building in villages and small towns; the great cathedrals belong rather to the middle of the period, and the exquisite chantry chapels, chapels of knightly orders, and college chapels, such as the Beauchamp chapel at Warwick, St George's, Windsor, King's College Chapel, Cambridge, and the chapels of the choir at Tewkesbury, to its close.

A MEDIEVAL CARPENTER
WITH HIS TOOLS

In the Rome of Numa Pompilius, as we have seen, there were goldsmiths, potters, and carpenters. In medieval England this last most useful craft had split into two

CARVED OAK CHEST
Thirteenth century

divisions. The carpenters undertook the heavier sorts of woodwork, and made roof-beams and doorposts and stakes for fences, while the joiners did the smaller jobs, and produced

window-frames, barge-boards for gables, stools, chests, cupboards, and shelves. In the days when most houses were
built of wood the carpenter had more to do with house-building
than had the mason. His tasks were almost as multifarious as
those of the smith; for he, or his 'opposite
number,' the joiner, might have to make a
gibbet for a felon, a pallisade for a tourna-
ment-ground, a coffer for a damsel's dower,
a perch for her bridegroom's hawk, a trestle-
table for a banquet, a pew for a church, or
a beam for a barn; and even then there were
many other quaint and necessary tasks that
only a carpenter or a joiner could tackle.
Closely allied—indeed, almost identical—
with theirs was the craft of the woodcarver.
The strong, instinctive craving for beauty
which seems to have thrilled through the
brains and the hands of medieval craftsmen
found nowhere a more delightful outlet than
in the woodcarver's handiwork. His material
was usually oak, and his conventional designs
were usually architectural—suggested, that
is to say, by the complicated tracery which
he saw in the windows and chancel-screens
of churches and cathedrals. When his imagination was allowed free play the result was
often charming. Look, for instance, at the
pew-end wrought by a fifteenth-century

PEW-END
Fifteenth century

carver of East Anglia, with its exquisite little ship and its neatly
curled waves, its huge fish plunging downward, and its sun,
moon, and stars all shining joyously together in the sky.

Many of the objects made by the carpenters and joiners
required, and received, an enlivening touch of colour from the
hand of another craftsman, the painter-stainer. Until the reign
of the first Tudor king the 'peyntours' and the 'steynours'

formed two separate crafts, but in the year 1501 they were "knyt, joyned, and unyd togiders." It is probable that in earlier times the 'peyntour's' was a rather more responsible and dignified employment. He would paint real pictures, as we now understand the term, portraits of notabilities and representations of saints and heroes. Whoever painted the portrait of Richard II which now hangs in the choir of Westminster Abbey, he was the direct spiritual and artistic ancestor of Van Dyck and Reynolds. The 'peyntour' worked for kings and for churchmen. He adorned crude grey walls with rich frescoes, and chancel-screens with bravely hued scenes from Holy Writ. In England he lagged behind a little, being outstripped by the Flemings and the Florentines, who got ahead of him in anatomy, perspective, and craft-methods. The English 'peyntour's' human figures are queerly stiff, his lions and dromedaries amaze the beholder, his paven walks and tiled floors seem to slant giddily up to the sky. More humble and even more primitive were the productions of the 'steynour,' who painted any sort of woodwork that wanted painting, and would bedaub with violent colour the sail of a ship, the sign of a tavern, or the back-cloth for a mystery play. As was the case with the carpenters and joiners, these two craftsmen, the 'peyntour' and the 'steynour,' were constantly invading each other's domains, and chiding each other for doing so. They linked hands, however, against the presumptuous plasterer when *he* ventured to work with plaster of many colours.

Another medieval English industry into which the arts of carving and painting entered was the production—at one time it was almost the mass-production—of sculpture in alabaster, tinted and gilt. Though the handiwork of the fourteenth- and fifteenth-century English sculptors seems to us quaint and crude rather than impressive or beautiful, it was in great demand, and was even exported to the Continent. Most of their output was absorbed by churches, big and little, and the private chapels of the rich. They did not work on a large

104

ALABASTER ALTAR-PIECE OF THE FIFTEENTH CENTURY

Victoria and Albert Museum

scale, nor did they attempt bold effects or strain after realistic representations of nature. As they concentrated upon retables and altar frontals, they often chose as their subjects scenes from the closing phases of Christ's earthly life: The Last Supper, the Way of the Cross, the Crucifixion, Resurrection, and Ascension. There is a curious charm and dignity about some of their slim, stiff images, and occasionally a touch of genuine beauty upon the face of a saint or an angel, though a certain uncouthness, angularity, and grotesque *naïveté* may provoke a smile.

Many crafts which under primitive conditions were practised at home, such as weaving and baking, became specialized and detached as life became more complicated. Tribal settlements expanded into villages, villages into towns, and the weaver and the baker make their appearance. Spinning continued to be a woman's task—whence the term

FRAGMENT OF BYZANTINE SILK
Twelfth century

'spinster,' denoting an unmarried woman, whose obvious duty it was to sit meekly at home and spin—but weaving was both too heavy and too intricate an art for the amateur to practise with success.

In England the early weavers used the fibres of the flax-flower and the fleeces of sheep on their rough looms. As we shall see later, more sumptuous fabrics of woven silk were imported, first from Byzantium and Cathay, and later from Florence, Venice, and Genoa. Saracenic influence at the Court of Charlemagne probably accounted for the skill of his daughters in the delicate art of silk-weaving.

The commoner sort of woollen cloth produced in England was called 'burel' or 'borel,' and was brown or grey in colour. Metaphorically the word came to mean a layman, as distinct from a clerk, and thence an unlettered person of homely wit. Chaucer's Frankeleyn, before he begins his story, says:

> But, sires, by-cause I am a burel man,
> At my bigynnyng first I yow biseche
> Have me excused of my rudê speche.

During the Irish campaign of 1172 the soldiers of Henry II were clad in this 'burel,' and large quantities were purchased by charitably minded potentates for distribution among the poor and needy. The garments of the villeins would be made of 'burel.' Very different was the fine scarlet cloth purchased at Lincoln for the use of the King's Majesty in 1182, costing 6s. 8d. an ell, equivalent in modern money to £7 a yard. In the wardrobe accounts of Henry III we read of "blues of Beverley, scarlets and greens of Lincoln, scarlets and blues of Stamford"; and though one never hears nowadays of Beverley blue or Stamford scarlet, the phrase 'Lincoln green' still calls up pleasing visions of archers and yeomen clad in tunics the colour of the forest trees.

The popular idea that the art of weaving was introduced into England by Philippa of Hainault is an erroneous one. What had happened was that the English weavers had lagged behind their Continental brethren. In the fourteenth century, what did the Englishmen do? Instead of girding themselves for the fray, instead of making—and keeping—stern resolutions to beat the Flemings and the Florentines at their own game, they adopted the policy now known as 'restriction of output,' or 'ca' canny.' To this Edward III objected vigorously. And to counteract the results he encouraged weavers to come from Philippa's own country to her adopted one. He even went so far as to suspend temporarily the rules governing the standard breadth of cloth, and to flout Magna Carta, which had decreed that dyed and russet woollen stuffs should be two ells wide from selvage to selvage.

As is the case with many other crafts, this craft of weaving did not stand alone, and was not sufficient unto itself. The red and black cloth of which the Countess of Ulster gave a pair of breeches to "Galfridus Chaucer" passed through many processes between the time that it left the sheep in the form of wool and the time that it reached the tailor in the form of cloth. It

A WOMAN WARPING WOOL

had to be dyed, fulled, stretched, and shorn, as well as woven; so here come the dyer, the fuller, the tenter-man, and the shearman. The dyer used a great deal of woad (*Isatis tinctoria*) to produce his blues and greens and purples; for scarlet he had recourse to a little insect, the Alkermes, Kermes, or Scarlet Grain insect, the female of the *Coccus ilicis*, formerly supposed to be not a beast, but a berry. (Hence the phrase 'dyed in grain,' meaning dyed with pure scarlet.) There was in London a well of which the waters were said to be particularly good for the preparation of this beautiful scarlet dye. When once the wool was dyed and woven the turn of the fuller came. He took the cloth, scoured it with the greyish-green clay known as fuller's earth to remove the grease, steeped it in a trough of water, and trampled upon it, or caused his assistants to trample upon it, till it was of the desired thickness and suppleness. In the thirteenth century a device was introduced by which a wooden bar was made to do the work formerly done by the human feet, but this bar had to be kept in motion on the principle of a mill, and where water-power was not available man-power—and very often woman-power—was used. On the outskirts of most medieval towns were fields known as 'tenter-grounds,' set apart for the stretching and drying of the fulled cloth. Where White-chapel now stands once lay the tenter-grounds of London. The phrase 'to be upon tenter-hooks' is a survival from the days when this process was commonly practised, and when the meaning of the metaphor would be plain to every one that heard it. Unscrupulous people were wont to impair the quality of the cloth by stretching it to excess. With the aid of a lever a length of thirty yards might be extended to thirty-five. Edicts and ordinances and royal statutes forbade this practice, but in vain.

After the luckless cloth had been thus racked it was combed all over with teazles, the burr-like heads of the *Dipsacus fullonum*, to draw out the loose ends. Here the work of the fuller ended and that of the shearman began. He took his sharp shears and trimmed the surface of the cloth, all shaggy from the teazles. It was now ready to be rolled in bales, and those bales were, in due course, sold,

> To such as chose to buy 'em.

In the reign of Edward IV a very curious political poem was written which throws a gleam of light upon the conditions then prevailing in the woollen trade and among the weavers. The writer is perturbed by the fact that the finest English fleeces are exported in such enormous quantities to foreign lands, and he urges that in future only the coarsest sort of wool should be "sowlde" to England's rivals. He would fain see the weavers of his own country as prosperous as those beyond the sea, and in particular he deplores the conduct of those merchants and cloth-makers who force their "spynners, carders, wevers . . . dyers and scheremyn" to take half their wages in merchandise,

The wyche makythe the poreylle [1] to morne and wepe :
Lytyll thei take for theyre labur, yet halff ys merchaundyse;
Alas! for reuthe, yt ys gret pyté.

Akin to the weaver were the capper and the glovemaker, but they had associations with yet another craft, that of the leather-worker, and he, in his turn, with yet *another*—that of the tanner, to whom, in his turn, the cordwainer or shoemaker was related. The tanner seasoned ox-, cow-, and calf-hides by steeping them in a preparation of oak-bark; his 'opposite number,' the tawyer's raw material was the skin of the deer, sheep, or horse, and he used alum and oil. Leather was second only to wool in its importance as an article of commerce. From it were made stout jerkins for the villeins and fine, close-fitting suits for the knights, scabbards and 'hangers,' or straps for swords, shoes, belts, girdles, purses, saddles, harness, even tankards to hold beer or wine. These leather tankards came to be known as 'black jacks,' and astonished foreigners, beholding them, hastily concluded that Englishmen drank out of their boots!

The cordwainer, or 'corveiser,' was so called because at one time most of the leather he required was imported from Cordova in Spain. During the Plantagenet period he had to keep
pace with various strange fluc-
tuations of fashion, notably when
the 'Cracowe' or 'Pologne' was

THE 'CRACOWE' OR 'POLOGNE'

introduced from Poland and won the favour of Richard II's dandified courtiers by its fantastic and exaggerated form. In the fourteenth century a shoemaker's apprentice received only eighteenpence a week, but he might claim as his perquisite eight pairs of shoes. What was the price of a pair of shoes of the simplest type we may gather from the fact that the beneficent, though not particularly strong-minded, Henry III in 1266 ordered a hundred and fifty pairs of shoes, at $4d.$ and $5d.$ the pair, for distribution among the poor.

[1] poor people.

109

The armourer had to keep pace with the corveiser, and to make the sollerets, or foot-pieces, of the plate armour in the form then favoured by the dandies of the day. To these sollerets in time of war, and to the 'Cracowes' in time of peace, were attached the spurs made by another craftsman, the spurrier. When the wearer of the spurs was a knight they were made golden with much gilt. If his horse were draped with heavy housings and thick they were made very long, so as to penetrate those housings and reach the animal's flank. By degrees the more beautiful, and more humane, rowel-spur, with its many-toothed revolving wheel, replaced the wicked little prick-spur of the early medieval period. Not only knights and huntsmen needed this means of inspiring their steeds to fresh activity. Chaucer tells us of the Wyf of Bathe that she had

On hire feet a paire of sporès sharpe.

CHAPTER VI
MERCHANTS AND MERCHANDISE

LONG before the soil of Britain had ever been scarred by the sandalled feet of the Roman legionaries the Britons were in touch with Rome by means of the Gaulish and Greek traders who frequented such centres of British life as Avebury and Stonehenge, and who brought into this semi-civilized land golden staters of Philip of Macedon and glass jars from Tyre. There was also an intermittent exchange of British bronze for Scandinavian gold between the

GOLD STATER OF PHILIP OF
MACEDON

Celts of the West and the Norsemen of North-eastern Europe. During the Roman occupation, when *fora*, or market-places, formed the centres of all the important towns, and when distinctively British coinage was minted at Eboracum (York) and Londinium Augusta (London), trade between Britain and the Continent flourished mightily, only to be partially—if not entirely—eclipsed during the earlier decades of the Anglo-Saxon period. As those coarse and fierce invaders became more civilized—probably by contact with conquered Britons, whose minds and customs still bore the imprint of Rome—the pulse of commerce began to beat again. It is certain that the early Britons had learned—or had taught themselves—how to make boats of a more elaborate type than the scooped-out tree-trunk and the hide-covered coracle, because when Cæsar was in Spain he ordered his soldiers to construct hurriedly some boats "after the fashion of those used by the Britons," with keels and ribs of timber, and hulls woven

III

of osier and covered with stretched skins. The whole course of English history might be expressed in pictures of the different sorts of ships and boats that have played their part in it,[1] from the galleys of the Phœnicians and the Romans, the transports of the Saxons, the dragon-ships of the Norsemen, the brightly painted fleet of William the Conqueror, the merchant vessels and pilgrim vessels of the Middle Ages, the cogs, and carracks, and caravels, the high-pooped ships that sailed to Virginia and went forth against the Armada, down to the black-and-

ANGLO-SAXON BROOCH OF GILT BRONZE

white timbered frigates and ships-of-the-line that harassed Napoleon.

Trade between England and the Continent was certainly beginning to revive when the Emperor Charlemagne wrote to Offa, King of Mercia, complaining that many English merchants were wont to pose as pilgrims in order to obtain safe-conducts through the Imperial dominions, whereas their real purpose was to smuggle their wares and dispose of them by the way. These wares were probably small articles of jewellery, in the making of which Anglo-Saxon gold-smiths had come to excel. During the reign of Athelstan (925–940) a law was made that every merchant who had fared thrice across the wide ocean at his own cost was "thegn-right worthy," and entitled to rank as a *thane*, a position lower than that of the *eorl*, but considerably higher than that of the *ceorl*.

This law shows that as early as the tenth century English

[1] See *The Sailing-ship*, by R. and R. C. Anderson (Harrap).

merchant-venturers were daring the perils of strange seas and strange lands in quest of gain and gold. In the *Colloquies* of Ælfric [1] we make the acquaintance of a merchant of the early eleventh century, who tells us, "I go aboard my ship with my goods, and go over sea and sell my things, and buy precious wares such as this country does not produce, and bring them hither—brocade and silk, gems and gold, various raiments and dyestuffs, wine and oil, ivory and brass, copper and tin, sulphur and glass, and so forth. And," he adds, with engaging simplicity, "I wish to sell them dearer here than I buy them there, that I may get some profit wherewith I may feed my wife, and myself, and my sons."

These goods came chiefly from Constantinople to Venice, thence overland to Flanders, and so by sea to England. Hides, ropes, tall tree-trunks for ships' masts, and ironwork of various kinds came from the Scandinavian countries, and the lands lying round the Baltic or eastward of the North Sea. English exports were seldom manufactured goods at this time. Cornish tin was still a valuable raw material, and so was lead from the Peak district in Derbyshire. The excellence of the fleeces of the English flocks was early recognized, and even before the Conquest the great weaving industry of Flanders drew its chief supplies from England. As time passed sheep-breeding for the sake of wool became so profitable that many great landowners transferred to pasture acres of land formerly used for corn and other crops, until under the Tudors it was said metaphorically that in this country you might see a strange sight—sheep devouring men.

Domesday Book, William the Conqueror's great register of his island realm, gives us many interesting glimpses of the activities of the Anglo-Saxons, and we learn there that salt was both a staple commodity and the basis of a flourishing industry. Salt-works to the number of 727 and 5000 salt-mills are

---

[1] For a further account of these *Colloquies* see *The Boy through the Ages*, by D. M. Stuart (Harrap).

mentioned in the Norman record. The export of manufactured articles developed slowly for more reasons than one. It must be remembered that the monasteries were busy centres of crafts-manship, and that mills, forges, masons' yards, and carpenters' shops were attached to all the principal monastic houses, where monkish millers, blacksmiths, masons, and carpenters were glad to work for the laity, either in exchange for a donation to the coffers of the abbey or priory, or simply "for the love of God and His saints."

The first effect of the Norman Conquest was to impoverish all the small centres of trade in the larger towns and villages, and to handicap and harass the traders. Soon, however, there came a great inrush of new influences and activities. The Normans had much to teach the Anglo-Saxons, and, half reluctantly, their lessons were tackled and mastered.

A SHOP IN THIRTEENTH-CENTURY PARIS

French and Spanish ships began to discharge and reload at the southern harbours of England. Craftsmen from France and from the Low Countries came in legions and settled in the country and plied their several callings unmolested. The towns—which means the trading communities dwelling in the towns—began to prosper, and to be jealous of their privileges, and to petition the king for charters, not often in vain. Then merchants banded themselves together into guilds, for their protection and to ensure fair dealing all round. Of these guilds we shall have more to say later. Theirs was a very important *rôle* in the Middle Ages, quite apart from their assigned sphere of trade and commerce, for they were the fosterers of many arts, the drama among the rest.

Till the thirteenth century the chief exports of England continued to be raw materials, and the agents through whom the export trade was carried on were not, as a rule, Englishmen. German merchants of the *Hansa*, a league formed for trading

TRANSPORTING MERCHANDISE FROM ASIA

purposes and later known as the Hanseatic League, were firmly established in London in the thirteenth century, and had as their headquarters a walled fortress—the Steelyard—on Thamesside, where, when their gates were bolted at curfew, they could bid defiance to all the King's horses and all the King's men. The first Hansa merchants hailed from Cologne and Lübeck and Hamburg; they were followed by others from Flanders and the Netherlands. Trade with Genoa began at the period of the Third Crusade, and flourished mightily. Russian tallows and Chinese silks reached Western Europe through the trafficking that went on between the Hansa merchants and them of Mus-covy and Cathay at the great fair held in Novgorod. The pioneers of international finance were the Jews, who, though persecuted and oppressed, were enormously successful as bankers and money-lenders, and introduced the system of bills of exchange long before the great Christian banking houses of the Medici and the Fuggers began their operations.

In England itself there were as yet no great manufacturing cities, no centres of world finance or of international commerce. The time was far distant when the introduction of steam-power should change the "green and pleasant land" into a partial wilderness of fuming chimney-stacks and huddling slums. Home trade was kept in circulation chiefly by means of weekly markets and annual fairs. Thus buyers and sellers were brought together, and foreign merchants were given opportunities to do business with their English brethren, already a not inconsider-able part of the community. The Roman *forum* had dis-appeared, and nothing equal to it in architectural dignity was seen in England until Tudor times, but already in the days of the later Plantagenets the merchants of London and other trad-ing centres had recognized meeting-places, sometimes adapted from existing buildings, sometimes planned and built for that express purpose. In 1445 Sir Simon Eyre, draper, destined to be the hero of a charming Elizabethan comedy, *The Shoemakers' Holiday*, adapted as a granary and market a large old house which in the reign of Edward I had belonged to one Sir Hugh Neville. Eyre had this house reroofed with lead, whence it came to be known as Leadenhall Market. On the east side he built a chapel dedicated to the Holy Trinity where Mass was sung every day for the benefit of the people working or trans-acting business in the market.

Another Plantagenet merchant who received the honour of knighthood and who enriched the City with a stately building was Sir John Crosby. This worthy citizen was a woolstapler, an alderman, and a Member of Parliament. Like most

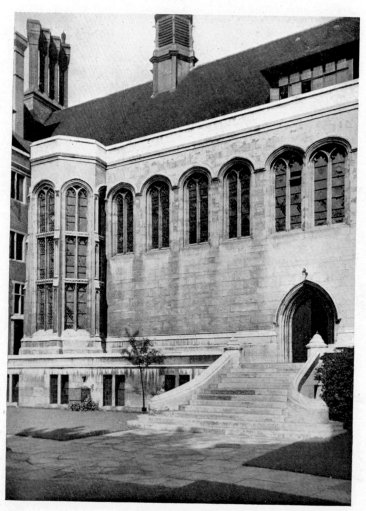

CROSBY HALL
As re-erected at Chelsea
Maud Shelley photo

116

Londoners, he wore the white rose during the Wars of the Roses, and stood stoutly for Edward IV.   During the summer of 1471, when Edward was in hot pursuit of the flying Lancastrians after his victory at Tewkesbury, a certain Thomas Neville, commonly called the Bastard of Fauconberg, seized the occasion to make a bold thrust at the capital.   Under Henry VI this man had been Vice-Admiral of the English Channel, but, finding his occupation gone, he turned pirate, and gathered round him, as an old historian puts it: "many Persons of desperate Fortunes."   Marching through Kent at the head of a motley army, he pitched his camp at Southwark.   Apparently he was not devoid of military talent, for the plan he devised was quite a good one.   He detached a portion of his troops and landed them on the north bank of the Thames, to the east of the City walls, with orders to attack Aldgate and Bishopsgate, while he himself, with the main body, attempted to take London Bridge by storm and burst into the City from the south.   Good though the plan may have been, it was brought to naught by the stubborn valour of the Yorkist Londoners, who repulsed the attack on their gates with such energy that Fauconberg and his followers were fain to recross the river and return whence they had come.

Foremost among the defenders of Bishopsgate was John Crosby.   He, indeed, had a strong personal motive for wishing to keep this violent rabble out of Bishopsgate Street, since only a year earlier he had leased a plot of ground there from Dame Alice, the Prioress of St Helen's, upon which he was building a house of stone and timber, "very large and beautiful," says Stow, "and the highest at that time in London."   How large and how beautiful this house was we may guess if we go and contemplate that portion of it which, having been demolished in 1908, is now re-erected in More's Garden at Chelsea.   When Edward IV returned in triumph from the West he knighted several of the citizens who had fought so manfully for the white rose, and John Crosby was of their number.   Such were the merchants of Plantagenet London, valiant and princely, dwellers in noble houses, wielders of doughty blades. Crosby's effigy upon his tomb in St Helen's wears the collar of suns and roses which was the badge of the Yorkist dynasty, and his armour would be appropriate to a knight whose knighthood was his sole profession and who had never either worn the robe of an alderman or plied the quill of a merchant.

Fairs were held under royal charter in such places as London, Chester, Oxford, Winchester, York, Hull, Cambridge, and King's Lynn, to mention only a few. While the fair was in progress all other trading in the neighbourhood was at a standstill. Streets of wooden booths, each assigned to some particular craft or calling, were erected on some suitable stretch of open ground, and thither hied a motley crowd, some

PILGRIMS' TOKENS
(1) The Compostella cockle-shell
(2) St Thomas of Canterbury

of them sober and solvent and honest, and some of them most decidedly the reverse. Foreign merchants, come to barter wines and spices, silks and fine cloths, were recognizable by their strange jargon and by certain peculiarities of costume. They came from places as far asunder as Hamburg and Genoa, Bruges and Florence, Rouen and Cologne. Some of them had been in strange, remote lands, and were tanned by the ardent Eastern sun or scarred by the bitter winds of the Baltic. Many had combined a little prudent piety with their quest of gold, and had made a point of visiting any famous places of pilgrimage that happened to lie upon their way. You could tell these pious merchants at a glance, because their hoods or cloaks would be decorated with pilgrims' tokens, in pewter, or lead, or, perhaps, in gold.

At the markets much of the business was between neighbours,

118

and much of it was exchange rather than sale. Thus, a farmer would barter a load of hay for so many barrels of salt or tar. People depended on the fairs for merchandise that was hard to come by, but the markets provided them with most of the simple necessities of their very rough and simple lives. One of the most famous fairs of the Middle Ages was held on the green and pleasant hill to the east of the ancient city of Winchester, the hill of St Giles, upon whose festival the fair began. Young monks from the monastery in the valley below were given a 'fairing' every year that they might supply themselves with fresh penknives, and it is interesting to realize that even in these far-off days the knives made in Sheffield were known to be excellent. Pedlars plied their irregular trade among the frequenters of the fairs, and even the poorest ploughman was not so poor that he could not bring home to his wattle-and-daub cottage a little brooch or button for his womenfolk.

Some idea of the enormous volume and variety of the merchandise passing over and under Old London Bridge may be gathered from the list of wares upon which Edward I levied toll for the "repairing and sustaining" of the bridge. These included such diverse items as wax and lead, sugar, liquorice, and ginger, musk and mace, red squirrel skins and grey, woad and wine, scarlet cloth, fustian, linen, and cloth-of-gold, lampreys, salted haddocks, and eels, arrow-heads and staves, pigs, sheep, and cows.

Certain English towns were distinguished by the name of *Staple* towns—a name that carried with it both responsibilities and privileges. It was at these places, and these alone, that *staple* commodities—wool, hides, leather, lead, and tin—might be sold to buyers from overseas. The wool-trade, one of the most vital, was controlled by a group of men known as the Merchants of the Staple. A wool-pack was their recognized badge or emblem, and appeared on the seals of certain of the Staple towns. The seal of Lincoln represents the Virgin and Child standing *upon* one, and on that of Boston we see St Botolph, the patron saint of the town, standing *behind* one of generous proportions. Edward III, whose bride, Philippa, was a Fleming, greatly desired to encourage trade between Flanders and England, and to this end made, in 1353, the Ordinance of the Staple, regulating transactions between foreigners and his own subjects in such a wise as to give a sense of security to the former. Many of these Flemish merchants deserted their own flat, reedy homeland for the eastern and southern shires of England. You see their monumental brasses, side by side with those of native-born neighbours, in ancient churches of East Anglia, and there is one in All Hallows, Barking, by the Tower. Very well pleased with themselves do all these worthy fellows look, with their neatly cropped hair, their furred gowns, and their rich chains. England could—and *did*—produce the finest fleeces, but not for many years were English weavers as skilful as they of Flanders. Chaucer mentions it as something quite remarkable about his Good Wyf of Bathe that she had such skill in cloth-making.

STAPLE SEAL OF BOSTON

She passèd hem of Ypres and of Gaunt.

The Merchants of the Staple dealt chiefly in wool; their great rivals, the Merchant Venturers, who came into prominence in the reign of Henry IV, exported woven cloth and miscellaneous merchandise.

BRASS OF A WOOL MERCHANT IN NORTHLEACH CHURCH

As trade increased seaports grew in importance. Those on the south coast had an especially momentous part to play, for they were the chief points of contact with France both in peace and war. Along the coast of Kent and Sussex runs a chain of seven ancient towns of which only two—Hastings and Dover—are still awake and astir to-day. The other five—Romney, Hythe, Sandwich, Winchelsea, and Rye—are tranquil and drowsy places now; the grass grows high among the cobble-stones that once clattered be-neath the hooves of pack-horses; the old belfries that once rang the alarm when French raiders landed, and English farms went up in flames, have long forgotten the very sound of a call to arms. Winchelsea and Rye are the most picturesque, but their five sister-towns were the original Cinque Ports. To them Edward I granted a royal charter, whereby they were exempt from taxation and from the

SEAL OF WINCHELSEA

jurisdiction of the law, in return for which they had to provide fifty-seven ships for fifteen days each year. This exemption seems to have been abused by the Cinque Ports, for they actually embarked upon piratical expeditions, and made treaties as if they formed an independent State. Billingsgate was the most ancient of the London wharves, and thither came ships from Normandy laden with dried peas and red wine, and fishing-vessels with cargoes of great grey cod from the North Sea. In the West Bristol was the most flourishing port, and thence sailed many a proud ship, with gilded fo'c'sle and painted sails, on a perilous voyage of discovery. Thence went John and Sebastian Cabot, in 1497, on a journey which lasted for two months, and ended on the wild and then unrecked-of coast of Labrador.

During the reign of Henry VI anxious observers in England began to fear that English merchants were less prosperous and triumphant at sea than they had been in earlier and more aggressive days under more forceful sovereigns, and that the maritime strength of the country was beginning to diminish. The Flemings, in particular, were regarded as dangerous rivals, despite the smallness of their country and their dependence upon England for supplies of wool to keep their weavers busy. One of these anxious observers "dropped into poetry" and composed an interminable but very energetic 'poem' "exhortynge alle Englande to kepe the see enviroun, and namelye the narowe see, shewynge whate profete commeth thereof, and also worschype and salvacioun to Englande and alle Englyshe menne."

The nameless author declares that the "trewe processe of Englysh polycye" is to

> Cheryse marchandyse, kepe th' amyralté
> That we bee maysteres of the narowe see.

In peace or in war he shows how the very life of the island depends upon her control of that "narowe see" dividing her from her traditional rivals and enemies, the Flemish and the French. He does not fall into the error of underestimating the strength or the wealth of the peoples competing with England in the fierce struggle for sea-power and international trade, and he gives long lists of the "commodytees" of Spain, Flanders, Portugal, Prussia, Genoa, Florence, Venice, and even Iceland, from whose "costes colde" the men of Scarborough were wont to bring large cargoes of cod for salting. Regretfully this patriot-poetaster looks back to the days of Henry V, when the King built great ships at Southampton, the *Trinity*, the *Grâce Dieu*, the *Holy Ghost*, and others. What, he asks, was Henry's purpose?

> It was not ellis but that he caste to be
> Lorde rounde aboute enviroun of the see.

Alas, that this gallant prince should not have lived to carry out his design, and that they who came after should have failed to follow whither he led the way!

The growth of commerce led indirectly to the spread of education. Merchants had either to keep accounts or to hire clerks to keep them, and if the Church held an absolute monopoly in learning it was obvious that trade must either wither away or lapse into priestly hands. Such hands were often both worthy and capable, as witness the practical business ability of many prelates, priors, and stewards of monastic houses; but, on the other hand, trade was the very life-blood of the nation, and in order that it should circulate freely one obstruction after another

TALLY-STICKS OF THE THIRTEENTH CENTURY
(*a*) A private tally ; (*b*) an Exchequer tally

had to be removed. Even so, well into the nineteenth century the unlettered people, the simple folk who would modestly describe themselves as poor scholars or none, were fain to check their buying and selling with the aid of notched sticks called *tallies* (French, *taille*, a notch), such as may now be seen in many museums.

Many arts and sciences owe much to the fostering and stimulating influences of commerce. Geography and navigation obviously do. When once the Crusades had established contact between the Eastern and the Western world a stream of merchandise began to flow from Asia and Africa to Europe. Alongside it flowed another, invisible, but none the less swift and strong—a stream of *ideas*. Those stout-hearted early merchants brought home in their square-sailed, high-prowed ships more marvellous cargoes than they recked of; together with casks of Spanish and Greek wine, bales of silk and barrels of spices, they brought legends and fables, tales of far, fantastic lands and peoples, and of even more fantastic birds and beasts.

123

And they were carriers of *words*, as we shall soon realize if we pause to think how many terms in common use are of Oriental origin, and must have been brought westward by the merchants of the Middle Ages. Spices were very valuable in the days when large quantities of meat and fish had to be pickled every autumn in anticipation of the needs of the winter; so, by way

of Greek, we get the Hebrew word 'cinnamon'; 'tariff' is not much unlike the Arabic *ta'rif*, a notification; 'scarlet' has a Persian source in *saqalat*, red cloth; 'muslin' came first from Mosul, and 'gauze' perhaps from Gaza; 'alcove' is Arabic, and 'awning' Persian, and both the science of algebra and its name travelled northward from Moorish Spain. In order to describe a man playing chess or eating an orange, or a lady putting jessamine in a jar, an English scribe had to use almost purely Persian words; but if, in addition,

CHAUCER'S MERCHANT
From the Ellesmere MS.

his hero or heroine happened to eat ginger he all unwittingly 'tapped' the language of a civilization even more ancient than that of Greece, Sanskrit, the mother of all the (so-called) Indo-European tongues; for in Sanskrit *kringa vera* means 'the horn-shaped thing,' and every one who has seen the root of the ginger-plant will understand how that name came to be given to it in Vedic India. With these Oriental words came Oriental fairy-tales and romances, which were retold under grey skies long before *The Arabian Nights* was translated into French in the eighteenth century. That is how it chanced that Chaucer's Yong Squiér began to tell the "story of Cambuscan bold"—that wonderful story of a brazen steed and an enchanted glass which, unfortunately, he "left half-told." "The Par-

124

doner's Tale" is another importation from the East, and so, in all probability, is the Merchant's. The Merchant himself, though his portrait fills only fifteen lines of the Prologue, is a lifelike figure, with his forked beard, his Flemish beaver hat, his neatly clasped boots, and his impressive talk about his rising profits, his bargains, and his journeys. Chaucer tells us, too, that

Wel koude he in eschaungé sheeldés selle.

These 'sheeldés' were not such as knights and heralds bore, but French coins, *écus*, stamped with the lilied shield (*écu*) of France.

Coinage and currency were subjects of much interest to the merchants of the Middle Ages. If unscrupulous kings tampered with the mint, and debased, clipped, or imperfect coins got into circulation, buying and selling became difficult, and profits uncertain. The English pound represented a pound's weight of silver, and the Hanseatic Mint at Lübeck, where the purest coins were struck, adopted this standard of value. The merchants were the bankers of early days, and spendthrift princes, eager to make war on their neighbours or to give dowries to their daughters, were glad to dip their royal fingers into the coffers of such men as Richard Whittington. And then the lender began to assert his power over the borrower, and merchants were knighted, and monarchs deigned to sit at meat in Guildhall. The first recorded Lord Mayor of London was Henry FitzAlwyn; like John Gilpin, "a draper bold was he," though probably not a *linen*-draper only. The city over which he held sway was moated like a castle, girdled with walls, tufted with trees, and bristling with spires and towers. He and his successors had many duties to perform besides guarding the rights and liberties of their city. They had to organize a sort of rough and ineffectual police-force, to persuade (or compel) their fellow-citizens to keep lamps alight before their doors after dusk, to abstain from flinging all household refuse into the middle of the road, and to prevent their pigs and ducks from wandering to and fro, and hampering the progress of passers-by, both mounted and on foot. Moreover, if a baker's loaves were under-weight, or a vintner sold bad wine, the culprit was haled before the Lord Mayor, who decreed some suitable penance, causing him, perhaps, to sit in the stocks, or to stand in the pillory, amid the jeers of his more virtuous fellow-citizens.

Though the story of Richard Whittington, mercer and four times Lord Mayor of London, has passed from the sober realm

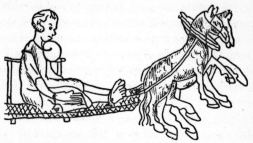

BAKER DRAWN THROUGH THE STREETS TO A PILLORY
From a manuscript

of history to the golden world of fairy-tales, what we know of the real man, albeit it is not much, is yet enough to give us a very good idea of the career, the activities, and the ideals of a great London merchant of the early fifteenth century. Richard was the younger son of a Gloucestershire knight, and, like many younger sons, had to turn to trade for a livelihood, since the more glorious calling of his father might not be his. Whether his immortal cat was a real animal, or the name of a ship in which he invested all his money, historians cannot agree, and it is improbable that anybody will ever know. But Richard is no misty myth, like King Arthur, as Henry IV and Henry V had reason to know when they borrowed from him the funds they needed for their wars at home and abroad. Many of the archers who fought so well at Agincourt, and of the bows and shafts with which they harried the French cavalry, were hired and purchased with coins from the coffers of Whittington. There is a legend, so picturesque that one hopes it may be shot through with truth, that when the great mercer, in the year 1421, feasted the victor of Agincourt and his queen, he "concluded the banquet" by flinging into the fire, instead of the aromatic spices which it was then the fashion to cast upon the flames, a wad of crackling parchments dangling with royal seals—the king's bonds to repay the modest sum of £21,000 lent to him by his host.

Whittington died a very wealthy man, and his manner of disposing of his wealth shows us what manner of man he was. The plight of the prisoners in the ruinous and reeking prison of Newgate, the sad case of the aged and friendless poor, the sufferings of "sick persons and young children," the hardships of needy scholars lacking books, had all touched his heart; and even the difficulties of Londoners who had to go far afield in quest of water, and to bring it home laboriously in heavy buckets or barrels, did not escape his keen and yet compassionate eyes. So with the ample funds that passed from his cold grasp to their living hands, his executors rebuilt Newgate, founded almshouses, repaired St Bartholomew's Hospital (already an ancient foundation), contributed to the glazing and paving of the 'new' Guildhall, and bore half the cost of building the library attached to it; and they also had conduits made, and 'bosses' set up, in Billingsgate and Cripplegate, whence the people of those thickly populated districts might draw supplies of pure water—or, at least, water as pure as the conditions of the time could afford! Well might it be written upon his long-vanished monument in the church of St Michael, Paternoster Royal:

> *Ut fragrans nardus*
> *Fama fuit iste Ricardus.*

> (Fragrant as spikenard
> The fame was of this Richard.)

In Whittington's century—the fifteenth—London had come into her own as the "flower of cities all," an almost unimaginable

London, fair and smokeless, with her belfries gleaming pearly white against the clear sky, and silver-winged swans floating on a Thames shaded by the apple-trees in the orchards of the riverside houses.

In towns where 'shops'—as the term was then understood—were open all the year round trade seemed to concentrate about the principal church. Thence developed those squares, surrounded by quaint old houses and under the very shadow of some tall belfry tower, which one sees both on the Continent and in England. Pious traders may have liked to "ply their music" under that shadow, just as the chafferers of prehistoric Britain liked to meet under the shadow of the grim triliths of Stonehenge. In London the nerve-centre of commerce lay—as it still lies—east of St Paul's and north of it.

A typical fourteenth- or fifteenth-century shop would occupy the front ground-floor portion of the house, open to the street, windowless, but closed with stout oaken shutters at will. At the back the workshop, where the various wares were produced for sale, might lie, or a store-room for surplus merchandise. Above a jutting upper storey of one or two rooms served as a dwelling for the merchant and his family, while the apprentices slept in the chamber below. The richer merchants, such as Whittington, Eyre, and Crosby, built themselves stately houses, but never lived outside the confines of the City, and seldom separated their place of abode from their place of business. A list of the belongings of a London vintner of the fourteenth century exists, and shows how meagre the furnishing of one of these shop-houses might be. This man, who was a member of the Vintner's Company and the owner of several tenements, possessed only one table and two chairs, one mattress, one candlestick, one frying-pan, one spit, six blankets, seven sheets, three basins, and two tubs; but he had also six silver spoons, and a cup made of a coconut with a cover and a foot of silver.

The streets in what we should now call the 'business

quarter' of the City were full of movement—and of noise. Beside the open booths, and under the projecting upper stories of the houses, leather-lunged 'prentices were calling out the

SHOP BOOTHS AT BLACK GATE, NEWCASTLE-ON-TYNE
Fourteenth century

merits of their master's goods, while wandering hawkers and pedlars added their voices to the din. A visitor from the country would find himself beset on all hands, one man offering him hot ribs of beef, another cherries still on the bough, another spectacles, another felt hats. There were bad characters about, then

I

as now. One such bewildered countryman (John Lydgate) has recorded his sensations when he lost his hood at one end of the City in the morning, and before sunset had recognized it ("I knew it as well as I knew my creed," says he) hung up for sale at the other.

A MERCHANT OF THE
THIRTEENTH CENTURY

CHAPTER VII

TRADE GUILDS AND COMPANIES

EACH year, in the month of November, when a new Lord Mayor of London is elected, we are duly informed to which of the great City companies he belongs. If we hear that he is a Fishmonger, a Merchant Taylor, a Stationer, or a Grocer we probably know better than to conclude that he spends much— or any—of his time weighing fish, or cutting out clothes, or selling notepaper, or dealing in sugar and spice; but we have a pretty clear idea as to what calling was followed by the founders of his guild or company. If, however, we learn that his lordship is a Loriner, a Whittawyer, or a Cordwainer we may— quite excusably—feel a certain amount of uncertainty on the point. The Loriners, by the by, were the makers of horses' bits and bridles and horse-furniture in general; the Whittawyers were the tanners of white leather; and the Cordwainers, as we have already seen, the makers of shoes.

There were, as we know, craft guilds in the Rome of Numa Pompilius, and there were certainly craft guilds in Roman and in Anglo-Saxon London. When William the Conqueror granted a charter to the citizens of his new capital he confirmed the rights and privileges which had been theirs "in the days of King Edward," when that saintly Anglo-Saxon with the lint-white locks had held his Court where afterward his shrine stood, on the place once called Thorneye, or Thorn Island, but then, and now, known as Westminster. Of all these rights and privileges the people of London were exceedingly tenacious, and the merchants of London, the heads of the great trade guilds, played a noble part in defending and maintaining the freedom of the City, and the integrity of its customs, against

131

any would-be meddlers in high places. Doubtless their motives were selfish in the main, and it was their own interest rather than that of the community at large which they had in mind; but London owed much to these stubborn and courageous merchants of hers, especially in the days before Parliament was, and when the monarchs with whom they had to deal were

HALL OF THE MERCHANT VENTURERS, YORK

men of alien blood and speech.   Guilds have always stood firm for ancient privilege against new tyranny.   Philip of Burgundy, in the fifteenth century, found the guilds of Ghent a very tough nut to crack, and even after he had won a temporary victory over them, and had forced them to deliver up their painted banners, and their leaders to walk barefoot in the snow beseeching pardon, he did not succeed in breaking their spirit, as his granddaughter, Mary of Burgundy, found to her cost.   Princes and their councillors must have looked with very mixed feelings at these powerful organizations.   On the one hand these guilds were troublesome and dangerous; they stirred up strife if they thought that their liberties were threatened.   On the other

132

hand they simplified the task of government by enforcing regulations as to just weight and measure, and good workmanship; and, most important of all, they were exceedingly wealthy. Many a monarch has found himself short of money; and a monarch who is hard up is an easier person for a merchant to deal with than a monarch would be who had no need either of gifts or of loans. So the medieval guilds, notably they of London, held more than one royal ankle in a noose of gold.

The status and scope of a City guild or company were usually fixed by a royal charter long after custom and tradition had established them. The charter itself would be a thing of no little stateliness and beauty, written in fair and symmetrical script upon tough vellum, adorned with a huge capital letter enclosing a coloured portrait of the sovereign by whom it was granted, and tipped with a heavy disk of wax bearing the impress of the royal seal. In some cases the granting of the charter belongs to a period so remote that the actual document has not survived to tell the tale. Henry I, the scholar-king, granted one such to the weavers of London, but the bakers and fishmongers were in the field before them. Thus it is clear that the crafts concerned with the feeding and clothing of the multitude early became powerful enough to claim regal recognition and special privileges. As conditions changed and trade expanded new guilds came into being, and new charters were sought and bestowed. The reign of Edward III witnessed the entire reconstitution of the London guilds, which then dropped the old name of 'guild,' and called themselves 'crafts' or 'mysteries.' This word 'mystery' has completely lost its medieval significance. In the fourteenth century it meant a handicraft or art, what we should now call a 'skilled occupation.' For example, the man who *chopped* wood was not exercising a 'mystery,' but the man who *carved* it was. If we go back to the very beginnings of this very ancient word we shall find that in the language of the Greeks there is a verb *myein*, which means to close the lips or eyes. Thus, when a novice was initiated into one of the secret rites of the goddess Demeter at Eleusis he had to promise never to reveal what he had seen and heard; thence came the word *mystes*, a person who *had* been so initiated. Many centuries later, in a very different world, the word was still associated with the idea of initiation. The

INITIAL LETTER OF ELIZABETH'S CHARTER TO THE CORDWAINERS

apprentice had to learn his trade, he had to be introduced by degrees to its various secrets, and thus the trade itself came to be called a 'mystery.'

Under Edward III [1] an Act was passed that "all artificers and people of mysteries" should each choose his own 'mystery' before the next Candlemas; and that, having so chosen it, he should thenceforth "use no other." The passing of this Act led to the expansion and multiplication of the London craft fraternities, which then for the first time began to elect Masters and Wardens to govern them. As the centuries rolled onward

---

[1] It was this king who granted the City companies the right of electing Members of Parliament, a right which remained theirs until the passing of the Reform Bill in 1832.

134

new trades sprang up, demanding new charters. The Fan-makers, Coachmakers, and Spectacle-makers are mere infants compared with the older City companies. The Barber-surgeons, who combined the duties of the hairdresser with those of the bloodletter, received *their* charter from Henry VIII, whom Holbein has depicted in the very act of granting it. The pinched and pallid features of his daughter Elizabeth appear at the beginning of rather a large number of these coveted documents. Her Majesty was always glad to oblige her loving people, when it could be done with little or no expenditure of coin on her Majesty's part.

In the Middle Ages a man's working week was not sharply divided from his day of rest and prayer. All his activities were coloured, and many of them were shaped, by his religion. Each 'mystery' had its patron saint. The iron-workers were under the patronage of St Dunstan, himself a blacksmith, and a doughty one; did he not pinch the nose of Satan once between his red-hot tongs? As Dunstan wrought in divers metals, the goldsmiths claimed a share of his attention, though they had a sainted goldsmith of their own in the person of St Eligius or Eloi, who, before he became Bishop of Noyon in the far-off days of King Dagobert, was himself a skilful worker in gold. St Crispin, himself

> a cobbler bold,
> Who wrought with hammer and with awl
> In Soissons-city once of old,

took the cobblers and cordwainers under *his* protection. Each guild or craft fraternity had, therefore, some link or association not only with some special saint, but also with some special parish church. To restless modern minds, absorbed by the pursuit of "the things that are seen," the preoccupation of the medieval mind with "the things that are unseen" seems strange and quaint. The merchants of the Middle Ages were not less fond of gain than are the merchants of to-day, and if the crafts-men loved their work a little better than does their twentieth-century successor it may be because their work was more interesting and less mechanical than his. No! The great line of cleavage between us and them consists in the difference of spiritual outlook. Just as the perspective of a medieval picture is different from that of a modern one, so the perspective of the medieval intellect was different from ours. The horizon, the point where earth ended and heaven began, was always nearer and higher to *their* vision. And, just as their earth was not our earth, their heaven was not our heaven. Not yet had Galileo and Copernicus startled and dismayed mankind by proving that this planet is not the centre of the universe, and that the sun and moon do not move meekly through the year in order that man, that noble creature, may have light. The abode of the blessed was above man's head—and not so very far above, either; the abode of the damned was below his feet—and not so very far below. Gates of pearl barred the sunset; surely Paradise lay just beyond. Gusts of flame rose from certain mountains; obviously hell lay just beneath. When all these things were clear and plain, is it surprising that few people, or none, should have paused to ask, "Whither are we bound?" The question would have smacked of impiety. According to your conduct upon the common level of living and breathing men, you were bound either upward or downward when your time came to die.

Since it is certainly better to move upward and toward the light than to move downward and toward the darkness, he is a wise man who so directs his doings that his own last step shall be in the right direction. So firmly had the medieval mind taken hold upon this simple idea that the whole fabric of medieval thought and action bore its impress. The most grasping merchant, the least industrious craftsman, was equally responsive to its appeal. Whence it followed that the two chief aims pursued by the great City companies and the humble village guilds were the same—the prosperity of their members in this world, and their eternal welfare in the next.

The duty of such a fraternity to its dead brethren was no less important than its duty to those who still lived. A proportion of its funds was set aside that Masses might be sung for the repose of the souls of departed members; chaplains were hired, chantries were endowed, altars were dedicated, or candles were offered, according to the wealth and importance of the guild. Very often, as in the case of the Merchant Taylors, a sumptuous pall was purchased for use at guild funerals. And all the

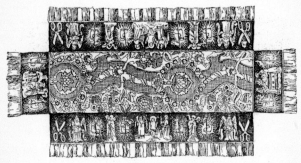

THE MERCHANT TAYLORS' PALL

members attended these funerals, clad in robes of the same fashion, and bearing lighted tapers in their hands. There are many ancient churches up and down England where a niche cut in a massy pillar marks the spot where once a guild altar stood. At Eastbourne, in Sussex, there are two such niches, sacred long since to St Margaret and St Bartholomew.

It was not only upon such mournful occasions that the brethren proceeded in a body to their own special church. There were occasions of rejoicing and thanksgiving, and there was the annual festival of their patron saint. From the custom of uniformity of raiment, observed whenever the guild went forth 'in force,' grew the "*Livery* Company" idea. The gowns worn by these good citizens were usually of two colours, but the particular colours might be altered from time to time, if such were the whim of the Master and Wardens. For example, in

1414 the Grocers wore scarlet and green; four years later they preferred scarlet and black; in 1428 scarlet and deep blue pleased them better; in 1450 these fickle and gorgeous Grocers chose a new livery, and wore gowns of crimson and purple 'in grain.' The Master of each company had, in addition, a rich chain and a pendant jewel to wear during his term of office, and with these insignia he was solemnly invested at his election. Was and still *is*, for the City of London clings stubbornly to her

LEATHER-SELLERS' CROWN

ancient customs, and the existing City companies follow much of the old ritual, and have let little of the old ceremony fall into disuse. The Masters of the Girdlers and the Leather-sellers had 'crowns' as well as chains of office. It was, perhaps, natural that the Goldsmiths should show a marked affection for gold and silver trimmings. When Anne of Bohemia, the youthful bride of Richard II, was welcomed by the citizens of London at her first coming among them in the year 1382 the word went forth that *all* the companies, irrespective of their separate and characteristic liveries, should be clad in plain black and crimson. Perish the thought! said the gallant Goldsmiths. So when the procession assembled it was found that *this* company, at least, had paid no heed to that decree. Gay and gallant the Goldsmiths of London must have looked that day, for their scarlet cloth was adorned with silver bars, and dotted with silver trefoils, and the black cloth was enlivened with clasps or knots of gold and silk.

138

Nine years later the City companies bore a prominent part in the pageants wherewith London greeted the return of the same feckless King after a quarrel during which he had actually threatened to rescind the charters granted to the City by his ancestors. The cause of the dispute was Richard's chronic lack of money and the firm refusal of the London merchants to lend him a thousand pounds. However little they may have liked the security offered by their would-be debtor the Londoners liked the results of his displeasure even less, and when, at the intercession of Anne of Bohemia, the breach was healed and the King intimated that he would make a State progress through London they vied with each other in devising magnificent shows wherewith to greet him. In Cheapside the conduit was made to gush with red wine and white, at St Paul's sweet music arose from a band of minstrels playing cymbals, psalteries, horns, lyres, and viols; at Ludgate the King and Queen were welcomed by angels swinging thuribles and scattering flowers; at Temple Bar there was a sort of menagerie of stuffed wild beasts and of men disguised as dragons, leopards, and lions in the centre of which sat St John the Baptist, the patron saint of those Hospitallers who now kept the courts where once the Templars gloried and drank deep.

By solemn vows the members of these fraternities bound themselves to be loyal to the craft, and obedient to its rules, and to bear them in brotherly wise each to the other. They held frequent meetings to discuss the affairs of the company, and public affairs too, in as far as the company was affected; and, as we have seen, they assembled, clad in their livery, upon certain pious and solemn or joyful and stately occasions. But there was another kind of assembly which from time to time drew them together and gave them a chance to show their magnificence, and this was when they held a great banquet. Then it was indeed a case of "Todgers's could do it when it chose." By the middle of the fifteenth century all the principal guilds had their own halls, Guildhall (it is quite incorrect to call it *the*

Guildhall) being the common meeting-place of them all. The Great Fire of 1666 swept away most of these halls, and many of them were rebuilt by the indefatigable Christopher Wren; but we can imagine pretty well what they must have been like in their glory. Their interior roofs would be of timber, perhaps not quite as beautiful as the roof—still remaining—of Westminster Hall, but very similar in plan and execution; their stone walls would be masked within by panels of carved oak, and on days of ceremony draped with tapestry, or with painted cloths. In all the decorations the badge or armorial bearings of the company would be kept much in evidence. The Grocers' camel did duty as a salt-cellar, while the stag of the Leather-sellers, the dolphin of the Fishmongers, and the pelican of the Poulters appeared and reappeared on banners and goblets. Sometimes the companies entertained each other at banquets, as the Skinners and the Merchant Taylors have done every year since 1483, but more frequently the guest, or guests, of honour would be royal or noble personages, or distinguished foreigners visiting England. Not only was civic pride unfolded in the adornments of the hall and the board. Each company vied with the other in the gorgeousness of the actual meats and wines. The Salters had their own recipe for a Christmas pie, and a prodigious pie it must have been, for it contained, among other ingredients, pheasant, hare, capon, partridge, pigeon, the hearts, livers, and kidneys of sheep, eggs, spices, mushrooms, and, of course, salt. The Brewers were famed for the excellence of the swans served at their feasts, and in 1425 no fewer than twenty-

THE MERCERS' CUP,
1499

140

one of those beautiful birds were sacrificed for the benefit of the Brewers' guests. (One hopes that Chaucer's monk [1] was among those invited!) About this time Richard Whittington, Mercer and Lord Mayor of London, was very much annoyed with the Brewers, whom he accused of what would now be called 'profiteering' in beer, and of overcharging the public. But the Brewers declared that Whittington's wrath was not purely righteous and disinterested wrath; it was, said they, the excessive splendour of their swan-banquets, not the excessive dearness of their beer, that caused him to fume and rage. Carving at such banquets as these was a grave and responsible task. The Lord Mayor's carver was a permanent official, who lodged in the chambers over Bishopsgate.

Many a 'prentice lad as he stood at the shop-door bawling "What d'ye lack?" or toiled away at the chasing of a flagon, or the grinding of colours in a mortar, or the glazing of a jar with thick green glaze, must have cheered himself with bright dreams of the day when he too might wear the particoloured gown of one of the great Livery Companies, and have a share in its banquets, perhaps sitting at the side-tables, with the other liverymen, or if fortune were kind, and if he himself became a Master or a Warden, sitting at the chief table, on the dais, and pledging royal guests as the two-handled loving cup went round.

Medieval London, like the London of to-day, was a great commercial centre, a city of many merchants, worthy and wealthy men, and of innumerable 'prentice lads and craftsmen and poorer folk, such as porters and wherrymen, who practised no 'mystery' and who for their livelihood depended upon the prosperity of the more fortunate. Provincial trading centres, some of them still flourishing, such as Bristol, Ipswich, and Coventry, others now shrunk into picturesque decay, such as Winchester and King's Lynn, had also their trade guilds and craft fraternities, highly organized, with rules, rights, and privileges similar to those of their 'opposite numbers' in the capital.

[1] See page 147.

As these guilds multiplied they did much to encourage the spread of education. Records and accounts had to be kept and a knowledge of those marvellous, mysterious, but very useful arts, reading and writing, became more and more desirable, and even necessary. Such knowledge, however, remained beyond the great mass of the people till a much later period, and shop-keepers, like tavern-keepers, found it necessary to hang gaily hued, conspicuous signs over their doors, by which illiterate passers-by might recognize both the building and the wares sold

If it plese ony man spirituel or temporel to bye ony pyes of two and thre comemoracios of Salisburi use enpryntid after the forme of this preset lettre whiche ben wel and truly correct, late hym come to Westmonester in to the almonesrye at the reed pale and he shal haue them good chepe.

Supplico set cedula

CAXTON'S ADVERTISEMENT

therein. Even Caxton, whose patrons might be supposed to have some inkling of letters, set up his presses and sold his books "At the Sign of the Red Pale." There was a great variety in the tavern-signs of the larger towns, but the country ale-wife was usually content with an ivy-bush, or a bunch of green twigs tied to a pole. By this signal the thirsty wayfarer knew that here was a 'pull-up' for him: and thence comes the proverb "Good wine needs no bush." Where the wine and ale were known to be excellent, there would never be any dearth of cus-tomers, whether the bush were hung out or no! In London shop-signs were not permitted to hang lower than nine feet above the road level, lest some passing horseman should knock his head against one of them.

If, upon some medieval highroad, or in some narrow medieval street, you had encountered a group of four or five men all wearing gowns of the same colours and fashion, you would pro-bably have concluded that they all belonged to the same 'mystery,' and in nine cases out of ten you would have been right. In the tenth case, had you questioned them, you would have found that though they followed different occupations, they were fellow-members of one of those numerous guilds, half social, half religious, which then abounded, and which took the place of the modern club, friendly society, insurance company, and church guild all in one. There were five such men among Chaucer's pilgrims, a haberdasher, a carpenter, a weaver, a dyer, and a tapestry-maker:

> And they were clothed alle in o [1] lyveree
> Of a solémpne and greet fraternitee;
> Ful fressh and newe hir [2] geere apikèd [3] was;
> Hir knyvès werè chapèd [4] noght with bras,
> But al with silver, wroght ful clene and weel,
> Hire girdles and hir pouches everydeel. [5]
> Wel semèd ech of [t]hem a fair burgeys [6]
> To sitten in a yeldehalle, [7] on a deys. [8]

Women were admitted to some of these societies, and the children of the brethren might share the benefits of membership, as at Ludlow, for instance, where dowries were provided from the common funds of the guild for virtuous young girls whose fathers were too poor to give them any. If the property of any member were damaged by fire or flood the guild came to his rescue; sometimes it even supported his widow and orphans if he met with an untimely death. These guilds were not incorporated under charters; they needed none. They were created and held together by the interest and profit of all the separate units thus welded into one. Many of their activities were purely pious; but the piety was seldom detached from the divine grace of charity. For example, a gentlewoman called Margaret Odom, who lived and died in Bury St Edmunds toward the end of the fifteenth century, bequeathed certain houses and lands to the Candlemas Guild of that town, so that a priest

---

[1] one.   [2] their.   [3] trimmed.
[4] capped or tipped.   [5] every whit, or every one.
[6] burgess.   [7] guildhall.   [8] dais.

should "say Mass in the chapel of the gaol, before the prisoners there, giving them holy water and holy bread, every Sunday," and so that seven faggots of wood should be given to "the prisoners of the long ward of the said gaol" from All Saints' Day (November 1) to Easter Day each year. As a large number of candles had to be kept burning at various altars on behalf of the members of the guild, both dead and living, fines for infringement of guild rules were often paid in wax instead of in money.

In spite of this constant mindfulness of death, and this all-pervading remembrance of the unseen and the unknown lying beyond the dear familiar things of every day, the medieval guild-brethren were by no means a gloomy tribe. They were too true to the national type, that sturdy, cheerful, indomitable type, whom neither alien kings nor English weather could daunt or dismay. Even the priests who sang dirges for their souls were not sombre-looking fellows, if we may believe the commentator on the *Constitutions* of Cardinal Ottoboni. The Cardinal desired that clerical dress should be simple and decorous; he remarked that some of the English priests looked more like soldiers. And the scandalized commentator added that some of them were conspicuous not only for their gay attire, but also for their open-mouthed laughter (*risus dentium*).

CHAPTER VIII
MEN OF DIVERS CALLINGS

A VERY important member of the household of a well-to-do merchant, a knight, or a noble was the chief cook. His duties were arduous, and his responsibilities were many. He had to direct operations in a vast, vaulted kitchen, with only the most primitive utensils, with a limited and precarious water-supply, and with spits and ovens served by smoky wood-fires. To aid him he had a regiment of scullions and turnspits, but it was he who received the reward of his master if the dinner were a success, and his rebukes if it were a failure. His raw materials, the ingredients of his various masterpieces, were of bewildering diversity, and on special occasions, such as wedding-feasts and complimentary banquets, he was expected to produce allegorical dishes and symbolical table-decorations, as well as the usual courses that went to the long-drawn-out medieval meal.

Among Chaucer's pilgrims was a cook who knew, among other things, how to "rooste, and sethe, and broille and frye," and how to make "poudrè-marchant tart" and "galyngale," "mortreux," and "blankmanger." Now, in the reign of Richard II the officers of the household of that gorgeous but ineffectual king drew up a sort of cookery-book, called *The Forme of Cury*, giving recipes for a large number of dishes, including those in the repertory of Chaucer's cook. Unfortunately these forerunners of Mrs Beeton did not trouble to state the quantities of the ingredients, nor the time necessary to bring them to perfection, so any attempt to produce one of these Plantagenet dishes to-day would be a bold one, and a perilous. Let us suppose that a fourteenth-century cook had been called upon by his noble master to make 'mortreux,' and that he had in his possession a copy of *The Forme of Cury*. These are the instructions which he would find:

> Take hens and pork, and boil them together. Take the flesh and hew it small, and grind it all to dust. Take grated bread, and mix it with the broth, and add to it yolks of eggs. Boil it, and put therein powder of ginger, sugar, saffron, and salt—and look that it be stiff.

If 'blankmanger' were to be the next course the cook's first proceeding would be to take "rys"—we do not know how much

PREPARING DINNER
Luttrell Psalter

—pick it, wash it, and boil it in milk of almonds until it "al to brest"—*i.e.*, till the separate grains were broken up. Then, while it cooled, he would take the livers of hens or capons, "grynd [t]hem smal," and boil them in white grease. Before this dish was served blanched almonds and saffron would be sprinkled on the top, giving an agreeable effect of silver dusted with gold. The tart-tasting 'poudré-marchant' was a spiced powder used to flavour certain concoctions; not less sharp and aromatic was 'galyngale,' the root of an East Indian plant. The cook depended much upon imported spices, pepper, ginger, cinnamon, the poetically named "grains of Paradise" (probably a sort of cardamom-seed), and sunflower-seeds. The usual sweetening medium was honey, but the importation of sugar was fairly general in the fifteenth century and not unknown a good deal earlier.

146

Not only had the medieval cook to provide elaborate dishes and fanciful table-decorations; he had to cater for patrons with incredibly large appetites, who spent many hours in what one can only call 'guzzling,' and whose feats at the board might have put some of the greediest of the ancient Roman emperors to shame. For example, when Richard Nevill, Chancellor of England under the gay and debonair Edward IV, celebrated his elevation to the Archbishopric of York by a banquet, he and his guests, by their united and unremitting exertions, disposed of one hundred tuns of wine (a tun amounted to two hundred and fifty-two gallons), one hundred and four oxen, six wild bulls, one thousand sheep, three hundred calves, two thousand pigs, four hundred swans, a hundred dozen quails, eight hundred bream, six hundred pike, twelve porpoises and seals, a hundred and four peacocks, and two hundred pheasants. Among the company were several men whose destinies were to clash darkly in the succeeding reign. Richard, Duke of Gloucester, with his clever, sardonic face and his uneven shoulders, sat near John Tiptoft, Earl of Worcester, whom we met before as one of Caxton's patrons; not far away would be the Earl of Warwick, acting as steward to his reverend kinsman, and Lord Hastings, comptroller of the feast, and the cupbearer, Lord John of Buckingham.

Several of the items in the menu would startle diners of to-day. We do not usually think of porpoises and seals, swans and peacocks, as 'likely starters' for the dinner-table. Yet Chaucer assures us that his monk loved a fat swan "best of any roost"; and we know that among the birds which a well-taught young "squiér" would "carf biforn his fader" bustard, crane, and heron were numbered, as well as peacocks and swans.

Many of the wines with which these mighty repasts were cheered had remarkably pretty names—vernage, vernagelle, malvoisie, muscadel, clarey, malmsey, pyment, osey, and tor-rentyne—yet it may be doubted whether any of them would appeal to a modern palate. They were, as a rule, very harsh, strong, and sweet, crushed from thick-skinned Tuscan grapes (with which the stalks were often fermented), or brought by perilous ocean paths from Epidaurus and Alicant, Cyprus and Sicily.

> The grete galees of Venees and Fflorence
> Be wel ladene with thynges of complacence,
> Albe spicereye, and of grocer's ware,
> Wyth swete wynes.

So wrote a fifteenth-century versemonger, and with good reason. As pure drinking-water was practically unobtainable—especially

DISHING UP
Luttrell Psalter

in towns—wine was a necessity, and vintners throve. In the cellars of these thriving vintners there were no bottles. The use of glass bottles with stoppers of cork did not become general until the eighteenth century, and the "swete wynes" were kept in casks and barrels.

A favourite beverage was hippocras, so called from the fanciful name given to the bag through which it was strained— "Hippocrates' sleeve." As befitted a wine which had for its godfather the founder of the Dogmatic School of Medicine, hippocras was believed to be exceedingly medicinal, and many ailing people were dosed with it, no doubt with their own full approval and ready consent.

The formula for making hippocras is given with great detail in a quaint old manual entitled the *Boke of Nurture*, written by

148

one John Russell, usher to another, an earlier, and a rather different Duke of Gloucester, "Umfrey . . . that prynce peerless," as he calls him. This was Humphrey, the bookish brother of that quite unbookish sovereign Henry V, the same Humphrey whose library, bequeathed to the University of Oxford, formed the nucleus of the famous Bodleian.

John Russell informs us that in order to prepare hippocras for some one of high degree you should take ginger, cinnamon, grains of Paradise, sugar, and sunflower-seeds, while for those of humbler rank the ingredients are ginger, canella, pepper, and honey. In either case two or three gallons of red wine are required. You will then need three clean pewter basins and three straining-bags of fine cloth. The powdered spices and the red wine are mixed in the first pewter basin and then strained off into the second. Before straining it into the third you must "feel it well both with mouth and tongue" to see if the flavour is correct. If it be, you may serve the hippocras with wafers, "both in chamber and cell."

In an age when most people ate and drank a great deal too much, when even a royal prince took a bath but seldom, and when all the Roman plans and practices of water-transport and domestic sanitation had been forgotten and lost, it was inevitable that there should be a tremendous number of epidemics and a tremendous amount of ill-health. Medical 'science,' though shot through with gleams of good sense, was in the main a very queer sort of science indeed, compounded of superstition, credulity, tradition, and prejudice.

The medieval doctor had no knowledge of most of the drugs and chemicals used in medicine to-day, many of which are brought from then undiscovered lands or created by processes then not invented. To atone for this poverty of materials, he had a vast number of herbs, and he used quantities of queer things, animal, vegetable, and mineral, in compounding his mixtures—things that nobody would think of eating or drinking in these less courageous and less enterprising times. In the libraries of the great monasteries were preserved ancient text-books and treatises on medicine, written by Byzantine-Greek and Anglo-Saxon experts, some of whose counsels sound eminently wise, while others are decidedly alarming.   Later there was a gradual diffusion of science, both the false and the true varieties, from the great University of Salerno, on the Gulf of Naples. The marvellous knowledge of drugs and their properties pos-sessed by the Spanish Moors and by the Greek, Sicilian, and Italian Jews penetrated to Salerno, which, owing to its geo-graphical situation, was in touch with the more ancient civiliza-tions of Northern Africa and of the Near East.   The university was wealthy, and grew wealthier through the gifts of the grateful patients who had been cured of various ills in the hospital attached to it.   Almost alone among the medical schools of the Middle Ages that of Salerno followed something approaching scientific methods of study and treatment.   There were women lecturers and women students at Salerno, and no doctor was licensed to practise unless he had a fuller knowledge of his sub-ject than could be derived from books.   At Oxford, on the other hand, books were the be-all and the end-all of the medical student, who was obliged to read the treatises of Hippocrates, the priest-physician who dwelt on the island of Cos in the sixth century before Christ, and those of Galen,[1] the philosopher-physician of Pergamos, Imperial healer to Lucius Verus and Marcus Aurelius in the second century of the Christian era. Between six and eight years had to be spent conning these vener-able text-books, but the student was in no danger of getting into an intellectual groove, for the course of study at the English university included astronomy, music, and logic.

Hippocrates was responsible for that long-enduring and far-stretching 'theory of humours' upon which the whole fabric of

---

[1] " There is nothing improbable in the supposition that men who had consulted Galen as to their health may have walked along the Roman cause-way in Cheapside on which, fifteen hundred years later, Wren placed the foundations of the present tower of St Mary-le-Bow," writes Dr Norman Moore in *The Study of Medicine in the British Isles*.

medicine rested for some two thousand years, the theory to which both Chaucer and Shakespeare allude more than once, and which embedded itself firmly in the imagination of mankind throughout Christendom. According to this theory there are four 'humours,' blood, phlegm, yellow bile, and black bile, composing the human body. When these exist in the correct proportions a man is in good health; but if any be present in excess he becomes ill. If the first dominate him he is apoplectic and full-blooded ('sanguine'); if the second, he is cold and indolent, whence the adjective ' phlegmatic'; if the third, he is simply bilious (and 'choleric'!); if the fourth, melancholy —a word which tells its own story when one remembers that it comes from the Greek *melas*, black, and *chole*, bile.

CHAUCER'S DOCTOUR
OF PHISIK

The Doctour of Phisik who rode to Canterbury with Chaucer's pilgrims was well acquainted with the Hippocratic theory, and had not confined his studies to the books of the university medical course. Chaucer gives a list of fifteen authorities with whom the Doctour was familiar, and of that fifteen six are Arabs, three are Asiatic Greeks, one is a Carthaginian, two are Greeks of classical times, one a Frenchman of (probably) Scottish origin, and two, John of Gaddesden (Gatesden) and Gilbertus Anglicus, are Englishmen. The library of St Augustine's monastery at Canterbury contained, at that time, no fewer than ten of the books mentioned by Chaucer. In the earlier Middle Ages the physician was very often in Holy Orders as well—John of Gaddesden was a Bachelor in Theology as well as a Doctor of Medicine— but by degrees the two callings diverged, and the layman-physician took the place of the physician-priest.

The Doctour of Phisik, that "verray parfit praktisour," was a layman. He knew, Chaucer tells us, "the cause of everich malade," and his patients profited greatly by his knowledge of astronomy and "magyk natureel." Astronomy in this instance does not mean the scientific observation of the nature and movements of the heavenly bodies, but rather 'astrology,' the study of their alleged influence upon, and association with, the lives of individual men. When it was firmly believed that each man's life was shaped and coloured by the movements of certain stars

TREPANNING

through the signs of the zodiac the duty of the physician was obviously to pay the closest attention to the doings of these stars, to relate their position to the patient's case, and to take care to prescribe and administer all his remedies in a way, and at a moment, when the starry influences were favourable. Here "magyk natureel" played a great part. The herbs of which some of the medicines were compounded were more effectual if they were gathered when the moon was at the full, or on the wane, as the case might be. No conscientious doctor would bleed anybody or trepan him or draw his teeth when the moon was in the sign of Taurus (the Bull) or Pisces (the Fishes), or fail to make sure that when the physic he prescribed was actually administered the moon was in Libra (the Scales), Scorpio (the Scorpion), or Pisces, with Saturn *not* in conjunction.

Among the more curious and costly ingredients in medieval physic were *aurum potabile*, gold-dust made drinkable, diamonds ground to powder, and pearls dissolved in wine. Chaucer remarks drily of his Doctour that he kept the money which he had earned during the Black Death:

> And yet he was but esy of dispence,
> He keptè that he wan in pestilence,
> For gold in phisik is a cordial,
> Therefore he lovède gold in special.

Yet this "verray parfit praktisour" does not seem to have been over-niggardly in his personal expenditure, for he was sumptuously clad in crimson and blue cloth

Lynèd with taffata and with sendal.[1]

To be richly and imposingly clad was, indeed, part of the professional etiquette of a Plantagenet physician. He relied upon his beauteous robes no less than upon his dignified, infallible air to impress both the patient and the patient's friends. Langland alludes somewhat bitterly to this practice, and seems to enjoy the idea that if men were wiser, and the world better ordered, these gorgeously clad 'doctours' would have to lay aside their splendour and work with their hands. But then Langland was always exasperated by the sight of goodly outer trappings, in which he descried the livery of "Lady Meed," that great power whom Shakespeare calls "tickling Commodity," and to whom all too many men pay service and homage still.

The good old fellows who wrote medical treatises sometimes chose very pretty and romantic names for them. Thus Bernard of Gordon, one of the professors at Montpellier early in the fourteenth century and one of the authorities known to Chaucer's erudite Doctour, entitled his book *Lilium Medicinæ* ("The Lily of Medicine"), while John of Gaddesden called his the *Rosa Anglica* ("The English Rose"), and John Mirfield, of St Bartholomew's Priory Hospital at Smithfield,[2] called his the *Florarium Bartholomei* ("The Flower-garden of Bartholomew").

John of Gaddesden died in 1361, so his life covers the first half of the fourteenth century and overlaps that of Chaucer for some twenty years. He studied at Oxford, grappling with the seven arts—grammar, rhetoric, logic, arithmetic, music, geometry, and astronomy—and with the three philosophies— natural, moral, and metaphysical. In 1309 he took the degree

[1] See p. 172 for an account of the silk fabrics in use in medieval England.
[2] See p. 191.

of Doctor of Medicine, and in 1314 he compiled the *Rosa Anglica*, a book of which he himself writes with engaging modesty, "As the rose excels all flowers, so doth this volume excel all treatises upon the practice of medicine." Master John borrows freely from Greek, Jewish, and Arab physicians, but there is much in his book which suggests that he himself was an active and highly esteemed "praktisour." Among his patients he numbered the highest in the land, including one of the king's sons. The king at the time would be Edward II, but we are not told whether the sufferer were his eldest son, afterward Edward III. At all events, John's treatment of his disease— smallpox—was eminently successful, for he records that the prince made a good recovery, and was unmarked. Not very many years ago superior persons, wise in their own conceit, might have smiled pityingly at John of Gaddesden's 'treatment,' which consisted chiefly in wrapping the patient in scarlet cloth, and hanging his bed, and the walls of his room, with stuff of the same mystic hue; but modern science has devised a plan whereby the skin of the sufferer from smallpox is exposed to certain red rays in order to prevent 'pitting,' so instead of laughing at Master John, we feel more disposed to doff our hats to him. It seems improbable, however, that his successors of the present day will ever revert to his prescription for tonsillitis —the beak of a magpie hung round the neck! To ease the pangs of toothache you are recommended to take a needle and prick "the many-footed worm which rolls up into a ball when you touch it"—*i.e.*, the isopod crustacean commonly known as the wood-louse, and then with that same needle to touch the raging tooth, while for that very painful affection called 'the stone' Master John favoured a paste of pounded crickets and beetles. Some of his medicaments are less disconcerting, and, like all medieval 'doctours,' he makes use of a prodigious number of herbs—outlandish herbs such as hyssop, cassia, and cinnamon; homely herbs such as nasturtium, sow-thistle, wood-sorrel, wood-sage, liverwort, wild parsley, fennel, and juniper. A

154

quaint and rather pleasing belief then prevailed to the effect that Dame Nature had kindly indicated which herbs were good for which diseases by imprinting upon their leaves or petals the image of the organ damaged by the disease. Thus, wood-sorrel, being shaped like a heart, was a remedy for cardiac maladies, and hepatica, or liverwort, resembling the form of the liver, could hardly fail to cure, or, at least, to relieve, hepatic, or liver, distempers. Under the term 'colic' a vast number of abdominal and intestinal affections was grouped, and the same treatment was meted out for appendicitis or peritonitis as for the common or garden 'tummy-ache.' Pains in the side were—or the sufferers believed that they were—cured by the application of a piece of jade, that beautiful mineral whose very name tells of the use to which it was formerly put, for it comes from the Spanish word *ijada*, meaning the flank.

When the Doctour of Phisik had exerted himself in vain, when all his skill in astrology and "magyk natureel" had not availed to save the patient's life, then came the turn of the members of two other honourable and learned professions—the priest and the lawyer. It was the priest's part to prepare the soul of the dying man for its passing into a world where gold and gear would profit him little; it was the part of the lawyer to help him to dispose of that gold and gear which he must now relinquish for ever. The medieval 'last will and testament,' whether it were dictated when the testator was in good health or on his last legs, always begins with a profession of faith, and by commending his soul to God (and perhaps to some special saint as well) and his body to some particular church. Then, as a rule, comes the provision of Masses for the repose of his soul, followed by certain legacies designed to propitiate St Michael when, at Doomsday, the Archangel should weigh the good against the bad deeds of each son of man. If the testator were wealthy these legacies might consist of substantial slices of land or of money assigned to some prelate, or to some monastic foundation; if his means were modest it might be that he could do nothing more than leave his best gown to his parish church, to be used as a second-best cope. John Alpeyngham of Walberswick, Suffolk, left money to provide for the Holy Ghost,[1] "goyng upp and down with a cheyne"; the men and women of Croscombe, in Somerset, were very mindful of their own particular church at the close of the fifteenth century. In 1476 "Jane Fenton at her det gaf to Our Lady a ring gylt"; Jane's gift would, of course, be dedicated to the altar of the Lady Chapel. A year later Thomas Blower not only gave "j vyolet long gowne in grayne," but "a ryng, gold with a torcus,[2] and a kerchef of Syper"—*i.e.*, Cyprus silk. To Old Chelsea Church a certain Margery Lynde in 1484 bequeathed small sums of money for the lamps and tapers at the high altar and the side-altars, and to "the Light afore Oure Ladye the Pyte [3] 3*d*. during 20 yeres."

If the patient of the Doctour of Phisik had neglected to make his will until the last possible moment he would, doubtless, glance round the room where he lay dying and take thought as to who should inherit its more costly contents. Let us imagine the poor fellow to belong to that station in life where some of the contents *would* be costly. Obviously poor Hob or Wat would not require the services of a lawyer to arrange for the disposal of their timber stools and pewter pots! A medieval bedroom would present few points in common with a modern one, but what it lacked in convenience and comfort was compensated in beauty. The floor, inlaid with chequered tiles, the leaded windows gay with heraldic glass, the oaken cupboard or press, the richly carved chest with an intricate lock of wrought steel, and, above all things, the bed itself, would appeal strongly to the eyes of an artist—and the pocket of a curio-dealer! The bed was a formidable affair, almost always a four-poster or else

---

[1] An image of the Third Person of the Trinity in the form of a dove, probably of silver-gilt.

[2] turquoise.

[3] Our Lady of Piety, the representation of the Blessed Virgin with the dead Christ in her arms, known in Italian art as the *Pietà*.

a canopied bed, much encumbered with curtains. The curtains
might be drawn round, so as to form a sort of tent or pavilion,
or else pulled up at each corner, and allowed to hang there in

BEDROOM SCENE
Reconstructed from a medieval manuscript.

four queer, unwieldy bundles. So rich and beautiful were
these bed-hangings that medieval wills are full of allusions to
them, and they would, indeed, appear to have ranked next after
the cups and flagons of silver and silver-gilt among the most
valued of worldly possessions. John of Gaunt bequeathed to

157

his son, Henry IV, his great bed [1] of white and red silk whereon was embroidered in gold a turtle-dove sitting upon a tree; Edmund, Earl of March, father of Harry Hotspur's wife, left to his son Roger his great bed of black satin embroidered with white lions, golden rose-trees, and heraldic escutcheons; Joan, Princess of Wales, the "Fair Maid of Kent," widow of the Black Prince, bequeathed to her son, Richard II, a bed of even more than common magnificence. It was of red velvet, embroidered with Prince of Wales's feathers and foliage in silver, interspersed with leopards' masks in gold.

Such would be the beds in which the Doctour of Phisik found his more distinguished patients when he went to examine them, and whereunto the Man of Law would be summoned sometimes to draw up a tardy testament. Perhaps as they jogged toward Canterbury Chaucer's Doctour and his Sergeant of the Lawė chatted apart together, and compared experiences and exchanged anecdotes concerning their respective clients, though always with due regard to prudence, discretion, and professional etiquette.

This discreet and accomplished lawyer arrayed himself in sober raiment for the road. His coat was of mixed woollen stuff, with a girdle of striped silk, but Chaucer tells us that

> Of fees and robės he had many oon.

The robe he would wear as a sergeant of the law would be a parti-coloured robe—that is to say, one half made of plain and the other of 'rayed' or striped material. It is rather an amusing idea that he may have made his girdle of a fragment of one of his old legal gowns! These parti-coloured gowns were usually of blue and green, but from a very early time the recognized trappings of the judge appear to have been scarlet and miniver. Upon their heads both judges and barristers wore close-fitting white hoods, called 'coifs,' fastened under the chin. The little circular patch of silk on the top of a modern judge's wig is a

---

[1] 'Bed' must be understood to mean bed-hangings.

relic of the coif, and the form of his robes has altered hardly at all since the days of the later Plantagenets.

PRISONERS AT THE BAR
From a law treatise of the time of Henry VI

Chaucer does not tell us to which of the four Inns of Court —Inner Temple, Middle Temple, Lincoln's Inn, and Gray's Inn—his sergeant belonged, but it is practically certain that he belonged to one of the four. These voluntary legal societies, which came into being toward the close of the thirteenth century, are active, flourishing, and powerful at the present time, and if the coifed and parti-coloured barristers of the Middle Ages were to revisit the glimpses of the moon in their former haunts they would find, along with many startling changes, much of the spirit and something of the substance of their own time, unaltered and alive. Until 1207, when the clergy were forbidden to act in the temporal or non-ecclesiastical courts, the functions of lawyer and priest were as closely interknit as those of priest and physician; hence the semi-ecclesiastical character of the judges' robes. It was this formal detachment of legal from spiritual activities which created not only the layman-lawyer, but the whole complicated fabric of common law, and, incidentally, the great Inns of Court which, as Mr F. W. Maitland remarks, "had about them a good deal of the club, something of the college, something of the trade union." Law students did not concentrate all their attention upon musty legal folios; singing and dancing were included in the regular course of study, and the Christmas revels of the young lawyers became famous for their gaiety, and even for their violence.

The medieval client did not, as a rule, betake himself to the Inns of Court when he was in quest of a lawyer. There were lawyers, "plentiful as tabby cats," waiting for patrons in Westminster Hall, and in the "parvise" or closed-in porch of St Paul's Cathedral. Lydgate tells us, in his lively poem *London Lickpenny*, how a simple countryman came up to London, and betook himself to Westminster Hall, hoping to find a lawyer to take charge of a lawsuit on his behalf. He besought one after another to act for him, "for Mary's love, that holy mayde," but, as he offered no other inducement, fee, or reward, none of these grave men learned in the law was willing to help him. It is the measure of the simplicity of Lydgate's countryman both that he should have offered so unsubstantial a return and that he should have felt some surprise when it was shrugged or pushed aside

160

with scorn. There is a disconcerted as well as a rueful note in his perpetual refrain:

> For lack of money I might not speed!

To the client who approached him with a well-filled purse the lawyer gave a very different reception. If the necessary 'peny' were forthcoming much might be done, and a cynical songster of the fifteenth century declares cheerily:

> Thow I have a man i-slawe [1]
> And forfetyd the kyngès lawe,
> I xal [2] fyndyn a man of lawe
> Wyl takyn myn peny and let me goo.

[1] slain.　　　[2] shall.

A COOK
Luttrell Psalter

CHAPTER IX
CHURCHES, PRELATES, AND PRIESTS

IT is a little difficult for us to realize the part played by the Church in the common life of the people of England before the Reformation. That life was a hard one, grim, laborious, and grey; almost the only source of rest, colour, and refreshment was to be found in the services and the festivals of the Church. The edifice itself was the centre round which revolved the spiritual and intellectual activities of the parish or village where it stood. But for the simple, and sometimes even meagre, instruction given by their priests, the ignorance of the mass of the nation would have been profound. Anything that they knew —and the most learned of them did not know much—about other times and other countries than their own, they had heard or seen within consecrated walls. One says 'seen' advisedly, for few churches were so poor that they boasted no carvings in stone or wood, no mural paintings, no windows with coloured panes: and the images represented not only the famous figures of sacred history, prophets, patriarchs, and saints, but dragons, lions, and dromedaries, and far-off cities in *this* world, and beautiful or terrible regions in the *next*. That wayward genius François Villon has given us a glimpse of the wall-paintings of a fifteenth-century French church in the *Ballade which Villon wrote at the Request of his Mother*. There he makes the good woman say:

> *Au moustier voy dont suis paroissienne*
> *Paradis paint, où sont harpes et luz,*
> *Et ung enfer, où dampnez sont boulluz;*
> *L'ung me fait paour, l'autre, joye et liesse.*

> (A painted Paradise in church I see,
> Where amid harps and lights the blessed dwell,
> And lost souls burning in a painted hell;
> Fearful is one, the other fair to me.)

To the medieval mind, unvexed by astronomical lore, nothing appeared more certain than that the golden-azure City of Peace was immediately above the heads of men, and the flaming pit immediately below their feet; nothing seemed more right and natural than that the sun, moon, and stars should have been expressly created to illumine and to direct the comings and goings of the dwellers upon this flat world in the precise centre of the visible universe. This conception of the nature and purpose of "all things visible and invisible" made the task of the priest an easy one when he began to instruct his open-mouthed flock. From him they would learn not only the first elements of their faith, but also fascinating legends of dragons and damsels, demons and saints. Just as in pagan times an elusive divinity, perhaps friendly, perhaps the reverse, was apt to lurk among the woods and waters, so in Christian Europe wells and caves, trees and pools, had their angelic or demonic guardians. Scoffers were few, but the bold fellow who laughed at such notions in the safe and comfortable light of day would be fain to cross himself and mutter an *Ave* if his way led him past the haunted spot after dusk had fallen and when the wind was high.

In England the Reformation was never the devastating tempest which it became on the Continent. Much loveliness was swept away, but much remains. It was not in the English character to set to work with the bitter and relentless energy of—for example—the Dutch and the Scots. Standing in a medieval English church, or in one of the great English cathedrals, you still have a sense of contact with the past, whereas in a grim Scottish kirk or a bleak Dutch *kapelle*, however venerable the walls themselves may be, you feel that the bridge between yourself and its long-dead builders has been rudely hacked asunder.

Only a modest amount of architectural knowledge is necessary in order to recognize the four chief orders of English architecture. These are: Norman (from the middle of the eleventh to the close of the twelfth century); Early English (from the end of the

163

twelfth to near the end of the thirteenth century); Decorated (from the end of the thirteenth to near the end of the fourteenth century); Perpendicular (from the end of the fourteenth to the middle of the sixteenth century). The Anglo-Saxon churches that remain are few, and, like the men who built them, they are simple and sturdy rather than beautiful; the thickness of the walls is remarkable, as is also the smallness of the windows. Much toil and much time were needed to build a worthy church, but neither was grudged in the days when both were dedicated wholeheartedly to the glory of God. When many years went to the making of one particular fabric it was inevitable that the ideas of the earlier generation should overlap those of the later. The result is that not a few of our most lovely cathedrals are masses of architectural patchwork. At Winchester, for example, the transepts or crossbars of the cruciform plan are pure Norman, the tetro-choir and the Lady Chapel Early English, the choir-stalls Decorated, and the nave Perpendicular. Massive strength and dignity are the first characteristics of Norman architecture. Columns are heavy, arches round. The walls are often circled with arcades of single or intersecting arches, adorned with elaborate moulding. Norwich, Durham, St John's Chapel in the Tower of London, and the church of St Bartholomew the Great, Smithfield, illustrate these features. The Early English architects loved high and narrow pointed windows (lancets); they planted delicate pinnacles upon the stalwart Norman towers; they replaced the stalwart Norman columns with clustered shafts of darker marble, making a sharp contrast with the paler and duller stonework above. As their walls were thinner, external buttresses became necessary, to resist the outward thrust. For ornament they loved what is known as 'dog-tooth' moulding on their pointed arches, and on blank wall-spaces they set carvings in 'diaper-work,' the design borrowed from that in the rich Oriental silk-stuffs then used so much in making the vestments of the priests. Salisbury Cathedral is the most unified and uncomplicated English

164

example of this style. Between the Early English and the Decorated came a time of transition, when one style had not quite arrived and the other had not quite departed. When the Decorated had declared itself arches and windows began to grow broader. Such windows had to be divided in the centre by a vertical bar of masonry, and this necessity led to the invention of the graceful and flowing tracery typical of the style. The capitals of the columns blossomed with stone flowers and fruits, the frames of doors and windows budded into the 'ball-flower'; wherever peaks rose from tombs, or choir-stalls, or pews, or screens, they ended in beautiful carved ornaments, of which the most attractive is known as the 'poppy-head finial.' The buttresses, instead of huddling closely against the walls, now spring outward in a graceful curve, and become *flying* buttresses. To this period belong the cathedrals of Exeter, Wells, and York. Then

A FLYING BUTTRESS

comes the Perpendicular, so called because as the windows broadened yet more, long upright mullions were introduced to divide them. Indeed, the greater space occupied by the windows is the most characteristic feature of this style of architecture. As the Perpendicular period wanes curious changes occur. The Norman arch—and, consequently, the Norman window—were round; the Early English arch and window were high, pointed, and narrow; the Decorated arch and window, though still pointed, were less sharply so; then, as the Perpendicular windows and doors continue to broaden, square arches, and doors either square or with square hoods above their pointed arches, make their appearance. The vaulted roofs now adorn themselves with exquisite fan-tracery, and, presently, from the

165

intersecting fans depend bosses, elaborately carved. To the later Perpendicular belong Henry VII's Chapel, Westminster; St George's, Windsor; and King's College Chapel, Cambridge.

NORTH TRANSEPT, GLOUCESTER CATHEDRAL

Of fan-vaulting in its earlier and more graceful phase there is no better example than the cloisters at Gloucester.

The always delightful pastime of repeopling an ancient church with long-vanished worshippers becomes much less hazy and haphazard if we take care not to evoke the figure of a knight in

166

chain-mail emerging from an arch which was not built until plate armour was the order of the day, and not to imagine a coifed or hooded Angevin gentlewoman telling her beads by the

THE CLOISTERS, GLOUCESTER CATHEDRAL

light of a window whose jewelled rays fell first upon Plantagenet headdresses, peaked and horned.

As windows grew broader more glass was required, and the art of the glazier kept pace with this need. In earlier times, when only small and narrow windows were seen, or lancets such as the "Five Sisters" at York, the glass was applied rather in

167

the manner of mosaic, dozens of small, intensely hued fragments being fitted together to form the design. Much of the fine old glass in Canterbury Cathedral is of this type. As the windows expanded the glass-workers grew more enterprising, and worked with a more free and generous touch; and then came the beautiful fourteenth- and fifteenth-century examples,

PAINTED-GLASS WINDOW

such as those at Gloucester and at Great Malvern, where figures and buildings are skilfully fitted in, but always subordinated to the general effect, which remains that of a mesh of rainbow jewels spun from point to point of the stone tracery. Such is the Tunnoc window at York, representing the pouring of bell metal into a mould. Later still this jewelled effect vanishes, and the windows become simply pictures painted upon large panes of glass, as are those in the cathedral-church of St Gudule at Brussels.

In the twelfth and thirteenth centuries the basic glass was never pure white. The sand used in its manufacture contained so much iron that even the clearest had a yellowish or greenish

168

tinge. The flakes of red colour, being held in suspension, had a gorgeous ruby glow. At the end of the fourteenth century, instead of the colour being thus held in the glass, it was applied in a layer upon the surface, and gained in brightness what it lost in depth. As the oxides with which the glass was stained were never chemically pure, the glazier could never tell beforehand exactly *how* a certain colour would 'come out,' and chance and guess-work played a large part in the production of his masterpieces.

The great abbeys and cathedrals became veritable treasuries of decorative art, where the loveliest achievements of sculptors and goldsmiths, embroiderers and glass-stainers, were gathered together, the piety and enthusiasm of each successive generation seeming to outstrip and over-climb everything that had gone before. Most of these buildings possessed the relic or relics of one saint or more, and many of them guarded in a shrine of fretted gold the complete—or *almost* complete—skeleton of some famous bishop, virgin, or martyr. Such possessions were a source of much wealth, as we shall find when we come to consider the fascinating subject of pilgrims and pilgrimages. Not only did prosperous pilgrims hang gorgeous gifts upon such shrines; proud lords and noble ladies desired passionately that their dust should lie near that of some famous saint, and to that end bequeathed much gold to the chosen shrine, and endowed chantries, that Masses might be sung for the repose of their 'sowlys' as long as the world should last. Sometimes it befell that a man who in his lifetime had astonished both his friends and his foes by his splendour and his pride would leave word in his will that he should, as a belated but probably quite sincere act of humility, be buried in the coarse woollen gown and cowl of a monk.

Royal sinners naturally liked to shelter beneath the shadow of a royal saint, and even some whose sins were not exactly as scarlet felt a pleasant sense of security in the immediate neighbourhood of haunted and holy sepulchres. In Westminster the stiff, golden-bronze Plantagenet kings and queens huddle nervously round the lofty tomb of Edward the Confessor; Henry IV may have felt a certain reluctance to thrust himself into the ghostly company of Richard II, for he and his queen rest at Canterbury, as does his valiant kinsman, the Black Prince, hard by the spot where the glorious shrine of Thomas Becket once rose like an ark of fretted gold above a surging sea of pilgrims' hoods.

One of the crafts to which the medieval Church gave the fullest encouragement was that of the worker in metals. For the high altars of the greater edifices huge candlesticks were

THE RAMSEY INCENSE-BOAT

needed, traceried tabernacles, many-rayed monstrances, cha-lices, and patens of pale and beautiful silver-gilt; for the cere-monies and processions jewelled crosses would be required, and incense-boats, and thuribles. The thurible (it is another name for a censer, or incense-burner) was often in the form of a pointed tower with elaborately pierced sides. The thurifer, or incense-bearer, swung it to and fro, with a rhythmic movement, upon its four slender chains, and spirals of fragrant blue smoke climbed to the intersecting arches high above. When the fum-ing embers began to fail the thurifer's companion lifted the roof-shaped lid, and with the aid of a long spoon added some fresh frankincense from the boat-shaped vessel which he carried. Nearly eighty years ago such a thurible and such a vessel were found in Whittlesea Mere, Huntingdon, and these are now in the Victoria and Albert Museum. They date from the four-teenth century, and once formed part of the treasure of Ramsey Abbey.

170

Obviously the richer churches would possess more costly and exquisite altar-furniture than the poorer and smaller ones. Gloucester Cathedral was proud of its marvellously wrought candlestick, a mass of writhing and intertwining foliage, thick-set with tiny figures of men and demons; but a parish church might have nothing finer than a pair of grey pewter prickets. (A pricket-candlestick is one upon which the candle is impaled, instead of being fixed into a socket.) Before the Reformation the priest alone drank from the cup during the Communion service: that is why medieval chalices have comparatively small and shallow bowls, though the stem and foot may be of great beauty, heavy with disks of coloured enamel or of crystal, or engraved with scenes from the Passion.

THE GLOUCESTER
CANDLESTICK

The vestments of the priests also varied in gorgeousness according to the size and importance of the church in which they were worn. When fully vested for Mass the priest wore: the *amice*, an oblong of linen passed over the head and then fastened round the neck with cords; the *alb*, a tight-sleeved linen garment, reaching from the shoulders to the feet; the *stole*, a narrow strip of fringed and embroidered silk worn round the neck, the two ends dangling beneath the *chasuble*, an oval, sleeveless mantle, ornamented with bars of embroidery, called *orphreys*, which are usually arranged so as to form a cross. To the left cuff of the alb is attached another strip of silk, smaller than the stole, called the *maniple*. The origin of this strip of silk is obscure, but, according to some authorities, it may be found in the ceremonial handkerchiefs with which the magistrates of pagan Rome used to give the signal for the opening of the *ludi*, or games in the circus. The outer mantle worn by the priest in processions, and at solemn ceremonies other than the Mass, is called a *cope*, and the design upon it is not usually arranged in bars, like the orphreys on the chasuble, but may be massed or scattered, or may consist simply of the pattern woven into the fabric itself.

Many of these silken fabrics used for priestly vestments in medieval times were of great beauty in themselves, apart from

the needlework with which they were enriched, and most of them came from distant countries: from China, Persia, Asia Minor, Mesopotamia, and Egypt. The five liturgical colours were white, red, green, violet, and black, and their use was related to the various feasts of the Church's year, and the particular ceremony during which they were to be worn.

Among the fabrics most in favour for priestly garments, altar-hangings, and so forth were sendal, baudekin, samite,

A FIFTEENTH-CENTURY CHALICE

taffety, sarcenet, diaper-silk, and velvet. Here again history is caught and held in a word. 'Sendal' comes from the Sanskrit *Sindhu*, which is also the root of the word 'India,' and means from, or of, the river Indus—*i.e.*, Indian; 'baudekin' is silk of Bagdad, from the Italian name, *Baldacco*, of Haroun al-Raschid's city; 'samite' has a Greek source in two words *hex*, six, and *mitos*, a thread, and may have been so called because in this fabric the weft-threads are caught only at every *sixth* warp-thread; 'taffety' is Persian, the root-word meaning to twist; 'diaper-silk' is not, as some good people once thought, *toile d'Ypres*, but in Byzantine Greek was called *diaspros*: *dia*, through, and *aspros*, white; 'sarcenet' is simply *drap sarrasinois* in old French, 'Saracenic cloth'; and the Low Latin *villus*, 'shaggy hair,' is the 'parent' of 'velvet.'

The demand for these costly and beautiful silks of the East

172

was constant and keen, as the far-seeing merchants of Venice and London, Genoa and Florence, soon perceived. In Italy, especially in the two cities last mentioned, dextrous weavers began without delay to copy the designs in the Persian and Chinese fabrics, but the less adaptable English were for the most part content to import them ready woven from the East and then have them "wrought wyth the nedel wyth ymages,"

THE SYON COPE

usually, in the case of church vestments or hangings, by the patient and skilful hands of cloistered nuns. It happens, however, that one of the most lovely of existing masterpieces of English ecclesiastical needlecraft is wrought not upon silk but upon linen. This is the Syon cope, so called because it belonged to a convent of Bridgettine nuns (nuns following the rule of St Bridget, a Swedish saint who, by the by, was not yet born when the cope was made) at Syon, near Isleworth, on the Thames. Being a cope and not a chasuble, it is covered entirely with figures of saints, archangels, and Apostles, and scenes from the life of Christ. The chief colours introduced are tawny brown, gold, green, and deep blue. This last tint appears rather startlingly upon the hair and beard of more than one Apostle! Some of the little figures are very graceful, especially the archangels and the seraphim, with their wings plumed with peacock's feathers. This monument of industry dates from the last years of the thirteenth century, so the nuns were busy upon it at the same time that the masons were busy upon the choir of Westminster Abbey, a little farther down the river. Much ingenuity and not a little humour were shown by the designers of such embroideries. Upon one fourteenth-century altar-frontal we see the angels appearing to the shepherds, and the scene is treated with delightful directness and more than a touch of childish gaiety. A shepherd is blowing so loud a blast upon his own bagpipe that he cannot hear the heavenly song, but several of the sheep hear it, as well as his fellow-shepherds, and from the manner in which the trusty hound is gazing upward with open jaws it looks as if the beast were unmannerly enough to howl in rivalry with the singing of the angelic messengers. Sometimes it happened that a lady would give or bequeath one of her best gowns, or a gentleman one of *his*, to the church, in order that the priests should have new copes. Thus we read that in 1477 Thomas Blower, of Croscombe, in Somerset, gave to his parish church "1 vyolet long gowne." Philippa of Hainault bestowed upon Simon, Bishop of Ely, the dress she wore when she went to give thanks for the birth of her eldest son, afterward the Black Prince. It was of mulberry-coloured velvet, powdered with golden squirrels, and ample enough to make no less than three copes.

In addition to the permanent adornings of each church—its candlesticks of pewter or of silver-gilt, its images hewn out of stone or carven in tough oak, its banners and frontals of needle-work—the interior would be beautified at certain seasons of the year with fresh green boughs and garlands of flowers. This was the case not only in country churches, but in those of the cities of London and Westminster. The churchwardens' accounts of St Margaret's, Westminster, for the year 1484, show that they spent fivepence upon red roses for Corpus Christi Day; those of St Mary-at-Hill in 1477 record a payment of eightpence "for Rose garlondis and wodrofe garlondis on St Barnabas' daye"; while St Andrew Hubbard expended two-pence on "bircche and lylies at Mydsomer" in 1485. Most picturesque of all is the note in the records of Thame Church, Oxfordshire, that in 1465 the churchwardens gave a penny "to Chyldryn to gadyr yvy."

Chaucer has left us an adorable and unforgettable portrait of the finest type of parish priest in fourteenth-century England—the Poure Persoun of a Toun.

> But riche he was of hooly thoght
>   and werk;
> He was also a lernèd man, a clerk.

PARISH PRIEST OF THE TIME OF
EDWARD III

This learned and holy priest was, as we should now say, 'a son of the people'; his own brother, one of his fellow-pilgrims, was a ploughman. His tastes were simple, his needs few; "He koude in lytel thyng have suffisaunce," and when a more worldly minded cleric might have threatened his flock with the thunders of the Church if they left their tithes unpaid he was patient, forbearing, reluctant to ask for what was in truth his own already.

> Wyd was his parisshe, and houses fer asonder,
> But he ne laftè [1] nat for reyn ne thonder
> In siknesse or in meschief [2] to visite
> The ferreste in his parisshe, muche and lite,[3]
> Upon his feet, and in his hand a staf.
> This noble ensample to his sheepe he yaf [4]

---

[1] omitted.   [2] trouble.   [3] great and small.   [4] gave.

That firste he wroghte, and afterward he taughte.
Out of the gospel he tho wordès caughte,
And this figùre he added eek thereto
That if gold rustè, what shall iren doo?

A restless, or a mirth-loving, or an ambitious man would
soon have grown weary of so arduous and austere a way of life as
his. Such men gravitated toward London, and, if no better
employment offered there, often became chantry priests at St
Paul's Cathedral, familiarly called "Powlys," where many little
side-chapels had been endowed by the pious departed in order
that Masses might be sung for the repose of their souls "as long
as the world should last." This was the fate of Chaucer's great
contemporary poet, William Langland, "Long Will," the gaunt,
grim, dissatisfied cleric-dreamer, author of *The Vision of William
concerning Piers the Plowman*. He lived meagerly and sombrely
in London, "feeding from a dead hand," as it has been strikingly
said, while the Poure Persoun, trudging through the mire from
one daub-and-wattle hut to another, had peace in his soul and
a smile in his eyes.

At the opposite pole, far from the parish priests and the
chantry priests, were the powerful prelates, princely in rank, in
wealth, and in magnificence, though sometimes as humble and
as pure of heart as the dear Persoun himself. These bishops
and archbishops of medieval England were not always—nor
even frequently—of ancient and noble birth. The word
'democracy' was never heard in those days—happier days for
that reason if for no other!—but the thing itself existed, in a
rough and irregular form, and was part of the very fabric of the
nation. Certain heights the humbly born might never hope to
scale; but within the compass of Holy Church there was no
peak so lofty that the son of a ploughman might not set his foot
upon it. The statesmen who advised the monarch and, through
him, virtually ruled the land were almost always churchmen as
well. The Chancellor of the realm was a priest just as inevitably as the Archbishop of Canterbury was one—and not un-

seldom the two offices were united in a single person. As 'Keeper of the King's Conscience' and royal confessor, the Chancellor had a difficult and delicate task to perform. Not until the reign of Henry VIII was the Chancellorship held by a layman. During the decrepitude of Edward III one of the

MITRE AND STOLE OF ST THOMAS BECKET

demands made by John of Gaunt and his malcontent followers was that the Chancellor of the realm *should* be a layman, but the effect upon the course of history was negligible. The layman in question was Sir Thomas More, and the sequel did not bode well for the success of the innovation. Till that distressful era of upheaval and transition, statecraft and priestcraft—to use neither term in a disrespectful sense—walked hand-in-glove, and the gloves were always episcopal gloves of crimson silk.

M

Becket and Wolsey, two crimson-gloved and crimson-robed phantoms, advance and fill the foreground of the picture with their triumphant splendour. They stand for ever as the supreme types and examples of the alliance between statecraft and priestcraft in England. Less familiar, but not less interesting, are the characters and careers of two other prelates, Robert Grosseteste and William of Wykeham.

Grosseteste was born toward the close of the twelfth century, in the little Suffolk village of Stradbrook. His father and mother were humble folk, tillers of the soil, and it is not known whether his second name, Grosseteste (big head), was a nickname or an inherited one. About his childhood we know nothing beyond what he himself has recorded, and that is little indeed. We are told that he took delight in studying, and in trying to imitate, the great figures in the Bible story. Now, the only teacher from whom he could then have gained even the most faint and fragmentary knowledge of Biblical history would be the "Poure Persoun" of Stradbrook. This good Persoun must have been quick to detect and to encourage the unusual intellectual gifts of the boy. Without some such encouragement little Robert would probably have been set to weeding or digging, or sent to scare the crows from the corn, at the time when he was actually commencing his studies at the University of Oxford. That he studied to good purpose we know. This child of a Suffolk peasant became one of the most brilliant 'all-round' scholars of his age. Dr Luard writes of him, in the *Dictionary of National Biography*: "Probably no one had a greater influence upon English thought and English literature for the two centuries following his time than Bishop Grosseteste." To skill in moral philosophy and in theology he added skill in medicine and music, agriculture and law. At an epoch when Western Europe was not only profoundly ignorant, but intensely distrustful of both natural science and exact science, he threw himself with ardour into the pursuit of knowledge by *experiment*. He studied—and taught—mathematics. With his

178

friends Adam de Marisco and the more famous Roger Bacon he made researches into the problems of heat, light, and colour, reasoned about rainbows, speculated concerning spheres and comets. Much credit has been given to Grocyn, Erasmus, and Cheke for bringing to England the *renewed* knowledge of, and enthusiasm for, classical Greek at the dawn of the sixteenth century; and they deserve much. But let it not be forgotten that early in the thirteenth century there was a small group of English pioneers who studied and taught not only Greek, but Hebrew, and who had the courage and the wisdom to place observation and experiment above tradition, and thus to anticipate by seven hundred years modern scientific methods and principles.

In 1224 Grosseteste, though not himself a Franciscan, became Rector of the recently established Franciscan school at Oxford. Ten years later he was appointed to the largest diocese in England—that of Lincoln—and enthroned in the beautiful cathedral whither, in 1220, the Kings of England and Scotland had borne the body of St Hugh upon their shoulders to its resting-place in the choir. The new bishop flung himself with enthusiasm into his pastoral duties. Indeed, many good easy men who had jogged along very comfortably under the lighter rule of his predecessor began to think that, though zeal was an excellent quality, you might have too much of it—in a bishop. There must, it seems, have been a streak of the Puritan in Grosseteste. It was his will that county folk should dance no more on consecrated ground, that the ancient buffooneries of the Feast of All Fools should be abandoned, together with all games, pastimes, and pursuits that might conceivably lead to brawling and profanity, that all mothers should personally direct the religious education of their young children; and, as he was a man of exceptionally strong character, it went ill with them who neglected his behests. About his disputes with the Vatican it is not necessary to speak at any length here. Though personally humble and courteous, he was a proud and passionate defender of the rights of the English Church, as he saw them, and his loyalty to the Holy See did not prevent him from protesting bitterly when Italians of tender years were appointed to English canonries.

Among the devoted friends of this Suffolk peasant's son was Simon de Montfort, to whose children Grosseteste acted for a time as tutor. It was probably through de Montfort that the brilliant churchman was introduced to the Court of Henry III and Eleanor of Provence. Henry was certainly not "a man of exceptionally strong character"; one chronicler called him the King with the Heart of Wax! But he was personally lovable, and few Kings of England, with the exception of Charles I, have had such a fervent and such an intelligent love for architecture and art as his. He was the creator of Westminster Abbey as we see it—of the choir and transepts, that is to say. When he enriched the amazing treasures of the Confessor's shrine with a relic of marvellous virtue, nothing less than a phial said to contain some drops of the blood of Christ, a solemn ceremony was held in the newly finished choir, and the sermon was preached by the eloquent and learned Bishop of Lincoln. When he sought enlightenment concerning the purpose and significance of the anointing of the sovereign at his coronation it was to the same bishop that he had recourse. The gifted but undependable Queen was also wont to seek spiritual guidance from Grosseteste, and it may have been some last, lingering trace of his influence which moved her to end her days as a nun in the convent at Amesbury. The fiery and warlike character of this great scholar-prelate entangled him in many troubles, and the last years of his life were spent under the constant shadow of excommunication. None the less, his death was so fair and so tranquil that legends soon arose that it had been accompanied by marvels, by heavenly music from invisible harps and shawms; efforts were even made to obtain the honour of canonization for him, and thus to set a fellow-saint beside St Hugh of Lincoln. These efforts were not encouraged at

Rome, so St Hugh was never called upon to share his splendour with a St Robert Grosseteste.

Rather different was the personality of another son of the people, who rose from obscurity to power in much the same way. In the Hampshire village of Wickham, or Wykeham, there was born in 1324, just one hundred years after Grosseteste became Rector of the Franciscans at Oxford, a boy who, like his father, took as a family name the name of the place of his birth. As was the case with Shakespeare, his mother was better born than his father, and, as is the case with many sons, he probably resembled her more than him. This boy was christened William, and when he was old enough to learn such lessons as were taught in the schools of the time, reading, elementary Latin, the grammar of Donatus, plainsong, he was sent to the Prior's school at Winchester. He must have been a devout child, for it is recorded that he loved to rise in the grey hush of dawn and creep to the cathedral to hear what was known as the 'Morrow Mass,' Mass sung for the benefit of such townsfolk and poor people, craftsmen

THE RICHENAU
CROSIER

and labourers, who had to set about their daily tasks betimes. Little did William dream that the time would come when he would wear a jewelled mitre and carry a crosier of carved ivory within those very walls. His first employment was as under-notary to the Constable of Winchester Castle; though a 'clerk,' he was not then a full-fledged priest, nor did he become one until 1362. In 1356 he entered the royal service, being appointed clerk of the King's works in the manors of Henley and Easthampstead. Five months later he was surveyor of the building operations then in progress at Windsor Castle. This does not mean that he had anything to

181

do with the *planning* of the work, but only that he had to pay the masons' wages, and see to the supply of raw materials. So well pleased was the King with his surveyor, honours and preferments, prebends, canonries, and deaneries, soon began to shower down upon Wykeham's head. In those days what is called 'plurality of benefices' was very usual, and though most

WILLIAM OF WYKEHAM

people—except the holders of them— agreed that it was both strange and wrong that one man should draw the revenues of so many posts at once and perform the duties of none, the abuse did not disappear till long after the Reformation. Wykeham was just as passionate in defence of national rights as Grosseteste had been, but he was far more temperate and tactful. His business ability, the quickness with which he fitted himself for the various tasks entrusted to him, his skill in pleasing his royal master, were so great that they aroused wonder in many minds and envy in not a few. "By him," writes Froissart, "everything was done, and without him, nothing." In 1366 he was, in accordance with the King's desire conveyed to the monks of the cathedral, elected Bishop of Winchester; in 1367 he became Chancellor. The ravages of the Black Death in 1348 and again in 1361 had led to such a serious shortage of priests, scholars, and clerks that people began to fear that the children then growing up, especially those far from towns, would be little better than barbarians, uncouth and untaught. With this danger before his eyes, Wykeham set about the noblest work of his life, the founding of New College, Oxford, and of "a college for seventy poor scholars who should live college-wise and study grammar near the city of Winchester." Great wealth was now at Wykeham's command, and he made use of it greatly. His experience as clerk of the works at Windsor had given him a profound knowledge of architecture and a keen enthusiasm for

182

beauty, and he willed that his poor scholars, both at Winchester and Oxford, should work and play in a stately and lovely environment of fretted stone and carven wood and painted glass. "Manners makyth Man" was the good bishop's motto, and it was surely a good one. Other benefactors followed his example, and left provision in their wills for the education of poor scholars, little dreaming that these bequests would still be administered to the glory of God and the advancement of learning long after the chantry chapels were dark and silent wherein they had willed that lamps should burn and priests should sing for their souls "as long as the world shall last."

CHAPTER X

MONKS, FRIARS, AND NUNS

THOUGH a hermit and a monk are not one and the same thing, the first hermits were, in a sense, the first monks. They were restless and yet meditative souls, who sought peace in the desert (Greek, *eremos*), and chose to dwell there, each one in stern solitude, far from the fever and the fret of human activity. That the word 'monk' should be derived from the Greek work *monos* (alone) is a little curious, since monks, properly so called, never live alone, but always in large or small companies. Their 'aloneness' is of another kind from that of the hermits; it is intermittent; but it is none the less real, and it is an important part of the spiritual discipline imposed upon every monk both by his own will and by the rules of his order.

The difference between a hermit and a monk is really less great than that between a monk and a friar. The typical monk is cloistered; even if he works in the fields, they are the fields of his monastery, and he may not stray beyond them. He must sleep always in the same cell, kneel always in the same chapel, eat always at the same board, until he die. The friar, on the other hand, moves about the world freely. It is his duty to do so. In the Middle Ages the friars were to be seen on every highroad, and in every village and town. They had their 'rounds,' just as the pedlars and the strolling minstrels had, and they were constantly in touch with the rough, gay, cruel, perilous, beautiful everyday world.

The first Christian hermits withdrew into the deserts of Egypt, but the *idea* of seeking peace and enlightenment in austere solitude is much older than Christianity. Buddhists and Hebrews had both conceived and practised it long before.

184

Indeed, Buddha himself spent five years among the barren hills of Rajagriha before he received his sudden revelation in the Deer Park near Benares. As Christianity spread westward the monastic habit of mind and body spread with it. In Anglo-Saxon England, and in Celtic Christendom, Scotland, Ireland, and Wales, thick-walled monasteries arose from the flowering meadows and from the grey hillsides, and these brotherhoods, varying in numbers from a mere dozen to several hundreds, praised God, worked with their hands, and led lives of primitive simplicity. When St Augustine came to Kent he brought with him an ideal of monastic life slightly different from that evolved by the Celtic Church—the Benedictine ideal. Before St Benedict wrote his *Rule* both Gaulish and Celtic monasticism greatly resembled the Egyptian type, and tended toward individualism. Each brother was a sort of self-contained unit, an 'island,' and there was no complete uniformity, no sense of the pervading community to which the individual must be subdued. All this was changed, and medieval monasticism was created, by that very remarkable man St Benedict. The place of his birth was Nursia, in Umbria, and the time 480. The Roman Empire was in the last distressful stages of decay, battered without and corrupt within. Benedict, sick at heart, fled from Rome itself, whither he had been sent to complete his education, and took refuge in a dark gorge of the river Anio, forty miles from the doomed city. There he remained for three years, and there he was sought out by the monks of a neighbouring monastery, who persuaded him, against his will, to place himself at their head. They soon regretted it, for his ideas were so much more severe than theirs that they attempted to get rid of him by the simple and picturesque device of a poisoned cup. The cup split asunder in his hands before he had raised it to his lips, and, with a quiet rebuke to their ingratitude, he rose and departed from their midst for ever. Near the source of the river Liris there stood, on a lonely hill called Monte Cassino, a ruined temple dedicated to the god of the golden bow, Apollo. In this place,

and on the site of this pagan shrine, Benedict spent the closing
years of his life. The old faith was not yet dead; the poor folk
of the valley still brought offerings to the old god. Benedict

PASSAGES IN THE LIFE OF ST BENEDICT
On the left monks persuading Benedict to leave his hermitage ; on the right, offering
the poisoned cup. From a fresco of the fourteenth century.

razed Apollo's temple to the ground, and built there two
oratories, one dedicated to St John the Baptist and one to St
Martin of Tours. Round these two chapels grew the great
monastery of Monte Cassino, the cradle of the Benedictine
Order. Not far away was a nunnery, founded by Benedict's
pious and devoted sister, Scholastica, with whom he spent one
186

day once a year. The great change introduced by Benedict into Western monasticism was the idea of unity, obedience, and labour as the basis of the holy life. No longer might each good brother 'gang his ain gait.' The abbot, or in smaller fraternities the prior, ruled them all in all things. No longer might each good brother meditate when he felt inclined, and do nothing but meditate, except when he was at prayer. Prayer and meditation were to be the duty of all the brothers, at certain fixed hours, and between times they were to work with their hands. To this last clause in the Benedictine rule the debt of Europe, especially England and France, could hardly be exaggerated. Thanks to the devoted toil of the black-robed brethren, shaggy

PRIOR REYMUND OF ST ALBANS

heaths were turned into green pastures, bleak wastes into fields of corn. Nor was this the sum of the debt. When there were no schools and no hospitals the great monasteries provided the equivalent of both. When, for lack of the still undreamed-of printing-press, learning might have perished the patient quills of monkish scribes kept records of history, ancient and modern, fabulous and true, of philosophy, sacred and profane, and copied, again and again, the psalter and the missal and the Old Testament and the New. The Benedictines were, above all things, scholars and builders. Canterbury, York, Westminster, Winchester, and Gloucester, to mention only a few, were Benedictine abbeys. These beautiful churches, now cathedrals, were simply the chapels attached to monasteries, though, as in the case of all those mentioned, special conditions, royal associations, shrines of saints, established contact between the monks and the outer world.

The monks spent the greater part of their time, when they were neither working out of doors nor praying in choir, in some

A SCRIPTORIUM OF THE FIFTEENTH CENTURY

part of the cloisters, the vaulted and traceried arcades running along all four sides of a quadrangle, in the centre of which was a plat of turf. One cloister would be set apart for those monks who were skilful penmen or illuminators, another for the studies of the young novices, another for the weekly washing of the brethren's heads and feet. At Gloucester the *lavatorium*, or washing-place, has altered hardly at all, and you can still see the troughs along which the water was directed, and the hinge-marks of the oaken cupboards where the towels were kept. In summer the flagstones were covered with hay and straw, in winter with rushes. When the stone tracery was unglazed the cold in the cloisters during the winter months must have been

188

almost unendurable, and the poor monks were no doubt glad
to bury their blue noses and numbed fingers in their ample
cowls and cuffs. In the refectory the brethren took their simple

THE WRITING-CELLS OF THE MONKS IN THE SOUTH CLOISTER,
GLOUCESTER CATHEDRAL

repasts. Chatting at table was not allowed, but, lest greedy
thoughts should fill any shaven skull, one of the monks read
aloud some portions of the Old or the New Testament in Latin
while the others dined.   The fare set before them was simple,
but eminently hygienic and—though they had never heard the

magic catch-phrase—'rich in vitamins.' Vegetable soup was the main item, and beans loomed large in the menu. Eggs from the monastery hens and fish from the monastery ponds were often seen, and meat, salted or fresh, appeared from time to time, though not frequently. It is pleasant to think that at Easter the good monks had lamb and mint sauce. Even pork was not unknown. At some monasteries, for example, at St Edmundsbury, staid married women of good repute were engaged from time to time to make puddings and tarts for the refectory table. The 'pudding-wives,' as they were called, had a special building to work in, the 'pudding-house,' and we can well believe that the younger monks rejoiced when the word went round that these good dames were busy inside. Courtesy at table was strictly enjoined, and at the conclusion of each repast two young monks brought a basket and collected any remains, crusts, odd pieces of bread, etc., for the use of the poor. The monk, as Cardinal Gasquet has reminded us, "was in no sense a gloomy person." *Angelic cheerfulness joined to monastic simplicity* summed up the monastic ideal at its sanest and best. The novices were allowed to play bowls and other games, even in the cloisters, where squares and circles neatly traced upon the flagstones still bear witness that the life led in that quadrangle of fretted stone was not all gloom and toil. Fishing was a duty and a diversion as well. Some abbots indulged in the pleasures of the chase; others kept pet animals, dogs, falcons, and monkeys. Sometimes the monks were so blithe and merry that people spoke a little ill-naturedly of them, or criticized their doings quite severely. In the main, however, the religious were liked by their neighbours, who had proof every day of the fidelity with which the divine words "Inasmuch as ye have done it unto one of the least of these My brethren, ye have done it unto Me" were remembered and translated into deeds within the monastery walls. Attached to many of the great abbeys—though by no means to all—were hospitals where the sick poor might be received and tended for the love of God; and even when the

ABBOT'S KITCHEN, GLASTONBURY

Frith photo

infirmary was not open to any but the brethren the good counsels of the infirmarian, the brother in charge, backed up by strong spices, ginger, cinnamon, and peony-seeds, were usually at the disposal of such as sought them at the abbey gate. At the hospital attached to the Augustinian priory of St Bartholomew the Great, Smithfield—a hospital which has now pursued its noble work without a pause for more than eight hundred years—the first patient ever admitted was a poor carpenter whose hands were crippled with rheumatism. Under the care of the monks he recovered; but such was his gratitude, and so happy had he been, he would not go away! Rather did he choose to spend the rest of his days in the priory, working at his craft as a carpenter for the benefit of his monkish friends, and ac-

THE INFIRMARIAN OF ST ALBAN'S
ABBEY

cepting in return only such simple food and lodging as they could give.

Next to the robe and the cowl, the distinguishing mark of the monk was his shaven head. The giving and the renewing of the tonsure (Latin, *tondere*, to shave or shear) was an important part of monkish practice. After the tenth century the initial tonsure could be bestowed only by a bishop or an abbot, and its bestowal was accompanied by solemn and elaborate ceremonies. It symbolized the dedication of the subject to some branch or aspect of the religious life. But because a youth or a man had

191

received the tonsure it did not follow that he must become either a priest or a monk. All 'clerks,' all men in 'orders minor,' and even all boys in the monastic schools were bound to have their

heads shaved. And the clerk, scholar, priest, or monk who omitted to repeat the process once a month thereby forfeited the rights and privileges which he had automatically acquired when he first received it. The exact origin of the custom is obscure; but it may well be that the circle of unshorn hair was meant to represent the crown of thorns. Every brother of every order, from the abbot to the youngest novice, wore the tonsure until his death.

YOUNG MONKS RECEIVING THE TONSURE

Monks who showed practical ability and proved themselves to be good organizers were not allowed to bury these useful talents in napkins, but given free opportunity to exercise them for the benefit of the community at large. Such men were appointed cellarers, refectorians, kitcheners, guest-masters, almoners, or chamberlains. The cellarer had charge not only of the beer and wine of the monastery—it must be remembered that pure drinking-water was hard to come by, and that the beer was *small* beer, of very low alcoholic strength—but of all the provisions necessary; he was, as Cardinal Gasquet says, "the 'Martha' of

192

the establishment." The refectorian's duties were with the table-linen and utensils; he had to see that fresh rushes, hay, or straw were strewn on the refectory floor, and sometimes in summer he added mint, fennel, and sweet-smelling herbs to purify the air. The kitchener looked after the pots and pans, had them mended when worn out, and replaced when past service; he also had charge of the poultry being fattened for the monastic table. The guest-master looked after the poor wayfarers to whom the guest-hall of the monastery was ever open, and also after the more prosperous visitors who sometimes came as 'paying guests.' The almoner's duties were many, and he had much to do besides dividing alms among the poor. In cold weather he distributed the old gowns of the monks to the needy, and gave presents of woollen stockings to "widows, orphans, and poor clerks." Here he and the chamberlain would take counsel together, as it was the chamberlain who had charge of the monastic wardrobe.

The daily offices said and sung in the monastic church were eight in number: *matins*, sung at midnight or soon after, and followed immediately by *lauds*; *prime*, at six o'clock in the morning; *terce*, at nine o'clock; *sext*, at noon; *none*, at 3 P.M.; *vespers*, toward sunset; *compline*, before retiring to rest. Six o'clock in the morning was reckoned as the *first* hour, so noon was naturally the sixth.

The Order of St Benedict was the most numerous and the most influential in medieval England, but there were many monks of other orders scattered up and down the land, wearing robes of different colours, and keeping slightly different rules. Some of these orders were themselves offshoots of the Benedictine. Such were the Cistercians, so called from the monastery of Cîteaux, in France. Their habit was white, and their practices were austere. Candlesticks of iron instead of silver-gilt appeared on their altars, and their priests sang Mass in chasubles of humble fustian instead of samite or baudekin. Even more austere were the Carthusians, founded by St Bruno among the mountains near Grenoble. Not for them were the roast lamb and mint sauce of the gentler Benedictines. They ate (and eat, for the order still flourishes) but one meal a day, and that had to be of pulse, bread, and water only. The habit was white, and the tonsure was more drastic than in other orders. Members of the Augustinian order were the clergy of cathedral and collegiate churches. They lived in communities after the manner of monks, and were known as Canons Regular, and also, from the colour of their gowns, as Black Canons.

Careless readers (and writers) often fail to distinguish between monks and friars. These latter were originally missionaries, sent forth by their founders to rekindle the fading fires of pious ardour both among the priests and among the laity. They were travellers, wayfarers, men of no abiding city, except when—as at Oxford—they founded schools. There were, of course, houses where friars gathered together, but they did not live strictly according to fixed rules and time-tables as the monks did, nor were they under the governance of abbots or priors, nor were they, collectively or individually, attached to one single place.

The two chief orders of friars in medieval England were the Dominicans and the Franciscans. The great aim of St Dominic was the stamping out of heresy. He was a Spaniard, fervent to fanaticism, yet so tender-hearted that he would shed bitter tears over the spiritual plight of the heretics whom he sought to bring back to the faith they had discarded. His Friars Preachers multiplied rapidly, and journeyed to the wildest and most perilous regions of the world—to Persia, India, China, Russia, Tartary, and even to Tibet. Their white robes and cowls and black cloaks were seen first in England when Peter de Rupibus, Bishop of Winchester, brought some of them in his train in the year 1221. When Henry VIII's rude hands pulled down the monastic system in England the Dominicans had fifty-eight convents, one being as far north as Bamborough, one as far west as Brecon, one as far south as Chichester. Their friary in London, where the trial of Catherine of Aragon took place, has long since

194

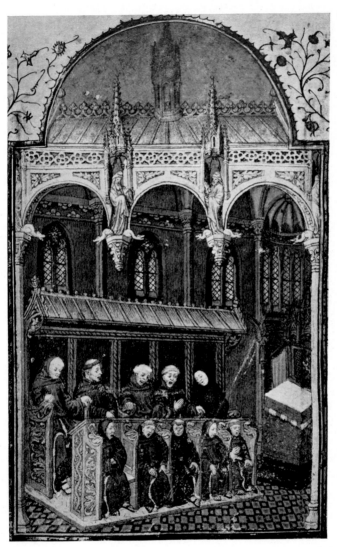

FRANCISCANS IN CHOIR
From the Psalter of Henry VI
British Museum   194

vanished, but the place where it stood is still called Blackfriars. The Franciscans, the other great order of friars, modestly dubbed themselves the Minorites, the Friars Minor, the *least* of the friars. Following their founder, the gentle Francis of Assisi, they vowed themselves to poverty, chastity, and obedience, and devoted themselves to missionary work (what would now be called 'propaganda'!) not only among the heretics and the heathen, but among Christians whose faith had grown cold. Their habit was at first grey, and from the knotted cord with which it was girt they were sometimes called "Cordeliers." In the fifteenth century, however, the colour was changed to brown, which it has remained ever since. The Franciscans reached England in 1223. At Oxford they founded the school of which Robert Grosseteste [1] became Rector, and where the chief glory of their order—though the heads of it did not realize it at the time—studied and taught. This was Grosseteste's friend Roger Bacon, whose experiments and researches gained for him the reputation of a dabbler in black arts. Mother Shipton and her prophecies belong to the borderland of fact and fable; Roger Bacon really did predict that men would fly in the air and travel swiftly in the depths of the sea. He has been described as "the first man of science in the modern sense." [2] He devised something in the nature of a telescope more than three centuries before Galileo was born; he was the first to give the formula for the production of gunpowder; and it was his arguments about the size and shape of the earth which helped to convince Columbus of the existence of a western continent.

The Carmelites were also known as the White Friars, and they too have given their name to a district in modern London. They originated in a company of hermits who dwelt upon the grim and inhospitable flanks of Mount Carmel. The third general of the order was an Englishman with the bluff and

[1] See Chapter IX.
[2] Dr Charles Singer in *Medieval Contributions to Modern Civilization* (Harrap).

breezy name of Simon Stock, and they were introduced into England by a Crusader, Sir John de Vesci, who is said to have ascended Mount Carmel during his wanderings in the Holy Land.

The nuns, on their side, played a very important part in medieval life, and introduced a gracious, tranquil, and civilizing

FRANCISCAN NUNS IN CHOIR
Fifteenth century.   From King Henry VI's Psalter.

influence in a world where such influences were all too rare. Within their convent walls the art of embroidery and the science of leechcraft were practised, and the young daughters of nobles, knights, and burgesses were received as pupils.   They had gardens as well as orchards, pastures, and fields of grain.   Their cloisters and their parlours were often oases of fragrance and quiet, set here and there in a grey and restless waste.   From the account-books of Dame Petronilla, a nun of the convent of Grâce Dieu in Leicestershire in the days of Henry V, we know that among the livestock of the sisterhood there were many pigs. Fish, salt and fresh, appeared with wearisome frequency at the board, served sometimes with mustard, sometimes—as a singular treat—with sugar. These nuns wore gowns of white wool, woven from the fleeces of their own flocks and within their own walls, and wimples of white linen spun from the blue-flowering flax of their own meadows. In addition to weaving and spinning, collecting and drying herbs and simples, looking after their farms and their tenants, and singing the offices of each day, these nuns—and others all over the land—employed themselves much with needlecraft. Most of the richly embroidered copes and chasubles, altar-frontals, banners, palls, and canopies that gave added splendour and solemnity to divine service were the work of their patient and skilful hands. Their stitchery is exquisitely fine, their silken and golden threads are grouped with wonderful judgment, and if the little figures of saints and seraphim sometimes make us smile, with their quaint, stiff outlines and their surprised faces, the charm of the good nuns' handiwork is not one whit the less for that. English ecclesiastical embroidery was famous all over the Continent, especially in Italy, where it was known as *opus Anglicanum*, or English work. The convents in which feminine accomplishments were cultivated were usually of the Benedictine order. Life was more strenuous and more austere in Franciscan and Carmelite nunneries. The Minoresses or Nuns of St Clare, sometimes called the Poor Clares, were founded by St Clare, the spiritual sister and devoted follower of Francis of Assisi. They wore the girdle of knotted cord, and went barefoot, or shod only with sandals.

The Bridgettine Convent founded at Isleworth by Henry V, to which we alluded when speaking of the famous Syon Cope, imposed upon its sixty nuns, thirteen priests, and eight lay brethren certain hours of strict silence every day, but as they were allowed to communicate with each other at such times with the aid of an elaborate code of signs the rule cannot have been particularly irksome in practice. This code has been preserved, and includes the signs representing such diverse things as apples, beds, bells, brooms, fish, ink, milk, mustard, water, and wine, proper nouns such as king, queen, abbess, priest, lay brother, verbs such as sleeping, eating, drinking, writing, chiming, singing, and standing. "Buttur or other fatness" was suggested by drawing the two first fingers of the right hand to and fro upon the palm of the left, "fisshe" by wagging the hand

ABBOT AND MONKS IN CHAPTER-HOUSE

sideways "in maner of a fissh taill," mustard by holding the nose in the right fist and rubbing it, sleep by putting the right hand under the cheek and shutting the eyes.

The conscientious monk who was aware of some lapse from duty on his part had an alarming ordeal to undergo when the brethren assembled in the chapter-house. This they did every day, immediately after morning Mass. A great variety of business, both pious and practical, was transacted in these beautiful buildings, placed on the eastern side of the cloisters. Where— as at Westminster and York—one of them remains in something like its former glory, it is possible to imagine most vividly the

198

abbot seated in his stall or chair, with his crozier in his hand, and the cowled and shaven monks silently taking their places, to the heavy tolling of a bell. A monk whose conscience was pricking now had an opportunity to unburden himself. Kneeling on a low stool before the abbot, he confessed his fault. If it were a slight one his superior signified by an inclination of the head that it was pardoned. If it were too serious to be thus mercifully remitted the culprit was stripped and scourged. In chapter-houses such as those at Westminster and Salisbury, where there is a central pillar supporting the roof, it was to this pillar that the monk was bound during his punishment. He suffered in singularly majestic surroundings, for the monkish builders lavished ornamentation on these council-chambers, illuminating them with vast jewelled windows, surmounting the stalls of the brethren with delicately wrought canopies and pinnacles, and making the walls gay with many-coloured frescoes. One of the most beautiful of all was—and is—the chapter-house at York, with its amazing wealth of carving, its heads and figures, some serious and some the reverse, its clambering and brimming-over masses of fretted foliage. Bogo de Clare, to whom the credit for building it seems to have been due, was not in every respect a praiseworthy person, but he certainly wrought well in this one thing, and perhaps the proud and grateful monks, gazing on their glorious chapter-house, were not disposed to be excessively severe upon his failings. In a cathedral which was simply the administrative centre of a diocese the chapter-house was used as a meeting-place by the bishop and his officers, who assembled there to discuss ecclesiastical and even secular affairs. Such was the very beautiful chapter-house at Wells.

We shall later have something to say about the pilgrimages which were such an important and interesting feature in medieval life, but here and now we may allow ourselves a glimpse at one or two immortal pilgrims, members of that motley company with whom Chaucer jogged along the road to Canterbury. There were among them a Monk, a Friar, a Host, a Prioress with a nun and a chaplain in attendance on her, and an Augustinian Canon. The Monk was as jovial a fellow as Prior Aymer in *Ivanhoe*, and the merry tinkling of his bridle-bells accorded well with his plump and rosy face and his restless, waggish eyes.

PILGRIMS LEAVING CANTERBURY
From a manuscript

No doubt his duties made it necessary for him to stir abroad and mingle with the jostling world, and no doubt he carried them out with alacrity. The saying that a monk out of his cloister is like a fish out of water appeared singularly foolish to him, and for the suggestion that holiness and hunting do not go together he did not give "a pullèd hen." To brighten the severity of his monkish attire he wore trimmings of grey fur on his sleeves, and fastened his hood under his chin with a curious gold pin in the form of a true lovers' knot. The Host was quick to see that here was   No pourè cloysterer, ne no novys;

and, when he calls upon him to tell a story to while away the time, he says admiringly:

> Upon my feith, thou art som officer,
> Som worthy sexteyn [1] or som celerer,
> For by my fader soule, as to my doom [2]
> Thou art a maister when thou art at hoom.

Both the Host and the other pilgrims were greatly disappointed when this burly monk, instead of amusing them with some merry tale, proceeded to "tell sad stories of the deaths of kings," and of other notable personages who came to a bad end, among them "Sampson, this noble almyghty champioun," Hercules, "Nabugodonozor," Zenobia, "of Palymerie queene," Pedro the Cruel, Julius Cæsar, and "riche Cresus whilom kyng of Lyde." At last the patience of one of the most polite pilgrims gives out.

"Hoo!" quod the Knyght, "good sire, namoore of this!"

The Friar pleases them far better with his lively tale of how a Somonour, an ecclesiastical officer, got the worse of a bargain with the Evil One. This Friar was a 'lymytour,' licensed to collect offerings and gifts for the benefit of his order, and Chaucer makes it clear that he performed that part of his duty most successfully.

> Ful swetely herdè he confessioun
> And plesaunt was his absolucioun;
> He was an esy man to yeve penaunce
> Ther as he wiste to have a good pitaunce; [3]
> For unto a poure ordre for to yive
> Is signè that a man is wel y-shryve; [4] . . .
> Therfore in stede of wepynge and preyères
> Men moote yeve silver to the pourè freres.

He was a cheerful fellow, who sang and played upon the 'rote' (a small harp), and whose hood was stuck full of little

[1] sacristan. [2] opinion.
[3] Where he knew there was plenty of money.
[4] shriven.

knives and pins intended as presents to the pious and open-handed dames upon his 'round.' As for the Host, at whose tavern in Southwark the pilgrims assembled, he was drawn from life, and even his real name—Harry Bailly—was given. A tactful, genial, and shrewd Host he was, though he appears to have been in some awe of his wife.

All the company, even the most boisterous, quarrelsome, and rough-tongued, unite in paying honour to the Prioress, and hers is indeed a gracious and charming figure. She has her little affectations, she counterfeits "cheere of Court," she speaks French, the Court language,

> ful faire and fetisly [1]
> After the scole of Stratford-attè-Bowe,
> For Frenssh of Parys was to hire unknowe.

From this Chaucer means it to be understood that his pretty, grey-eyed Prioress was educated at the Benedictine convent of Stratford-le-Bow, where Anglo-Norman French was taught long after the more up-to-date "Frenssh of Parys" was used elsewhere. It was probably at the same convent that Madame Eglentyne—her name is as pretty as herself—learnt to sing

> the servicè dyvyne
> Entunèd in hir nose ful semèly.

She was compassionate, gentle, and so full of pity that the sight of a mouse in a trap would bring tears to her grey eyes, "if it were deed or bledde"; and great was her wrath if any man dared strike one of the little "houndès," which she fed on

> Rosted flessh, or milk and wastel breed. [2]

Dainty and coquettish and coy was Madame Eglentyne; and that she was fair to look upon as well Chaucer convinces us. Her neatly folded wimple would serve only to emphasize the beauty of her broad brow, her delicately cut nose, her eyes "greye as glas," and her mouth small, soft, and red. The monk

---

[1] daintily.   [2] cake of fine flour.

allowed himself a touch of finery in the form of a gold brooch; the Prioress's innocent vanity found expression in a coral bracelet with green beads from which hung a pendant of gold, with an 'A' surmounted by a crown, and the motto *Amor vincit omnia*—Love conquers all things.

That nuns were allowed to possess—and so, presumably, to wear—jewels is proved by the Will of Elizabeth of Hainault, sister of Queen Philippa, who spent the last years of her life as a boarder in St Leonard's Convent, Bromley-by-Bow, and who bequeathed to the Lady Abbess "a gold ring with two stones, to wit, a ruby and an emerald." The ladies who lodged in nunneries without actually taking vows appear to have made themselves very comfortable,

THE PRIORESS

and to have practised few—if any—austerities. Elizabeth of Hainault had robes of various colours—green, tawny, and blue—gold rings, beads, brooches, and tablets, mantles edged with fur, prayer-books bound in red, and blankets and curtains of colours not specified. We may imagine Chaucer's Prioress enjoying the society of any great lady who boarded in her convent, and perhaps inheriting from her some of the little trinkets which she loved to wear.

The Black Canon did not set out with the pilgrims from Southwark, but overtook and joined them at Boghton-under-Blee. Under his black habit he wore a white surplice, and under his hood he had put a burdock-leaf

> For swoot,[1] and for to kepe his heed from heete.

His yeoman, or attendant, was an odd-looking fellow with a face strangely smudged and discoloured. Presently the pilgrims learnt the reason of his odd looks. His master dabbled in alchemy, and it was by dint of blowing the fire upon which he

---

[1] sweat.

heated his divers weird and mysterious chemicals that his unfortunate assistant had 'chaunged' his colour.   It is by way of a
'Canterbury Tale' that the yeoman relates his various hardships
and adventures in the service of this priest-alchemist.   The
Prioress tells the story of little St Hugh of Lincoln, and

> When seyd was al this miracle every man
> As sobre was that wonder was to se.

CHAPTER XI

THE MIRACLE PLAYS

ET les vignerons barbouillés de lie, debout dans leurs chariots, échangeant avec les passants la moquerie et l'invective, inventaient la tragédie.[1]

In these vivid words Anatole France describes how Greek dramatic art began. It began with the festivities held every year in honour of Dionysos, the god of the vine, him whom the Romans later invoked under the name of Bacchus. Crowds would naturally gather round the cart where stood the cultivator with the readiest wit and the most nimble tongue. Then two of the 'performers' would exchange chaff with each other, instead of with the audience; and then, in order to make their dialogue more effective, the two would invent and rehearse their respective parts beforehand. From these rustic dialogues, from dances and songs in honour of Dionysos, and mimic representations of his death and his coming to life again, were born Greek comedy and Greek tragedy. Their beginnings, like those of the art of dancing, and like those of the children's games played in a ring, were purely religious.

The Romans borrowed their drama from the Greeks; but medieval Christendom did not borrow its drama from the Romans.[2] The Dark Ages, the ages when barbarians from North-eastern Europe overwhelmed the ancient civilization of the West, intervened. Goths and Vandals and Visigoths, these

---

[1] " And the vine-growers, their faces dabbled with wine-lees, perched on their carts and bandying quips with the passers-by, invented the drama."

[2] The Roman *tradition* was never wholly effaced. Hroswitha, the dramatist nun of Gandersheim in the tenth century, bears witness to the popularity of Terence among educated readers ; but Terence was not the ancestor of the medieval drama of the people.

barbarians cared as little for "the glory that was Greece" as they did for "the grandeur that was Rome." In a blind, blundering way they realized that both the glory and the grandeur were far beyond their reach; they could attain unto neither. When Christendom emerged, slowly and painfully, from the thick gloom of the Dark Ages all the dramatic tradition of the antique world had been lost. Yet the connecting-link between religion and drama was found to be unbroken when, not less slowly and painfully, literature and art revived. The liturgy and the ritual, the ceremonies and the language, of many of the sacred offices of the Roman Church were, in their very essence, dramatic. The word 'drama' comes from the Greek *draein*, to do, or to act. At the most holy moment of the Mass the officiating priest, in a sense, *acted* the part of the Saviour at the Last Supper. When, on the Thursday in Passion week, princes and prelates solemnly washed the feet of poor men they too were actors in a religious drama. The element of dialogue entered in when the clergy chanted alternately from opposite sides of the chancel. Thus, at Christmas, the question *Quem quæritis in præsepe, pastores?* ("Whom do you seek in this stable, O Shepherds?") was asked by one group of chanting clerks, and answered by another group, who sang, *Salvatorem Christum Dominum* ("The Saviour, Christ the Lord"). In order to impress the main outlines of the Gospel story upon the memories of her simple worshippers, the medieval Church very wisely emphasized and developed this dramatic quality in her ceremonial. At Easter the dialogue between the angel and the three women at the Holy Sepulchre afforded an opportunity for 'acting a story' which the priests were not slow to seize. The annual ceremonies of the Boy Bishop,[1] and the gorgeous and elaborate processions in which the laity were allowed to join upon various pious anniversaries, all tended to the development of a drama that, however sacred its origins might be, very soon became thoroughly secularized. Meanwhile another influence

[1] See *The Boy through the Ages*, by D. M. Stuart (Harrap).

was at work, that of the jesters, *jongleurs*, and strolling mounte-banks, a large part of whose patter consisted of tales and songs cast in a dramatic form, sometimes grave, but more often gay.

These forces were making themselves felt simultaneously on both sides of the English Channel. It is interesting, however, to notice that while among the French secular subjects soon crept in, tales from history and romance, popular legends, the adventures, joys, and sorrows of famous knights and ladies, in England the Bible narrative and the lives of the saints continued to hold the foremost place. Plays borrowed from the Bible were usually called 'mystery plays'; those from the lives of the saints 'miracles'; but the two terms were interchangeable, and it was not until the second half of the fifteenth century that the allegorical dramas known as 'moralities' or 'morals,' such as *Everyman* and *The Pride of Life*, thrust themselves into the centre of the stage.

The people loved the dramatization of Holy Writ which, at certain seasons, took place within the walls of the church itself. After a time the performance—for such it had become—was given on a scaffold or platform in the churchyard, where a larger audience could assemble, and where the action and dialogue were unhampered by the sacredness of the surroundings. In-side the church Latin only might be said or sung; outside patches of the common speech, the language "understanded of the people," soon appeared. The principal performers were the clergy, the choristers, and the parish clerks; but the laity were permitted later to play minor parts—and also to share the expenses of the production. Then austerely minded prelates began to be alarmed at the popularity of these pious shows, and, by discouraging them, broke the bond linking the drama to the Church. The transition from the churchyard play to the craftsmen's pageant was gradual, but it was steady. The plays passed from the hands of the priests to those of the people. New elements crept in—dance, song, stage properties, fanciful costumes, pathos, farce, buffoonery. The guilds of the various crafts made themselves responsible for the annual representation of the miracle plays, in which the principal *rôles* were acted by the craftsmen themselves, and there came into being a national drama, crude, simple, and quaint, but full of colour and energy, and the direct ancestor of that supreme glory of the English race, the drama of the age of Elizabeth.

The characters, plots, and actions of the plays remained almost entirely Biblical, and the association between the drama and the Church survived as late as the time of Chaucer, when Absolon, the parish clerk of Oxford, played the part of Herod "on a scaffold hye." When the parts were being allotted there was no doubt brisk competition as to who should enact Herod, for it was a most exciting *rôle*, demanding much stamping, roaring, and glaring, and the donning of gorgeous attire, with crown, sceptre, and glittering crest. In *A Midsummer Night's Dream* we see a group of Athenian craftsmen planning a performance of *Pyramus and Thisbe*; but the men are as English as their names—Bottom, Quince, Snug, Flute, Starveling, Snout—and the "wood near Athens" where they meet to rehearse is very much more like a wood of Warwickshire. Just after this fashion, though perhaps in less delightful surroundings, must the craftsmen of the guilds have met each year to discuss their forthcoming pageants. We can imagine Nick Bottom clamouring for the part of Herod, or, failing that, for the part of Pilate. For Pilate was another part that demanded good lungs. Chaucer's Miller, in his most boisterous mood, shouted "in Pilátes voys."

As a boy Shakespeare had probably been taken by his father to see the famous Coventry plays, which survived the Reformation, and were not abandoned for good till the year 1580. Many allusions in his own plays seem to be inspired by childish memories of these gorgeous and yet alarming spectacles.

> 'Tis the eye of childhood
> That fears a painted devil,

says Lady Macbeth. And we know from the Coventry accounts that there were 'painted devils,' and fearful ones, to be seen there. And there were 'painted devils' at Stratford-on-Avon, painted on the wall of the Guildhall, and now, unfortunately, effaced. (See illustration on p. 213.) When Hamlet is giving his instructions to the strolling players he bids them beware of tearing a passion to tatters, and adds that he would "have such a fellow whipped"—that is to say, a fellow who overacts and rants and roars—since he "out-Herods Herod." A familiar figure in the later miracle and morality plays was the Vice, often an attendant upon some mimic sovereign. He flitted to and fro, he brandished a wooden dagger, he cried "Ah, ha!" in blood-curdling tones. So, in *Twelfth Night*, the Clown rattles off:

> I am gone, sir,
> And anon, sir,
> I'll be with you again,
> In a trice,
> Like to the old Vice,
> Your need to sustain;
> Who with dagger of lath,
> In his rage and his wrath,
> Cries, Ah, ha! to the devil.

During the epoch of transition, when the sacred drama was neither entirely in priestly hands nor wholly absorbed by the laity, it seems that the 'book' of each play was written by some priest or clerk for performance by a mixed cast, clerk and lay. Indeed, in the earlier stages of its development this drama could not have lived otherwise, for the arts of reading and writing, quite apart from the more complicated craft of the verse-maker, were beyond the ken of the multitude. Presently, however, the guilds began to employ their own scribes and their own 'tame poets.' The text of the plays became a queer patchwork, in which expert eyes can detect the hands of various authors belonging to different periods, yet all unified by a sort of rough kinship in conception and treatment. The writer of a miracle or mystery cycle (for none of the plays stood alone) had a vast

o

field to cover—nothing less than the Creation, Perdition, and Redemption of mankind. He must begin before the beginning of the human race, when the Three Persons of the Trinity are represented as discussing among Themselves the future destiny of the newly created world; he must end after the world itself had come to an end, with a vision of the Day of Judgment. Between these two points the whole pageant of the Old Testament and the New is unrolled: Noah builds and launches his Ark, Abraham prepares to sacrifice Isaac, Moses crosses the Red Sea, Gabriel salutes Mary, Christ is born, the shepherds and kings adore Him, the Innocents are slain, and thus by progressive stages we reach Doomsday. Each episode in the long-drawn-out cycle was enacted by members of a different craft or fraternity. At York the Shipwrights most appropriately represented the construction of the Ark, while the Fishers and Mariners showed how the Ark and its crew fared during the Flood; the Chandlers were the shepherds, the Goldsmiths the Three Kings. At the Last Supper the chief actors were Bakers, while the terrors and splendours of the Last Judgment were set forth by the Mercers. At Coventry the Shearmen and Tailors played the Annunciation, Nativity, Adoration of the Shepherds, Epiphany, and Massacre of the Innocents, while the Weavers were responsible for the Presentation in the Temple, and for Jesus disputing with the doctors. At Norwich the Bricklayers and Plasterers played the Creation of Adam and Eve and the Tailors the Descent of Christ into Hell.

At one time there must have been in existence the manuscripts of an enormous number of these curious old plays. Only a small number are known to-day. It is most unfortunate that the London cycle, played every year at Clerkenwell, should have been entirely lost. There remain four cycles, not complete, but yet not so fragmentary that their outlines and colours cannot still be discerned. These are the York, Chester, Wakefield (or Towneley), and Coventry plays, to which must be added the even less complete plays of the Digby Manuscript in the

Bodleian Library, and scraps and patches of those once acted at Beverley, Lincoln, and other towns in provincial England.

To the reader whose mind is not attuned to the peculiar and characteristic harmonies of the Middle Ages the miracle plays must seem strange and grotesque in their mingling of gravity and gaiety, of the most heart-searching ideas, the most tear-compelling spectacles, with wild buffoonery and horseplay. To the medieval mentality these abrupt changes of mood were both natural and easy. The same good citizen who, at one moment, was roaring with laughter at the sad plight of the henpecked patriarch Noah would the next moment shed tears over the art-less pleading of young Isaac. Sometimes the farce and the pathos would overlap in a single scene, as in the Coventry play where Herod's soldiers come to slay the Innocents. Here one of the indignant mothers, learning their errand, and preparing for single combat with one of them, exclaims:

> Sytt he neyver soo hy in saddull,
> But I schall make his braynis addull,
> And here with my pott-ladull
> With hym woll I fyght.

But resistance is vain. The babes are killed, and the first soldier, with an almost audible shudder, asks:

> Who hard eyver soche a cry
> Of wemen thatt there chyldur have lost?

As the popular drama expanded and developed the method of its presentation altered. Instead of a "scaffold hye" in the churchyard the players had a movable platform on wheels, which was dragged from one recognized halting-place to another, that the play might be given at various points and before many people. Instead of borrowing from the church copes of em-broidered sarcenet and baudekin wherein to array their prin-cipal *dramatis personæ* the players then had costumes and stage properties of their own, paid for out of the subscriptions of the craftsmen, and furbished up from time to time as they grew

211

shabby and old. The waggon upon which the plays were performed was itself called the pageant, padgand, or pagond. Sometimes it had four wheels, sometimes six; sometimes eight stout fellows, and sometimes ten, were needed to pull it from one halting-place to another, and they, together with the minstrels who cheered them on their way, had to be liberally refreshed with "met and drynk." In 1462 one of the Coventry pageants was provided with a pair of new "whelys," which cost eight shillings; grease or soap to make the "whelys" turn more smoothly, nails and hooks, tallow and rushes, had occasionally to be purchased. The Grocers of Norwich owned an impressive pageant described in their records as "a Howse of Waynscott with foure whelys," surmounted by a gilded griffin. The lower part of these cumbersome, two-tiered vehicles was curtained off, and served as a robing-room for the players. The upper part was the stage, but a very small one, which must have been painfully overcrowded when more than two performers had to appear upon it at a time. Indeed, strenuous characters, such as Herod, were apt to find it impossibly small, for in the Coventry Shearmen's play, after Herod had exclaimed:

I stampe! I stare! I loke all abowtt!

we encounter the stage direction, *Here Erode ragis in the pagond and in the strete also.* The scenery cannot have been elaborate, and probably consisted as a rule of coloured curtains, but startling effects were sometimes aimed at, as when "Hellmouth" was seen vomiting flames, or an image of the world itself was set on fire. The Norwich Grocers had a fascinating tree, hung each year with "orenges, fyges, allmondes, dates, reysens, preunes, and aples." Stage properties were numerous. In scenes representing the Creation a "Rybbe colleryd Red" was necessary, so that Eve should be extracted in a convincing manner from Adam's side. Kings had crowns and sceptres gay with gilt, and all the principal performers, including Satan, wore gloves. At Coventry Herod was made gorgeous with "silver

212

papur" and "gold papur," gold foil and green foil, and "blowe bokeram." God the Father appeared in a garment of white leather, painted and gilded; Christ wore a wig of gilded hair. It would be interesting to know of what colour was the "bockram" in which the Coventry Cappers arrayed the "Spret of

HELL-MOUTH
From a fresco at Stratford-on-Avon

God." In 1478 sevenpence was paid for the mending of the garments of Procula, Pilate's wife, and in 1480 Pilate's hat required—and received—the same attention. The part of Procula was taken by a man, but a certain good dame of Coventry, "Maisturres Grymesby," was rewarded in 1487 with the handsome sum of twelvepence "for lendyng off her geir for Pylatt's wyfe."

Though all the performers were what would now be called 'amateurs,' and (with the solitary exception of the minstrels)

213

no 'professional' person took part, their exertions did not go unrewarded, and each received a small sum of money for his services. In the Smiths' pageant of the year 1490 it is recorded that the following payments were made:

> *Imprimis*—to God, ij*s*., to Heroude, iij*s*. iiij*d*.—to Pilatt is wyffe ij*s*.

It will be noticed that "Heroude" receives one shilling more than God, but this may have been because his stamping and staring *rôle* demanded greater energy. In the Weavers' pageant several decades later "Josoff" received fourteenpence, "Marè" tenpence, and the "letell chylde" fourpence. In the Coventry Drapers' pageant, which showed forth Doomsday, there were white (or saved) and black (or damned) "sowlys." Oddly enough, the white souls received only eighteenpence each, as against the two shillings paid to every black one. Perhaps there was a certain reluctance among the worthy Drapers to disguise themselves as spirits beyond hope of redemption.

What of the plays themselves, what of the words recited and the songs sung by these rough, ardent craftsmen upon their creaking stage? All the dialogues and soliloquies are in rhyme, and the varying length of the lines gives them a lyrical quality which preserves them from heaviness. Some of these old playwrights have an extraordinary affection for long, impressive, sonorous words; others can, under the influence of strong feeling, write with poignant simplicity. The story of Abraham and Isaac made an especially powerful appeal to the medieval mind, and was retold many times, amid much weeping. Of the comparatively small number of miracle plays which survive no less than six are devoted to this theme. In a fifteenth-century manuscript known as the Brome Manuscript, from the name of the Suffolk manor-house where it was preserved, the story is unfolded with a most engaging mixture of simplicity, pompousness, and real pathos. When "Ysaac" has learnt that it is God's will that he should be sacrificed he exclaims:

> Now, I wold to God my moder were here on this hyll!
> Sche would knele for me on both hyr kneys
> To save my lyffe!

Abraham laments, weeps, wrings his hands, but dares not disobey the divine command. Ysaac, with a nobility of soul equalled only by that of Casabianca more than three centuries later, prepares to meet his doom:

> I prey yow, fader, make ye no woo,
> For, be I onys ded and fro yow goo,
> I schall be sone out of yowre mynd.
> Ther-for doo owre Lorde's byddyng,
> And wan I am ded, than prey for me;
> But, good fader, tell ye my moder no thyng,
> Sey that I am in a-nother cuntrè dwellýng.

The agony is relentlessly prolonged, for both audience and players enjoyed it to the full. Ysaac asks his father's blessing, asks him to blindfold him that he may not see the stroke of the "scharpe sword," asks him not to "tery" not once, but several times. His thoughts turn again to his absent and all-unwitting mother:

> Now, far-wyll, my moder so swete,
> Wee too be leke no mor to mete!

At last the perturbed patriarch screws his courage to the sticking-place, but at the critical moment the angel takes the sword "in hys hond soddenly." The angel has been sent by God, Who thanks Abraham

> an C. sythe [1]
> For the kepyng of hys commawment,

and Who has provided a "fayr ram" to take Ysaac's place in the sacrifice. Poor Ysaac is incredulous when his father joyfully tells him to "Arysse up," and ejaculates:

> A! fader, full glad then wer I,
> I-wys, fader, I sey, i-wys,
> Yf thys tale were trew!

---

[1] a hundred times.

The sight of the luckless ram in the thicket convinces him, however, and when he is sent to fetch the creature he prattles to it in this strain:

> A! scheppe, scheppe, blyssyd mot thou be,
> That ever thow were sent down heder,[1]
> Thow schall thys day dey [2] for me,
> In the worchup of the Holy Trynytė,
> Now cum fast and goo we togeder
>
> To my Fader of Hevyn;
> Thow thou be never so jentyll and good,
> Yet had I lever thou shedyst thi blood,
> I-wysse, scheppe, than I!

Then to his father he says:

> Loo! fader, I have browt here full smerte
> Thys jentyll scheppe, and hym to yow I gyffe;[3]
> But, Lord God, I thank thee with all my hart,
> For I am glad that I shall leve![4]

It is pleasant to find the boy sparing a morsel of pity to the "jentyll scheppe," but we like him still better when, in response to Abraham's urging:

> Cum on with me, my owyn swet sone,
> And hom-ward fast now let us goon,

he exclaims:

> Be my feyth, fader, therto I grant,[5]
> I had never so good wyll to goon hom
> And to speke with my dere moder!

So much for pathos and naturalism. Humorous scenes were everywhere received with delight, but nowhere more than in York, where simple jokes, within the comprehension of the least subtle intellect, were highly popular. The good folk of York year after year heard Mrs Noah scolding her meek husband, the shepherds striving in vain to imitate the singing of the angels, and Cain 'ragging' Abel, and each year the familiar fun seemed funnier than the last. It is very necessary in reading these

---

[1] hither.   [2] die.   [3] give.   [4] live.   [5] I agree to that.

curious old plays to distinguish between conscious and uncon-
scious humour. Some of those passages which make us laugh
most were, doubtless, received with the utmost seriousness by
fifteenth-century audiences. It may well be, as M. Jusserand
says in his delightful *Literary History of the English People*, that
the playwrights felt a "sly pleasure" in caricaturing kings and
princes; but it seems less certain that the audiences grasped
the force of the ridicule. Did they laugh, or were they deeply
thrilled, when Herod informed them at the top of his voice that
he was "cawse of this grett lyght and thunder," that the whole
Orient was under his "obbeydeance," and that with a "twynk"
of his eye not one of his foes would be "lafte alyve"? The more
intelligent among the spectators *may* have laughed; but it seems
probable that the more numerous among them were struck
with awe. Indeed, a marginal note on the manuscript of the
Towneley mysteries records that when the Emperor Tiberius,
after a characteristic bragging and boasting speech, turned to
the crowd and asked:

> Is it nat so? Sey yow all with on [1] showte!

all the "pepul" responded in unison, "Ya, my lord, ya!"

Summer was, naturally, the favourite season for the presentation of these open-air dramas, and the great festival of Corpus
Christi, observed throughout Western Christendom on the
Thursday after Trinity Sunday, was very often the time chosen.
Other days in favour were St John the Baptist's Day, June 24,
St Anne's, July 26, and St Bartholomew's, August 24. There
was no need for the medieval players to appeal to the audience,
as Shakespeare did, to "piece out our imperfections with your
thoughts." The thoughts of those good folk were exceedingly
supple and responsive. Even on a vivid June day, when the
gilded "papur" glittered in the sun, and God the Father panted
under his gorgeous wig, they could shiver during the Nativity
play, and pity the plight of the shepherds watching their flocks

[1] one.

on the cold hills outside Bethlehem. Of all the plays none has so wistful a charm as the Nativity play, to whichever group or cycle it belongs. Such a play has something of the round-eyed *naïveté* of a primitive Florentine or Flemish picture, where the perspective is impossible, the figures are stiff, but the line and colour are exquisitely clear and pure.

The pastors of the Coventry play listen with pious joy to the angelic song. "Harke!" cries the third to his fellows,

> they syng abowe in the clowdis clere!
> Hard I neyver of soo myrrè a quere.[1]
> Now, gentull brethur, draw we nere
> To here there armony!

But the pastors also can sing, though not in Latin, as the angels do. In homely English they raise their song as they go toward Bethlehem to worship the Babe of whom the angels sang:

> As I out rode this enderes night
> Of thre joli sheppardes I saw a sight,
> And all a-bowte there fold a star shone bright;
> *They sang terli-terlow;*
> *So mereli the sheppards ther pipes can blow.*

When they reach Bethlehem and find the young Child with Mary his Mother they kneel down and worship. Then the first shepherd offers a gift to the Babe. He has nothing to give but his pipe, wherein he himself has found "moche pleysure"; he says:

> Hold, hold, take yt in thy hond!

The second shepherd also makes offering:

> Holde, take thow here my hat on thy hedde!
> And now off won thyng thou art well sped,
> For weddur thow hast noo need to complayne,
> For wynd, ne sun, hayle, snoo, and rayne.

The third shepherd, perhaps the youngest and the poorest, now draws near and says:

---

[1] so merry a choir.

THE ADORATION OF THE SHEPHERDS

A mystery play at Coventry

Honor Appleton

> Hayle be thow, Lorde over watur and landis !
> For thy cuming all we ma make myrrthe.
> Have here my myttens to pytt on thy hondis,
> Othur treysure have I non to present the with.

Mary thanks the three gently; she will pray her child, "asse he is heyvin kyng," to bless them all.   Then, as the stage direction decrees, *the scheppardis syngith ageyne and goth forth of the place.* The people are hushed; softly in the distance the singing dies away, and the faint sound of

> *terli-terlow;*
> *So mereli the sheppards ther pipes can blow.*

SHEPHERD WITH
PIPES

CHAPTER XII

PILGRIMS, PILGRIMAGES, AND FESTIVALS

THE motives of the first pilgrims to Palestine were of extreme simplicity. They desired to behold with their own eyes Bethlehem, Calvary, and the Holy Sepulchre. The reward of such a journey lay in its accomplishment, and of no other reward did they dream, in this world or in another. Soon, however, this selfless devotion was coloured by somewhat different ideas. Men began to promise themselves—and each other—definite and tempting prizes at the end of the arduous voyage. Might not the pilgrims hope to be healed of bodily and spiritual ills, released from guilt, assured of bliss hereafter, without any interval of purgatory or any peril of everlasting damnation? When these questions were answered in the affirmative the stream of pilgrims swelled into a flood. Shipmasters prospered greatly; something not unlike a 'tourist' service of passenger vessels was 'run' from suitable harbours in France, Italy, and Spain. Tavern-keepers flourished. So did pirates and bandits. Against the first pilgrims learnt to protect themselves by sailing in groups, or even in fleets, of ships; against the second they were defended by the Knights Templars, an order called into being for that especial purpose in 1118. For such as were sick, or poor, or both, Christian charity raised up hostels and guest-houses along the route. In 1092 certain merchants of Amalfi founded a guest-house or hospital (Latin, *hospes*, a guest), hard by the Holy Sepulchre, and dedicated it to St John the Evangelist. Thence arose the Knights Hospitallers, whose order, much changed as to its outward trappings, survives to this day in the Order of St John of Jerusalem.

220

Though Jerusalem was—and remains—the focus of Christian enthusiasm, the supreme place of pilgrimage, other centres sprang up, and were much frequented by pilgrims too poor, too lazy, or too feeble to undertake the long and perilous journey to Palestine. The tombs of Apostles, saints, and martyrs, and then the churches which possessed even small relics of saints, attracted to themselves an ever-increasing number of pious and

THE CHURCH OF THE HOLY SEPULCHRE, JERUSALEM

hopeful people. Rome, the burial-place of the Apostles Peter and Paul, and the scene of so many martyrdoms, ranked next to Jerusalem in popularity; next to Rome came St James (Santiago) of Compostella, in Spain, where the shrine containing the Apostle's bones was an object of profound and passionate veneration.

Presently the great Christian communities of both Eastern and Western Europe began to set up little shrines within their own borders. These were often, as if by the operation of some mysterious natural law, erected upon spots once sacred to the old pagan gods. To these old gods a stubborn believer would sometimes erect a modest altar to prove that *he*, at least, had not abandoned them. There is one such, dedicated to the *Dii*

Veteres, in the British Museum. It was vain for these pious pagans to dig in their heels. With gradually increasing impetus the new faith swept all before it. Where heathen divinities had been honoured of yore, saints and sages, virgins and martyrs, became the centre of pious devotion and of unreasoning hope. Of both these elements was compounded the true pilgrim mentality.

PILGRIM WITH
WALLET AND STAFF
From a manuscript

The pilgrims who in the Middle Ages thronged the high-roads of England were drawn from all classes of the community, and their motives, manners, and morals were as varied as their garments. Chaucer has painted twenty-nine strongly contrasted types in the immortal Prologue to *The Canterbury Tales*, where he tells us how they set out from the Tabard in Southwark:

> That hooly blisful martir for to seke
> That hem hath holpen whan that they were seeke.

The "hooly blisful martir" was, of course, Thomas Becket, St Thomas of Canterbury. Very soon after his canonization he acquired a reputation for helpfulness and good nature. It is recorded that there was a gentlewoman once who held him in such esteem that she even taught her pet bird to cry aloud, "Oh, St Thomas, have pity on us!" Now, one day a fierce hawk swooped upon this bird, and bore it high into the air. Immediately the frightened creature uttered its favourite call; the astonished hawk relaxed its hold, and, by the grace of St Thomas, its might-have-been victim fluttered unhurt to the ground.

Many pilgrims sought healing either of bodily or spiritual ills; many went to return thanks for graces received, or in fulfilment of a sick-bed vow; many went to acquire credit, and some went in the hope of picking up a little profit on the way; others, again, were prompted simply by a love of adventure and travel,

222

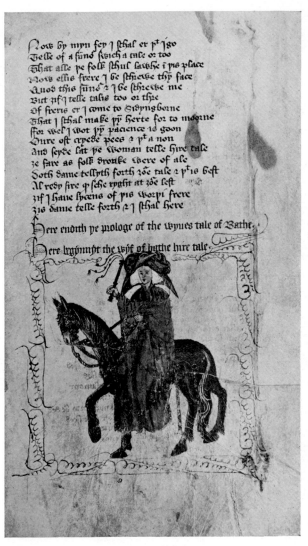

THE WYF OF BATHE

From a manuscript of *The Canterbury Tales* in the University Library,
Cambridge

a restless desire to see strange places and mix with strange people. Chaucer shows us all these types except the first. And this is a little curious, for one imagines that they must have formed the most numerous class. The Knight has obviously made a vow to wend to Canterbury if he should return safely from his "viage"; perhaps the Squiér intended to ask St Thomas's aid to win the hand of his lady-love; the Merchant, the Shipman, the Man of Lawe, and the Frankéleyn may have been either acknowledging benefits or seeking them; the Doctour of Phisik may have had gain as well as piety before his eyes. Certainly the Somonour and the Pardoner were on business bent. Piety, pure and undefiled, inspired the Poure Persoun and his

CHRISTCHURCH GATE, CANTERBURY, THROUGH WHICH THE PILGRIMS FROM LONDON ENTERED THE CATHEDRAL

brother; the Wyf of Bathe was simply in quest of variety, amusement—and possibly a sixth husband. Of none of the pilgrims are we told that he was seeking to be cured of any bodily ill, though it may be that when the Cook reached Canterbury he asked St Thomas to remove the "mormal," or sore, which Chaucer tells us he had "on his shyne."

The cathedral of Canterbury, one of the most beautiful in the world, was planned and built so as to form a vast shrine for the murdered archbishop. His actual sarcophagus was approached

223

by two flights of stone steps, ascended by many pilgrims on their knees, and had stone niches below, like those in the surviving shrine of St Edward the Confessor, into which diseased and crippled suppliants might crawl. When the cover of the shrine itself was raised by a pulley, and the great gold-cased coffin was revealed, the eyes of the kneeling multitude were dazzled by the splendour they beheld. Among the rich offerings hung there upon a network of golden wire was the glorious diamond, the "Regale of France," given by King Louis VII, and afterward so far degraded and profaned as to adorn the fat thumb of Henry VIII. Erasmus, who visited the cathedral shortly before it was looted by Henry's myrmidons, remarks of the high altar that "you would say Midas and Crœsus were beggars if you saw that vast assemblage of gold and silver." Fortunately none of the simple folk who frequented the shrine had any prophetic knowledge of its fate. Nothing could have seemed more certain to them than that the saint would sleep tranquilly there, under an ever-growing mountain of rich gifts, until doomsday.

When I think of Domèsday, full sore I am a-dread!

exclaimed an Early English poet—so early that it is quite necessary to alter his spelling a little. Such thoughts must have troubled many pilgrims. But a pilgrimage was an excellent way of easing the pangs of remorse, and priests often prescribed one to a worried penitent as a sort of spiritual 'cure.' Whether such a journey were a distressful or an agreeable adventure depended chiefly on the worldly wealth and rank of the pilgrim. When, for example, Richard Beauchamp, Earl of Warwick, betook himself to the Holy Land things were made as comfortable for him as the rigours of the time allowed. He proceeded to Joppa in a fair and goodly ship, and his land-travelling was done either in a silk-curtained litter or upon an easy-pacing steed. He would hardly have cared to change places with Sir Ingoldsby Bray, who, it was decreed, should never

> wash himself, comb or shave, . . .
> Nor indulge in a pipe, but dine upon tripe,
> And blackberries gathered before they were ripe.

For those who could hope to reach them Jerusalem, Rome, and Compostella remained the favourite destinations, but there

PILGRIMS PAYING TOLL ON LANDING AT JOPPA
From a manuscript of the fifteenth century

were many famous shrines which English folk might visit without crossing the sea. There were Our Lady of Walsingham in Norfolk, with its wonder-working image of the Blessed Virgin, St Edmund at St Edmundsbury, St Cuthbert at Durham, St Hugh at Lincoln, St Etheldreda at Ely, St Frideswide at Oxford, to name only a few. Every pilgrim took care to provide himself or herself with a token, to be sewn on the hood or cape, showing to what shrine a journey had been made. From the Holy Land branches of palm were brought—hence the name 'palmer'; a vernicle, a representation in lead or pewter of St

P

Veronica's handkerchief, indicated that the wearer had been to Rome ; a cockle-shell that he had reached Compostella. Devotees of St Thomas flaunted leaden or pewter models of that *ampulla*, or flask, in which the monks were wont to circulate small quantities of water sanctified by the immersion in it of a fragment of fabric stained with the martyr's blood; another

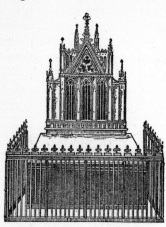

recognized Canterbury sign was a rough representation of Becket's mitred head, or of the whole of him, mounted on a queer, angular little steed. But profane people whispered that *some* 'pilgrims' whose hoods bristled with tokens, and whose talk was remarkable for its variety and vividness, had never gone farther afield than Canterbury—if so far !

Londoners had two saints in their midst, and one at Westminster, round the bend of the

THE SHRINE OF ST ERKENWALD

river. These two were St Mellitus and St Erkenwald, an Italian and an Anglo-Saxon. Erkenwald was the greater favourite of the pair, and his shrine was one of remarkable grace, wrought of delicately pinnacled and traceried goldsmiths' work, and dangling with goodly gifts. Thomas Samkyn gave his own silver girdle to St Erkenwald, and Richard de Preston, grocer and citizen of London, gave his finest sapphire, a very kindly gift, as this jewel was believed to possess the power to cure diseases of the eye.

It sometimes happened that popular sympathy and enthusiasm invested certain tombs with marvellous powers against the teaching and against the will of Holy Church. The very unsaintly Simon de Montfort was invoked after his death as *Protector gentis Angliæ*, and though Edward II was never within a mile of being canonized, the offerings at his grave were so abundant that they enabled the monks of Gloucester to rebuild their choir. Human nature being what it is, a mass of contradictions and imperfections, it follows that most human inventions, however good in themselves, however pure in their beginnings, change and deteriorate with the passing of time. So it was with pilgrimages. Yet even when their first seriousness and ardour had spent themselves these pilgrimages probably did more good than harm. They saved people from becoming mere clods, without imagination and without enterprise. They touched with colour lives that might otherwise have been dull and dim. And, indirectly, they encouraged certain civic and communal virtues upon which depended the security of the nation itself.

The anniversary of the dedication of a church was often the occasion for much merrymaking, and for such plentiful quaffing of ale, that the festivities came to be known as 'church ales.' The fairs associated with the festal-days of certain saints, such as Bartholomew Fair in London, and St Etheldreda's (St Audrey's) at Ely, were also centres of more-or-less harmless junketing. It is rather interesting that our word 'tawdry' comes from St Audrey, and no doubt the wares which the pedlars sold at her annual fair were well described by that adjective. We have seen how Grosseteste, Bishop of Lincoln, forbade the village-folk to dance in the churchyard—that is, upon consecrated ground; but most of their mumming and jigging must have been performed within sight of the church, for the natural scene of such performances was the village green.

On the first day of May the ancient Romans had been wont to hold festivals called *Floralia* in honour of Flora, the goddess of flowers. These were probably the source of the medieval May Day ceremonies, when the maypole was set up and decked with hawthorns, and maids went a-maying while the dew was still on the grass, and the windows of houses were decked with fresh boughs, green and white and rose-hued. There was probably a trace of primitive tree-worship in the maypole dance. The Puritans frowned upon it as pagan and popish both, and remorselessly hacked into faggots the great, mast-like poles that had once been the centre of so much joyous prancing and twirling. The church of St Andrew Undershaft, in the City of London, takes its name from the fact that the 'shaft' was set up hard by each May Day, and kept on hooks in a neighbouring alley (still called Shaft Alley) from one year to another. As the pole was taller than the church-steeple, the church itself came to be dubbed '*Under*shaft.' There was also a maypole in the Strand, a fine one, no less than a hundred feet high, which raised its garlanded head where the church of St Mary-le-Strand stands now, while at Kennington Green, despite the Puritans, another maypole remained erect till 1795.

May Day was the special festival of the morris-dancers, who, with ribbons and bells on their knees, danced the lively measures said to have been introduced by John of Gaunt from Moorish Spain, and replayed the old pageant of Robin Hood and Maid Marian, where the hobby-horse curvetted so proudly on its two human legs, and Maid Marian tried to trip as gracefully as if 'she' wore long petticoats, instead of doublet and hose, on all the other days of the year. So strong a hold had Robin Hood upon the affections of his countrymen that it needed all the bitter zeal of the Puritans to stamp out his yearly festivals. These continued right up to the Civil War. Their exceeding popularity in early Tudor times is amusingly illustrated by a sermon of Bishop Latymer, who, preaching before the pale, sandy-haired, prim little Edward VI, complained that when he came to a certain town on May Day, expecting to preach to a large congregation, he found the church door locked, and the parishioners nowhere to be seen. When he had tarried there for half an hour "one of the parish" came to him and said, "Syr, this is a busy day with us; we

228

cannot hear you; it is Robin Hoode's day." There was no more to be said. The bishop's rochet,[1] as he himself ruefully remarked, "was faine to give place to Robin Hoode's men."

[1] A linen vestment, resembling a surplice, worn by bishops. (German, *Rock*, a coat.)

THE CANTERBURY AMPULLA

CHAPTER XIII

THE POETS: I. THE TELLERS OF TALES

WHEN, in medieval Scotland, a poet was called a 'makar' there occurred a very interesting contact between the thoughts of two nations far apart in time and place. For the Scots, consciously or unconsciously, were borrowing from the ancient Greeks, in whose language the parent-verb *poiein* means to make, fashion, or create. Rome had taken the noun *poeta* long before, and had passed it on to the Italians, the Spaniards, the Britons, and the Gauls, who use it to this day. In the England of the Plantagenets and the Tudors a poet *might* be called a 'maker,' as Chaucer and Philip Sidney bear witness; but it was in the Scotland of the Stuart kings that the crude and homely Anglo-Saxon rendering of the Greek idea passed into common currency and familiar speech. And a 'maker' is just what a poet is: a maker not only of verses, but of the raw material whereof his verses themselves are made. A poet must plant a whole grove of trees and build and launch a whole fleet of ships fashioned from their timber, before he can begin to sing of Robin Hood and Sherwood, or Richard Grenville and the *Revenge*.

At the first glance one might have expected another verb to lie at the root of the word 'poet'—the verb to sing. Men sang poems long before they wrote them, and listened to them long before there were any to read. But it must be remembered that the epic, the long-drawn-out narrative that 'tells a story,' came earlier into existence than the lyric, the brief song sung of old time to the music of the seven-stringed lyre. The wandering bards, by whom these epics were kept alive and handed on from generation to generation, had to 'make' the familiar characters and incidents anew, not only in their own minds, but in the

230

minds of their hearers, every time they plied their craft. The Anglo-Saxons, the Normans, the Scandinavians, were all lovers of epic poetry, and all three peoples left the imprint of that love upon the poetry of England. When the bardic age had passed away, and men began to write verses instead of merely improvising or reciting them, the epic poet had a far better chance of being honoured in life and remembered after death than had the singer of little songs. The names that stand out, like lofty peaks above the valley mists—Layamon, Chaucer, Langland, Gower—are all names of men who produced long narrative poems.

At the period when these giants lived and wrought there lived also many singers of little songs to whom our debt is only one degree less great, and whose names no man knows. They sang, as the birds sing, spontaneously, instinctively, from the heart. Sometimes, as with the birds, it was the return of the green spring to the grey earth that set them singing. Sometimes—indeed, very often—they were inspired either by happy or by hopeless love. Piety moved others to compose carols and hymns. Preserved by pure chance, in faded and half-illegible manuscripts, there remains a vast mass of such songs. Some are in the British Museum, some in the library of Lambeth Palace, others in the Bodleian at Oxford and the Fitzwilliam at Cambridge. Many of them are enchanting things, quaint in form, pure in colour, sweet in sound; for in the thirteenth and fourteenth centuries England, France, and Germany were like three forests full of fluting and piping birds.

By the fifteenth century, however, English poetry had begun to lose the freshness and fragrance of that songful dawn. Two events, one national and one international, were looming ahead, both destined to have for a time a blighting influence upon the art of the 'maker.' These were the Wars of the Roses and the Reformation. Political and partisan feelings now found an outlet in vigorous but rough-hewn verse, and perturbed thinkers upon whom the cold wind of Lollardy had blown gave vent to their doubts and fears in dreary doggerel. People were gloomily conscious of each other's sins—and of their own. This was, however, the century of the great English ballads, when the Robin Hood cycle assumed its existing form, and when the ale-house fiddler first sang of Chevy Chase.

Let us look up for a moment at the great peaks before we explore the mists of the valley. The first peak is the least lofty, but not the least interesting.

When the thirteenth century, the flowering-season of Gothic architecture, the century of the great cathedrals, was yet young there lived upon the bank of the river Severn a priest whose mind was haunted by tales of olden chivalry. His name was Layamon, and he was parish priest of Arley Regis, in Worcestershire, a beautiful corner of England—"it seemed to him good to be there," as he himself says. You may still see fragments of the walls of the "noble church" where he ministered, embedded in masonry of a later date, and in one very ancient little window-opening there is a stained-glass portrait of Layamon himself. It is, of course, a purely imaginary portrait, for we have no way of knowing what was the personal appearance of this poetical priest. About his mind and character we know a great deal. He was first and foremost an Englishman, passionate and unafraid. Two centuries had now elapsed since the Norman Conquest, and during the earlier of those two centuries the conquered people had felt small inclination to burst into song. Almost all the literature of that time—and there was much—had been written in Latin or in Norman-French. Such English verse and prose as was written between the reigns of William the Conqueror and Henry of Winchester was rude and uncouth, and tinged with the double gloom of Saxon melancholy and Anglo-Saxon defeat. And then arose Layamon, parish priest of Arley Regis by the Severn.

Layamon's lot had fallen unto him in a fair ground, near the Welsh Marches, near the legendary scenes of the exploits of Arthur and his knights. Geoffrey of Monmouth had retold the

232

Arthurian stories in Latin, and in 1155 Wace, a Norman clerk, had translated them into the Norman-French of the Court, adding touches of fresh colour in the process. The air was full of the legends of these shadowy and yet imposing Celtic heroes. In Wales itself popular enthusiasm for music and poetry would have kept their memory alive, even without the assistance of monkish scribes or courtly 'editors.' To Layamon, who loved all these romances and regarded them as sober and solid history, it seemed strange and sad that the noble deeds of British knights and princes should be sung in alien speech. The story of Britain was ancient, illustrious, honourable, reaching back to the Flood, and richly adorned with noble figures and epic scenes; and he, Layamon, would retell it.

As his source, foundation, and authority Layamon states with candour that he has taken the Venerable Bede and a "Frenchis clerk" named Wace, "who could well write." It was a pretty gesture to introduce Bede, but it was nothing more, for Layamon neither borrows nor adapts anything from the *Historia Ecclesiastica Gentis Anglorum*. With Wace the case is different, for the Anglo-Saxon priest follows the main lines of the Norman's narrative, and even deigns occasionally to translate and appropriate whole passages. None the less, Layamon adds much new material, incident, and dialogue. He takes a most un-Christian delight in battle, murder, and sudden death. His heroes exult in the most unsportsmanlike manner over their prostrate foes. Arthur, "that noble king," laughs when he sees his enemy, Colgrim, at his feet, and says "playfully" (!):

> Lien nu there, Colgrim,
> Thu were iclumben haghe;
>
> . . .
>
> Thu clumbe a thissen hulle
> wunder ane hæghe,
> Swulc thu wuldest to heaven—
> Nu thou shalt to hell.[1]

---

[1] " Lie now there, Colgrim, thou wert climbed high; thou climbedst on this hill wondrous high, as though thou wouldest to heaven—now thou shalt to hell."

Layamon borrowed from Wace even the title of his great epic, *Brut*. According to the legend, which they both firmly believed, the first King of the Britons was a prince of Trojan blood, Brut by name, a great-great-grandson of that Anchises whom his son Æneas bore upon his back from the flaming ruins of Troy. Belief in the Brut legend had not died out when Spenser wrote his *Faerie Queene*, and recorded how

> noble Britons sprong from Trojans bold
> And Troy Novant was built of old Troye's ashes cold.

In Roman times the territory north-east of the Thames estuary was occupied by a tribe called the Trinovantes or Trinobantes, and their chief stronghold came to be known as the Civitas Trinobantum. The word managed somehow to survive, but its real origin and meaning were lost, and another and a far more picturesque pedigree was devised for it. Brut, as we have seen, was a prince of Trojan race who founded the kingdom of Britain. What could be more natural than that he should call his new capital after the ancient home of his family, Troy Novant, Troie la Nouvelle, New Troy? Just after that fashion did the early settlers in the United States call their places of exile New Hampshire and New Orleans. (New York is not a parallel, since it was called after a *person*—James, Duke of York.) Matthew Paris, the thirteenth-century chronicler-monk, drew the quaint little sketch of London reproduced here, and above his drawing retold the legend of its foundation in his queer, cramped French. Old St Paul's holds the centre, with the "tour" on the left, Lambeth, Westminster Abbey, and St Margaret's on the right, and the old city wall in the foreground. In 1236, when Matthew wrote and drew, nobody doubted the solid historical reality of

> Brut that baron bold of hond,
> The first conqueroure of Englond.

Baron Brut shared the favour of gentle and simple folk, together with Alexander the Great, Judas Maccabæus, Julius

234

Cæsar, Roland, Charlemagne, and Arthur. All these heroes wear the garments and wield the weapons, think the thoughts and speak the speech, of medieval England.

When Layamon undertook the great task of retelling the story of his country from the days of Noah he wrote in a language that was still Anglo-Saxon in fabric, in cadence, and in colour. Sixteen thousand lines of his contain only fifty words of Latin origin. His heart is loyal to the alliterative (or 'Peter Piper') system of verse-construction, which is essentially un-Latin and un-French, and faded out of English poetry in the century of Chaucer. Yet he is conscious of new influences, and cannot wholly exclude them from his work. Rhyme, the rival and supplanter of alliteration, creeps

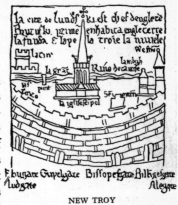

NEW TROY
From a sketch by Matthew Paris

in, as does also the French method of measuring the line. And, closely though he follows Wace, Layamon does deserve the noble name of 'maker.' It is in his pages, too, that Cymbeline, Cloten, and Arviragus, Locrine and Lear, make their first English *début*. Four of these names were destined to reappear in Shakespeare, and the fifth, that of Locrine, did not soon die out of English poetry. An Elizabethan tragedy woven round his semi-mythical career was long attributed to Shakespeare, and the nymph of the Severn, "Sabrina fair," who intervenes so happily in Milton's *Comus* is there apostrophized as

> Virgin daughter of Locrine,
> Sprung of old Anchises line!

In order to reach the next peak upon the horizon we must take an enormous stride—from the year 1205 to the nineties of the

235

fourteenth century. This enormous stride will bring us to John Gower, who would have ranked as the first English poet of any importance if Geoffrey Chaucer had never been born. In Southwark Cathedral, on the Surrey shore of the Thames, hard by the site of the Elizabethan theatres and bull-rings, may be

RICHARD II

seen the monument of good Master Gower. There he appears as a bearded gentleman of severe aspect, crowned with large and clumsy roses, his head rather uncomfortably supported by three massy books. He himself was the author of all three, of the *Speculum Meditantis* ("The Mirror of the Meditative Man"), written in French; the *Vox Clamantis* ("The Crying or Clamouring Voice"), in Latin; and the *Confessio Amantis*, in English. With the first two, one concerning "vices and virtues . . . and the various conditions of men in the world" and the other describing "the evils which befell England in the time of King Richard II," we need not tarry; it is the *Confessio Amantis* ("The Confession of Love") upon which Gower's claim to rank as an English poet and a teller of tales in the tongue of England is based.

John Gower was neither a poor clerk, like Langland, nor a hanger-on of the Court, like Chaucer. He was an esquire of Kent, "a man of propertee," a Tory before either Whigs or Tories were, tenacious of the rights of his class, and greatly perturbed by the spread of Lollardy and what would now be called 'Socialism.' He was conservative and conventional to the very bones, a stalwart stickler for the 'correct thing,' no dreamer of dreams, no seer of visions, but, measured by the standards of his time, a cultured and high-minded gentleman. (Low it be spoken, he had also in his composition a slight touch of the prig!)

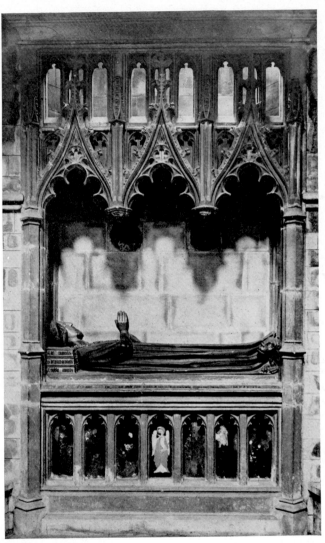

TOMB OF JOHN GOWER IN SOUTHWARK CATHEDRAL

Frith photo

236

Rather pleasingly Gower tells us how the *Confessio Amantis* came to be written. One fine day, when the poet was disporting himself in a small boat on the silver Thames, the royal barge, with King Richard on board, hove in sight. The young King was, as Froissart bears witness, a lover of poetry—and of love. Whenever he recognized Master Gower he called him into the silk-curtained barge, and bade him write "some new thing" concerning the oldest of all things, which is love. And so it befell that toward the year 1393 John Gower wrote

> A boke for King Richardè's sake.

It was a hefty "boke," this *Confessio Amantis*. In it we are told how a certain lover betook himself to a priest of Venus, Genius by name, and sought counsel of him. This Genius was quite ready to impart, in large quantities and at interminable length. For the edification of his disciple he retells one hundred and twelve love-stories. He borrows his plots with a free hand from the pagan Ovid and the Christian Augustine, the Jew Josephus, and the Florentine Boccaccio, as well as from the *Historia Troiana* of Guido delle Colonne and that great compilation of legends called the *Gesta Romanorum*. The works of Ovid and Boccaccio, together with these quaint medieval versions of the deeds of the Romans and the tale of Troy, were indeed the quarry from which most of the fourteenth-century epic poets obtained their building materials.

Gower lards his tales with many improving and some rather unexpected maxims and reflections. No wonder that his friend and fellow-poet, Chaucer, apostrophized him as the "moral Gower"! There is a constant desire upon Gower's part to 'improve the occasion,' to warn his royal hearer and his humbler audience against homicide and perjury, forgetfulness and sloth, to mention only a few of the sins, great and small, whereunto he finds that monarchs and men are prone. When Richard was yet young, the fair-faced and high-hearted youth who had defied Wat Tyler and had promised reforms to the followers of the "traitor," Gower hoped much from him, and half believed that his reign would usher in another Age of Gold. But disillusionment followed. Richard's follies and failures lost him the allegiance of men like Gower. The name of the gorgeous, foolish King has vanished from the later version of the *Confessio Amantis*, replaced by that of his supplanter on the throne, Henry of Bolingbroke.

There are few threads of pure gold in the vast woof of Gower's work, but there *are* moments when he ceases to be a mere mechanical weaver of rhymes. Such a moment comes when he is relating, through the mouth of Genius, the story of the sorceress Medea, and here, as Professor Saintsbury says, "the glamour of the legend itself has acted as a spell on Gower, and has warmed him up." Medea, deceived and deserted by Jason, comes forth when there is "noght but sterrèliht," and invokes the magic aid of Hecaté. In the description which follows Gower rises to heights of imaginative energy seldom attained by his somewhat heavy feet.

> With open hed and fot al bare
> Hir her tosprad,[1] sche 'gan to fare;
> Upon hir clothès girt sche was,
> Al spechèles, and on the gras
> Sche glod[2] forth as an addre doth,
> Non otherwisè sche ne goth,
> Til sche cam to the freisshè flod,
> And ther a whilè sche withstod.[3]
> Thriès sche torned hir aboute,
> And thriès eke sche gan doun lout;[4]
> And in the flod sche wette hir her,
> And thriès on the water ther
> Sche gaspeth with a drecching onde,[5]
> And tho sche tok hir speche in hond,
> Ferst sche began to clepe[6] and calle
> Upward unto the sterrès all,
> To wynd, to air, to see, to lond,
> Sche preide, and ek hield up hir hond

---

[1] her hair spread out.   [2] glided.   [3] paused.
[4] bend.   [5] a dreary or distressful breath.   [6] cry.

To Echates,[1] and gon to cry
Which is goddésse of sorcerie ;
Sche seidè, "Helpeth at this nede,
And as ye maden me to spede
Whan Jason cam the Flees to seche,
So helpe me now, I you beseche."

These last four lines show the struggle then proceeding in the minds of educated Englishmen between the French and the Anglo-Saxon forms of speech. Gower uses the Anglo-Saxon imperative in 'helpeth,' the Anglo-Saxon imperfect in 'maden': then he adopts the more modern and more 'Frenchified' imperative 'helpe,' and closes with a 'French rhyme,' a rhyme formed by *repetition* of an identical syllable—'seche,' 'beseche' —instead of by a *resemblance* in sound.

In the year 1378 a friend of John Gower's was sent by King Richard II on a diplomatic mission to Italy, and during his absence the Kentish poet-squire acted as his legal representative. The name of that friend was Geoffrey Chaucer. The worldly position and estate of the younger and greater poet did not resemble those of Gower. He was described as an 'esquièr' only by courtesy, and his father was no knight, no gentleman with "lands and beeves," but a worthy wine-merchant of the City of London. John Chaucer enjoyed the honour of supplying wine [2] to the royal table, and it was probably owing to this connexion with the Court that he was able to place his son as page in the household of Elizabeth de Burgh, wife of Edward III's son, Lionel, Duke of Clarence. Entries in the household accounts of that princess for the year 1357 show that an entire suit of clothes, consisting of a short cloak, red-and-black breeches, and a pair of shoes, was provided for "Galfridus Chaucer" at a cost of seven shillings—about five guineas in modern currency. Geoffrey served his royal patrons in many ways, and though his absent-minded tricks must sometimes have led him into odd predicaments it seems that in the main he served them well. Two years after he received his red-and-black breeches from

[1] Hecaté.   [2] For an account of medieval wines see Chapter VIII.

the Duchess of Clarence he followed her redoubtable father-in-law on an inglorious military expedition to France. Chaucer was not the stuff of which warriors are made. It is impossible to believe that it was owing to excessive valour and recklessness on his part that he was taken prisoner by the French. On the other hand, he cannot have acquitted himself very badly, for the King contributed £16 (about £240 in modern currency) toward his ransom, and shortly after granted him a pension, or annual salary, of twenty marks (£13 6s. 8d.) for life. He became 'valet of the chamber' to Edward, and enjoyed the privilege of making the royal bed, holding torches, and running errands. It was certainly not as a fighting-man, or by reason of his bodily prowess, that Chaucer made himself serviceable to his royal master. The *valettus* was a man of gentle speech and manners, a good linguist, familiar with the poetry of France and Italy, discreet, adroit, a born diplomatist. And Edward, a shrewd judge of men, was not slow to discern these useful qualities, and to exploit them. Many and long were the journeys which Chaucer made, and fair were the far-off lands which he beheld. At Genoa he haggled with the Doge over a commercial treaty; in Lombardy he had dealings with one of the most romantic figures of the Middle Ages, the English soldier of fortune, John Hawkwood; at Padua he met Petrarch, prince of sonnet-spinners, and heard from him the story of Patient Griselda. When, in 1374, he settled in London, in a house built over the gate known as Aldgate, he was appointed comptroller of the customs and subsidy of wools, skins, and tanned hides, an arduous and most unpoetical job, as he had to spend many hours at the docks, superintending the weighing and taxing of bales of wool and leather. The poor poet must have been devoutly glad when, from time to time, he was called away and set jogging upon the highroads of France, Flanders, and "Ytaile." Later he sat in Parliament, and later still he acted as Clerk of the King's Works at the Tower of London and at St George's Chapel, Windsor. Yet, despite royal favour, Chaucer seems frequently to have been hard up, anticipating his pension, or borrowing money on the strength of it. His plight might have become even worse had it not been that, as Justice Shallow said of old Double, "John o' Gaunt loved him well." It was to commemorate John of Gaunt's love and sorrow for his first wife, "Blaunche the Duchesse," that Chaucer wrote one of the most delightful of his longer non-narrative poems.

Chaucer's mind is the mirror in which we see the England of the Plantagenets reflected with all its gay colours, its sunny lights, and its grim shadows. There is more light than shadow in the reflection, however. Birds sing, daisies unfold, men laugh and play pranks, tell tales and make love. The Black Death, the French wars, the Peasants' Revolt, the fall of Richard II, scarcely leave even a passing blur upon that bright mirror. There is just as much shadow as the solidity of his figures makes necessary.

Chaucer was a singer of songs as well as a teller (and a re-teller) of tales, but his songs are not the best of his time, and his tales *are*. Apart from his *Troilus and Criseyde* and his delectable pilgrims and their narratives, he wrote divers long poems that one can rank neither as songs nor as stories. Most of these begin, in the orthodox, correct medieval manner, with a dream. Some poets, such as Langland, chose wild hills and woods to slumber and see visions among. Not so Chaucer. He goes cosily to bed. Before he can write of Duchess Blaunche, or the House of Fame, or the Parliament of Fowls, that is the necessary proceeding. Certainly, he often gets up again, now roused by the "smalé fowlés" and the "noyse and swetnesse" of their song, now anxious to see his beloved daisies greeting the sun; but in the background there is always the image of Geoffrey in his four-poster.

In order to realize the freshness and originality of Chaucer's genius, and the greatness of our debt to him, one must understand the rather complicated technique of English prosody. He delivered us from the clumsy, creaking measures of Gower

Q

and Gower's more obscure forerunners and contemporaries, and from the sonorous but inflexible and overwhelming alliterative system of the Anglo-Saxons. He taught the hitherto rather awkward-hoofed English Pegasus not only to amble pleasantly, but also to break sometimes into a gallop, and even to rise into the air. In the eyes of a modern reader the quaintness of his speech, the gay colours and fantastic perspectives of his style, may handicap Chaucer a little, though not for long. The difficulties seem much more formidable than they really are, and many of them disappear if the knotty passages be read aloud. And even were they twenty times greater they would be well worth tackling, and the reward of the persevering reader would be a goodly one.

Chaucer's pilgrims have appeared and reappeared in almost every chapter of the present book, never, I think, without demonstrating yet again how matchless a painter he was of men's souls and bodies both. It is elsewhere than in *The Canterbury Tales*, however, that we must seek for the welling up of the deep inner springs of true poetry. Such a welling up occurs at the end of *Troilus and Criseyde*, when the heartbroken Troilus laments over the faithlessness of his beloved. He gazes upon her abandoned house, with its barred doors and blank windows, and exclaims:

O paleis desolat,
O hous, of houses whilom best y-hight,
O paleis empty and disconsolat,
O thou lantérne of which queynt [1] is the light,
O paleis, whilom day that now art night,
Wel oughtestow to falle and I to dye,
Sin she is went that wont was us to gye ! [2]

O paleis, whilom crowne of houses alle,
Enluminèd with sonne of allè blisse,
O ring fro which the ruby is outfalle,
O cause of wo, that cause hast been of lisse !
Yit, sin I may no bet, fayn wolde I kisse
Thy coldè dorès, dorste I for this route : [3]
And far-wel, shrine, of which the seynt is oute !

---

[1] quenched. [2] to guide or rule. [3] dared I for this crowd.

Chaucer's contemporaries and successors were swift and ardent in their appreciation of his genius. His name, garlanded with words of praise, crops up again and again in English poetry, and poets, good, bad, and indifferent, have paid him homage now for six hundred years. To Dunbar, the Scottish 'makar' of the fifteenth century, he was "the noble Chaucer, of makaris flour"; to Spenser he was the "sweet well of English undefiled." He was admired, imitated, remembered, all through the Plantagenet period and, though a little less fervently, until the Tudor dynasty died in the fierce and gorgeous person of Queen Elizabeth. While he yet lived he had pious disciples, to the piety of one of whom we owe the best existing portrait of the dapper "Galfridus." This portrait was made at the behest of Thomas Hoccleve or Occleve, one of the clerks in the Privy Seal office, a plodding fellow who *would* write verse, though Apollo had touched neither his ears nor his fingers. Poor Hoccleve found his official work exceedingly monotonous; he envied the labourers who could chat and sing as they toiled.

CHAUCER
Drawn from a contemporary manuscript

> This artificers se[e] I day be day
> In the hottéste of al her bysynesse
> Talken and synge, and maké game and play,
> And forth his labour passeth with gladnésse;
> But we labóure in traveillous stilnesse,
> We stowp and stare upon the shepé's skin
> And keepé must our song and wordés in.

Poor dears!

To refresh himself after this silent drudgery Hoccleve pursued various paths, not all of them particularly creditable. Sometimes he haunted taverns, and disported himself in very doubtful company. At other times he visited the little house under the shadow of Westminster Abbey where Chaucer spent the closing months of his life. Hoccleve laments that this "universal fadir in sciénce" could not bequeath his genius to any living man. Chaucer was forbearing with the would-be poetical clerk; he would "fayn" have taught him the craft of the poet, "But," Hoccleve confesses, with an almost audible groan, "But I was dul, and lernèd lite or naght." [1] It is undeniable that the poor fellow was "dul": his verses creak and thump with most intolerable monotony. Only one sentiment could thrill him into something like grace and energy of style; and that was not love, or avarice, or discontent, but enthusiasm for Chaucer. Fervently he apostrophizes his "master," declaring that Death

> myghte han taryed her vengéance a while
> Til that some man had egal [2] to the[e] be;
> Nay, lat be that! Sche knew wel that this yle
> May never man forth bryngè lyk to the[e]!

It was God's will that Death should do her fatal office; therefore it must have been best. As a Christian and as a philosopher Hoccleve is forced to believe that it was so. But he ends with a touchingly spontaneous cry of farewell:

> O, maister, maister, God thi soulè reste!

Between Gower and Chaucer, and then between Chaucer and most of the English poets of his and the succeeding generation, there were definite and demonstrable points of contact. The other great poet of medieval England stands apart from him and from them, a lonely, sombre figure. William Langland, tonsured clerk, son of the people, dreamer of dreams, had nothing in common with Chaucer, though their lives ran almost side by side, and the same gay, grim, many-coloured England gave each his cradle and his grave. Langland was, perhaps, the greater poet of the two, with an intense and narrow greatness less easy to understand. The sin and sorrow of the world roused in him a passion of pity and revolt. The symbolic figure of Piers the

---

[1] little or nothing. [2] equal.

Ploughman which he created, and which, with slightly changing aspects and meanings, pervades all his visions, took a strong grasp upon the imagination of the English people. He loves allegory, and uses it, as fervently and as well as Bunyan did three centuries later. He rails against "Lady Meed," by whom he means self-interest or worldly gain, and of whom he makes a living woman, beautiful, alluring, perilous. Reason appears, and has much to say, all to the point; but Reason is a rather tiresome fellow—he would be! Langland does not jog merrily along the highroad as Chaucer does; he goes into smoky taverns, where beggars and tinkers gather; into wattled huts, where children weep for hunger; to the King's Court at Westminster, where "Lady Meed" is all too much in favour. There are no sharp outlines and few bright colours in Langland; but there are a grim intensity of life and action and a terrible throb and pang of human suffering and perplexity made audible and articulate.

Langland disdains such 'Frenchified' innovations as rhyme and stanzaic structure. He cleaves to the Anglo-Saxon alliterative system, with its long, rolling rhythm, and its perpetual pulse of recurring consonants. But he does not disdain the convention of sleep and dream as a basis for a long poem. Instead of tucking himself into bed or lying down on a fenced-in grass plat, like Chaucer, he climbs up on to the Malvern Hills, those beautiful, craggy, bosky hills whence he could see the rich and wide plains on one side, and on the other the distant silver gleam of the Wye and the faint blue profile of the mountains of Wales. And so begins his great Vision; as he tells us himself:

> I was weori of wandringe and wente me to reste
> Undur a brod banke bi a Bourne [1] syde,
> And as I lay and leonede [2] and lokede on the waters
> I slumberde in a slepyng hit sownede so murie.[3]

---

[1] brook (*cf.* Scots 'burn').   [2] leaned.   [3] merry.

CHAPTER XIV

THE POETS: II. THE SINGERS OF SONGS

THE medieval writer who took himself, or who hoped to be taken, very seriously was almost compelled to write tales in verse. These tales might be allegories, they might be fables, romances, farces, histories, but they must have bulk and substance, and they must satisfy the almost universal cravings of a practically bookless world. As John Barbour, the Scottish prelate-poet, the biographer of Bruce, saith:

> Stories to read are delectable,
> Supposen they be nought but fable:
> Then should stories that soothfast were,
> If told on a good mannér,
> Have double pleasure in telling.

The desire of the average reader, or listener, was usually for some story "told on a good mannér"; but there were poets whose own desires sought a less ambitious outlet, and who felt an irresistible impulse to sing—not to sing the deeds of heroes, but to sing of their own emotions. One might, indeed, say that epic poetry is objective and lyric poetry subjective. In so far as *any* poet can project his imagination *outside himself*, the epic poet does—or tries to do—it. The lyric poet works wholly *from within*; his songs are shaped and coloured by the 'me' in him.

The emotions which the medieval poet most often panted to express in song were love, piety, and political prejudice. To these were sometimes added conviviality and good-fellowship. The first two gave birth to the most beautiful lyrics, the third to the most vigorous. The earliest existing English song

246

La on qui premiere la passa
Quant ses naunes compassa
pour la toyson dealer querre
Bien cuida estre bien y querre

JASON IN QUEST OF THE GOLDEN FLEECE
From a fifteenth-century manuscript in the British Museum   246

wedded to contemporary music, *Sumer is i-cumen in*, gives utterance to an emotion often poetically associated with that of romantic love, but even more ancient—if that be possible. This is the emotion felt by man when the green spring returns to the earth. It wells up again and again in the poetry of the world; and maybe primitive man sang uncouth, grunting lays in honour of the budding trees before he began to sing them in praise of some shaggy and low-browed primitive lady.

The names of the medieval singers of little songs have perished utterly. Concerning them we know only what the songs themselves will tell us.

Since reading and writing were rare and marvellous accomplishments, the singer was probably a clerk. He may have been a full-blown priest as well, or only in minor orders, like Langland, or a scribe and a layman both, like Hoccleve. If he was, or had been, a student at one of the two great English universities, he had had some contact, though slight enough, with the wisdom and poetry of the antique world. Until the Renaissance unsealed the hidden springs of Greek literature not even the wisest of men had—or could have—any just sense of literary values. Aristotle was known chiefly as the raw material for the philosophic system of Thomas Aquinas; Virgil was honoured as a magician rather than as a poet. The *Odyssey* and the *Æneid*, and the stories of Jason and Hercules, had been transmuted by slow and curious processes into chivalric romances, whose heroes wore knightly battle-harness, swore by Christian saints, and were even familiar with the doctrines of the Fathers of the Church. These pleasant absurdities are far more insistent in the epic than in the lyric poems of the Middle Ages. The brevity, the spontaneity, and the simplicity of the lyric saved it from such clogging and complicating influences. Take, for example, one of the earliest and loveliest, the famous *Alisoun*. The exact date is uncertain, but it probably belongs to the opening years of the fourteenth century. When it was first written Edward Longshanks was struggling to suppress Scottish

247

independence, the nave of Westminster Abbey was not built
and the choir and chancel were still gleaming in their primal
white and gold, French was spoken in the Law Courts and at
the king's Court, and there were men still living who could
remember the stir caused in Christendom by the death of the
crusader-king, St Louis of France, at Tunis in 1270. The
language of the poet is strongly tinctured with Anglo-Saxon, but
his mood and manner are brightened and lightened by Norman
and French influence. His pronouns are still hazy; he writes
'he' for 'she,' and 'hire' for 'her,' and cannot decide between
the rival claims of 'Ich' and 'I'; he clings to the awkward
Saxon infinitive terminating in 'en'; but he sings like the most
sweet-voiced of all birds, none the less.

> Bytuene Mershe ant Averil
>   When spray biginneth to spring,
> The lutel foul hath hire wyl
>   On hyre lud [1] to synge;
> Ich libbe [2] in love-longinge
> For semlokest [3] of alle thynge,
> [S]he may me blisse bringe,
>   Icham in hire bandoun. [4]
> An hendy hap ichabbe y-hent, [5]
> Ichot [6] from hevene it is me sent,
> From alle wymmén my love is lent [7]
>   Ant lyht [8] on Alisoun.
>
> On heu [9] hire her is fayre ynoh,
>   Hire browe bronne, hir eye blake;
> With lossum [10] chere [s]he on me loh, [11]
>   With middel smal ant wel y-make;
> Bote [12] [s]he me wolle to hir take
> For to buen hire owen make, [13]
> Long to lyven ichulle forsake,
>   Ant feye [14] fallen adoun.
> An hendy hap, *etc.*

---

[1] In her language.	[2] live.	[3] seemliest.
[4] servitude, vassalage.	[5] A gracious chance I have grasped.	
[6] I wot. [7] given.	[8] alighted.	[9] colour.
[10] lovesome. [11] laughed.	[12] unless.	[13] mate.
[14] As if about to die.		

Nihtes when I wende [1] and wake,
    For-thi [2] myn wonges [3] waxeth won;
Levedi, [4] al for thine sake
    Longinge is i-lent me on.
In world is non so wyter mon [5]
That al hire bountè tellè con;
Hire suyre [6] is whittore than the swon,
    Ant feyrest may [7] in toune.
An hendy hap, *etc.*

Icham for wowyng al for-wake, [8]
    Wery so water in wore; [9]
Lest eny reve me my make
    Ichabbe y-yerned yore. [10]
Betere is tholien [11] whyle sore
Then mournen evermore.
    Geynest under gore, [12]
    Herkne to my roun [13]—
An hendy hap, *etc.*

In *Alisoun* there is a background of budding branches, but what one may call the spring-*motif* is not insistent. In another song of the same period, *Lenten is come with Love to Toune*, we catch the very breath and colour of the spring, and the love-*motif* makes itself only faintly heard. Men make merry with maidens, lovers whisper together, saith the poet, and "wym-men wax wonder proude"; but for the greater part of his three long stanzas he is shouting with joy at the myriad signs of spring.

Dayès-eyes in these dales,
Notes swete of nyhtegales
Each foul song singeth.

All the birds exult, "away is their wynter wo"; they are so many, and they sing so loud

That al the wode ryngeth.

---

[1] turn.   [2] For this cause.   [3] cheeks (*cf.* modern German *Wangen*).
[4] Lady.   [5] no man so wise.   [6] neck.   [7] maiden.
[8] wakeful, by dint of wooing.   [9] weir.
[10] I have long been perturbed.
[11] to endure (*cf.* modern Scots 'thole').
[12] Fairest under woman's garments.   [13] song.

This poet cannot disregard the conventional lily and rose of poetical botany, but he is sensitive to the beauty of wildflowers as few of his successors were until Shakespeare sang of lady's smocks and cowslips. He glances aside from the rose in her crimson array and the lily lovely to behold in order to rejoice in

THE RETURN OF ODYSSEUS
Homer's hero and heroine in fifteenth-century Italian costume

the return of woodruff, fennel, and thyme. It is possible that the singer of these two songs was the same man, but the sound of a different, though not less ardent, voice is heard in a little lilt of the same period where the north wind is urgently besought to send the poet his "swetyng." Five stanzas tell of the beauty of the "swetyng," her long hair, her brow "blysfol under hode," her fingers "feyre for to folde," and of the despair of her adorer; and each ends with the swift, breathless, *staccato* refrain:

> Blou, northerne wynd !
> Send thou me my swetyng !
> Blou, northerne wynd ! blou, blou, blou !

Among the Harleian manuscripts in the British Museum is a curious collection of devotional Latin prose interspersed with brief fragments of English verse. Most of these fragments are devotional also, but here and there earthly love pushes its way into the heart of the scribe, as when he ejaculates ruefully:

> Love, thou art of mikel mit!
> Mi day thou tornis into nit
>   And dos me sikè sore;
> And al for one so swete a wit
> That onis [1] throw love me trouthè plit
>   To ben myn evere more.

At the first glance this language looks almost as wild and uncouth as the English of Layamon, but the first glance is deceptive. If a 'gh' be inserted before the 't' in all the words ending in 'it' the worst difficulties will vanish: 'tornis' is not much unlike 'turnest,' and the close relationship between 'onis' and 'once' will be perceived if the fifth line is read aloud. 'Sike' for 'sigh' is a little less obvious, but a recollection that the French verb *faire* means both to do and to *make* explains the third line completely.

The simple fellow who wrote these halting lines lacked the bubbling and thrilling lyrical gift possessed by many of his fourteenth-century contemporaries. Though there may be an element of justice in the charge so often levelled against the English, the charge that they are not naturally a musical people, they have certainly a sense of the music of *words*, and it is this sense which gives to English lyrical poetry its exquisite and inextinguishable charm. Added to this instinct for delicate and lightly poised rhythms there was in the heart of the English medieval poet a profound love for the open air and for the greenwood. Heaths and mountains left him uninspired; they were too grim and perilous. But he delighted in the daisied meads, the shaggy oaks and dark hollies of the woods, as much as he delighted in the fluting of the throssel and the lark. The song

[1] once.

which follows was written down as it stands, in the fifteenth century, but is probably older.   It describes a dispute between the rival merits of the holly and the ivy, those two venerable evergreens wherewith doors and windows and walls were decked toward the season of Yule.   Clearly the sympathies of the poet are all with the holly.   He begins and ends his little song with a stout rejection of ivy's claims, reiterating after every stanza:

> Nay, Ivy, nay,
>   Yt shal not be, I wys ;
> Let Holy hafe the maystry,
>   As the maner ys.

Then he proceeds to contrast the happy lot, the gay humour, the beauty, and the pleasant associations of the holly with the ivy's cold cheer, dark looks, and gloomy companions.

> Holy stond in the halle
>   Fayre to behold ;
> Ivy stond wythout the dore,
>   She ys ful sore a-cold.

> Holy and hys mery men
>   They dawnsyn and they syng,
> Ivy and hur maydenys
>   They wepyn and they wryng.

> Holy hath berys
>   As rede as any rose,
> The foster and the hunter
>   Kepe [t]hem from the does.

> Ivy hath berys
>   As blake as any slo ;
> Ther com[s] the oule
>   And ete [t]hym as she goo.

> Holy hath byrdys
>   A ful fayrè flok,
> The nyghtyngale, the poppynguy,
>   The gayntyl lavyrok.

THE SINGERS OF SONGS

Gode Ivy,
  What byrdys [h]ast thu ?
Non but the howlat
  That kreye[s] " How, how ! "
Nay, Ivy, nay,
  Yt shal not be, I wys ;
Let Holy have the maystry,
  As the maner ys.

It is a little surprising to meet the 'poppynguy,' or parrot, in the company of the nightingale and the lark, since at no time can that bright-plumed babbler have been a denizen of English woods. If he was seen in England at all it was probably upon a gilded perch in some fair lady's bower.

To the second group of nameless and delightful lyric-singers belong those who sang Christmas carols and other pious lays. The story of the Nativity appealed as strongly to them as it did to their brethren of the painters' craft. Fra Lippo Lippi in Florence and Jan van Eyck in Flanders did not love more dearly to paint the Virgin and Child than the poets of medieval England loved to sing about them. One of the loveliest of these carols, and one of the best known, is among the most simple. It has the cool colours, the quiet yet luminous tints, of that dewy morning hour wherein the mind of the poet lingers. There is a sort of hush and awe in the very rhythm.

I sing of a maiden that is makèless ;[1]
King of All Kings to her son she owes,[2]

He came all so still
Where His mother was,
As dew in Aprill
That falleth on the grass ;

He came all so still
Where His mother lay,
As dew in Aprill
That falleth on the spray ;

---

[1] mateless, without peer.   [2] as her son she owns.

He came all so still
To His mother's bower,
As dew in Aprill
That falleth on the flower.

Maiden and Mother
Was never none but she ;
Well might such a Lady
Goddis Mother be.

The painters, the sculptors, and the goldsmiths loved to show Mary as Queen of Heaven, clad in azure, surrounded by adoring seraphim and "bright-harness'd angels," or with dusky-visaged kings kneeling to offer her frankincense and myrrh in jars of silver and gold. The poets seem to have turned rather to the vision of a young mother rocking her baby in her arms; the stiff-robed figure holding the rigid Child in an angular and per-functory embrace did not touch their hearts. They sang of Mary as if they had heard *her* sing; they wrote little lullabies for her, and invented little dialogues between her and her Son ending with the homely refrain of "By, by, lully, lulley."

Jhesu my son, I pray ye say
As thou art to me dere,
How shall I serve ye to thy pay [1]
And mak thee right good chere ?

asks Mary, and when her Son has prayed her to dance Him in her arms He adds this engaging entreaty:

And yf I wepe,
And will not slepe,
Then syng " by, by, lully, lulley."

One particularly genial carol, which offers a sturdy welcome to "Yol" (Yule) and all the holy joys of the season, has also a "Wolcum" for

Stefne and Jon

and for the

Innocentès everychon.

---

[1] pleasure, satisfaction (Anglo-Norman).

THE VIRGIN AND CHILD
Hans Memling
W. F. Mansell photo

Stephen was a great favourite, and he is the 'hero' of this delightful carol which is almost a ballad as well:

Seynt Stevene was a clerk
  In kyng Herowde's halle,
And servyd him of bred and cloth
  As ever kyng befalle.[1]

Stevyn out of kechon [2] cam,
  Wyth boris hed on honde ;
He saw a sterr was fayr and bryght
  Over Bedlem stonde.

He kyst [3] adoun the borès hed
  And went into the halle :
" I forsake thee, kyng Herowde,
  And thi werkès alle."

" Quhat eylyt [4] thee, Stevene ?
  Quhat is thee befalle ?
Lakkyt thee eyther mete or drynk
  In kyng Herowdes hallè ? "

" Lakit me neyther mete ne drynk,
  In kyng Herowdès halle ;
Ther is a chyld in Bedlem born
  Is beter than we alle."

" Quhat eylyt thee, Stevyn, art thu wod ? [5]
  Or thu gynnyst to brede ? [6]
Lakkyt thee eythar gold or fe[e]
  Or ony ryche wede ? "

" Lakyt me neyther gold ne fe[e],
  Ne non ryche wede ;
Ther is a chyld in Bedlem born
  Xal helpyn us at our nede."

" That is al so soth, Stevyn,
  Al so soth, I wys,
As this capon crowè xal
  That lyth her in myn dych."

---

[1] As it is always the way with kings.   [2] kitchen.   [3] cast.
[4] What ails ?   [5] mad.   [6] to lose one's wits (?).

That word was not so sonè sayd,
    That word in that halle,
The capon crew *Cristus natus est !* [1]
    Among the lordès alle.

" Rysyt up, myn turmentowres,[2]
    Be to and al be one,[3]
And ledyt [4] Stevyn out of this town,
    And stonyt hym wyth ston."

Tokyn [t]hem Stevene
    And stonyd hym in the way ;
And therfor is his evyn
    On Cristès owyn day.

The boar's head thus unceremoniously "kyst adoun" by
Stephen was a very favourite Christmas dish, and itself the subject of a carol, the famous half-Latin, half-English *Bore's heed
in hand bring I*, printed by Caxton's successor, Wynkyn de
Worde, and still sung every year at Queen's College, Oxford,
with the appropriate processions and ceremonies. The last
stanza, all in English, is perhaps the cheeriest of all :

Be gladde, lordès, both more and lasse,
    For this hath ordeyned our stewárde,
To chere you all this Christmasse—
    The borès heed with mustárde.

Late in the fourteenth and early in the fifteenth centuries a
new influence made itself felt in England—Lollardy. Exactly
why the followers of John Wycliffe should have been called
Lollards is not quite certain. Some people derive the name
from the Latin *lolium*, tares ; others from the medieval German
lollen, to sing softly. They were earnest and restless idealists,
dissatisfied with the state of the Church and of religion, critical
of their superiors among the clergy, and anxious to replace
what they regarded as corrupt and confused customs and ceremonies by a simpler form of worship, to be strengthened by a
purer moral code. They were, indeed, the forerunners of the

---

[1] Christ is born.   [2] torturers.   [3] By two and also by one.
[4] The Anglo-Saxon imperative—lead.

Reformers of the sixteenth and the Puritans of the seventeenth centuries. Their enemies were more powerful than numerous, for the sympathy of the great mass of the people was won by the ardour of the Lollard preachers. The fellow-pilgrims of Chaucer's Poure Persoun suspect the good man of being a "Loller," and indeed he was much unlike the typical proud and gold-loving prelate of the period. Prelates of that type bestirred themselves to stamp out Lollardy, and might have succeeded had not the struggle become a political one, and had not Parliament and certain of the great nobles backed up the Lollards against the Traditionalists. With this struggle and its causes and results we are not concerned here, except in so far as the new ideas were reflected in the poetry of the time.

Both sides employed the 'poetical' weapon freely, and poured scorn in rhyme upon each other. While the Lollard rhymester ridiculed the worse type of priest or monk, the anti-Lollard laughed at the uncouth reformers, and at the men of higher degree, who would "jangle of Job and Jeremye" instead of doing their duty and sticking to the good old way. One of these anti-Lollards exclaims:

> Hit is unkyndly [1] for a knight
> That shuld a kyngès castel kepe
> To bable the Bibel day and night.

Some of these knights, after being temporarily lured away from orthodoxy, repented of their lapse in sackcloth and ashes, and died in a mood of extreme humility and remorse.

The Lollards seem to have conceived very early the idea, later elaborated and emphasized by Calvin and Luther, that *faith alone* will save a man's soul, however ill he may behave. In 1450 we find a remorseful and rather timorous poet imploring heaven to have mercy on his "myse-dede." True, he speaks of mending his ways, and asks for an opportunity to prove his good intentions, but it is quite clear that he trusts

---

[1] This does not mean 'unkindly' in the modern sense ; it means 'not after his kind,' not right, natural, or appropriate.

R

257

more to belief than to behaviour to pull him through. It is
God's part to pardon—and his to *need* pardon.

> It is of thee for to forgyfe
> Alkyn [1] tryspas both more and mynn ; [2]
> It is of me whyles I here lyfe
> Or more or lesse eke day to synne.

The fountain of pure poetry had now sunk very low in England, where not long before it had filled the land with its silver
sound. The rhymes creak and stumble; most of the rhymesters
are dull dogs. Only here and there is there a faint echo that
reminds us of the old music. We hear such echoes in the stilted
and wordy lament for Edward IV, with its recurrent refrain:

> All men of Englond are bounde for hym to praye.

The claims made by the 'poet' on behalf of the comely but
indolent Edward are fantastic. He was the "most dred prince
that was under the Sun "; his action in consenting to be 'bought
off' by Louis XI is represented as a great victory won over the
French "without stroke."   But in two stanzas there is a note of
genuine feeling, of genuine love and sorrow, that sends a thrill
of music through the dreary plodding of the verse:

> O noble Edward, where art thowe become
> Which full worthy I have seen goyng in estate ? [3]
> Edward the iiijth I menė, with the soune, [4]
> The rose, [4] the sounė-beme which was full fortunate ;
> Noon erthly prince durst make with hym debate.
> Art thou agoo, and was here yestirday ?
> All men of Englond are bounde for thee to pray.

> The well of knyghthode, withouten eny pere,
> Of all erthely pryncces thou wert the lode-sterre !
> Be-holde and rede ; herkyn well and here !
> In Gestis, [5] in romansis, in Cronicles nygh and ferre,
> Well knowen it is, ther can no man it deserre, [6]
> Pereless he was—and was here yestirday ;
> All men of Englond are bounde for hym to pray.

---

[1] All sorts of.   [2] great and small.   [3] going forth in State.
[4] Allusions to Edward's badge, the rose and sun.
[5] *Chansons de gestes*, tales of the great *deeds* (Latin, *gesta*) of heroes.
[6] deny.

CHAPTER XV

WOMANKIND

DURING the three hundred and thirty-one years that separated the accession of Henry II from the death of Richard III the position of woman in England underwent a very slow but very momentous change. And all the time, from *her* point of view, it was a change for the better. Though in the antique world goddesses had been worshipped and queens obeyed, the great mass of women were doomed to subjection and servitude. Among the wealthier classes the subjection was softened by luxury and refinement; but among the poor the servitude was both bitter and hard. As is still the case in many Eastern countries, the heavier share of the field labour fell upon the woman, and often while the unpitying husband rode ahead on his ass the laden wife was fain to trudge behind.

That this state of affairs should have been gradually altered in the West is due almost entirely to the rise and spread of Christianity, especially in its Roman form. The cult of the Virgin Mary, the worship offered to her, the multiplication of her images and altars, could not fail to influence the thoughts and deeds of Christian men. And when once the chivalric system had taken colour from this cult, and human as well as divine love inspired romantic dreams and heroic actions, it became clear that the old order was doomed.

Under ancient Roman law no woman could give evidence as a witness in a court of law, enter into a contract, or make a will, and many queer survivals remained even after the double influence of Christianity and of chivalry had made itself widely felt. For example, under the law of Ethelbert the man who had carried off a freeman's wife must, at his own expense, *provide him with another!* In medieval England a woman might receive homage, but could not render it; she could be constable of a castle or a town, but not sheriff of a county: and in medieval Scotland a woman committing a trespass without her husband's knowledge was liable to be "chastised like a child under age," or, in the language of the vulgar, spanked.

For the greater part of this three-hundred-year period the mind and the manners of the typical woman were what the will of man made them. His prejudices, his preferences, his misgivings, ruled her way of life. Education—even as it was then understood—liberty, enlightenment, were not for her. She might use her hands, but not her brain. And her plain duty was to be first beautiful as a maiden, secondly, meek as a wife, and then to be the mother of as many infants as the saints would vouchsafe to send. Only in two ways, neither of them very dignified or worthy, might she hope to wield any power over men in general or her husband in particular—either by coaxing or by scolding. She who had neither a fair face nor a sharp and tireless tongue stood little chance of getting her own way in great things or in small. This applies, of course, to the women of the middle and upper classes. Among the tillers of the soil there was probably a sort of rough equality, and a sort of uncouth but kindly comradeship between men and women in the toils, hardships, and rewards of their laborious existence. Indeed, in *La Court de Baron*, already referred to, the villein charged with stealing a perch from his lord's pond offered as an excuse that his wife had been in bed for a month, able neither to eat nor drink, and that it was to satisfy her sick craving for a perch that he went to the pond.

One result of the narrowness of the gently born woman's

BRASS OF A LADY
Fifteenth century

activities was to reduce the great majority of them to a sort of dead level. No doubt their individual characters were as sharply differentiated as are those of their descendants to-day; but they had no scope, no means of self-expression, and a medieval woman had to be either exceptionally holy or exceptionally sinful in order to make an abiding mark upon the page of history. At this distance they of whom we read in the old chronicles seem almost as stiff and lifeless as their images on their sepulchral brasses or their carved Purbeck tombs. Look at these slim-flanked, tight-waisted, blank-visaged ladies, with their folded hands and their heraldic gowns. Did rebellious hearts beat under those rigid kirtles? Did wild

NOBLE AND LADY AT PLAY
Luttrell Psalter

dreams haunt the heads under those horned and peaked headdresses? Was the Lady Aveline in truth *exactly* like the Lady Ysabel, even to the number of kinks in her hair and the number of pearls on her coif? Were the mouth and nose, the eyes and eyebrows, of the Lady Blaunche absolutely identical with those of the Lady Elianor? And what did they think about and talk about all the long day, those medieval ladies who look incapable of thought or speech?

As to their conversation, we have the evidence of one of the most gifted of medieval women, the poetess Christine de Pisan. Ladies, says Christine, talk about "Honnour"—that is to say, about chivalry, tournaments, and wars.

261

Et de beaulx livres et de dis,
Et de balades, plus de dix,
Qui mieulx, mieulx chascun devisoit,
Ou d'amours.

(Of goodly books and stories then,
And of ballads more than ten,
Each vying with each, of these they spake,
Or else of love.)

The education of the medieval girl, especially in the twelfth and thirteenth centuries, was even more meagre than that of

JOSYAN PLAYING
From an illuminated
manuscript

the medieval boy, but there is abundant evidence in the old romances that reading, and especially *reading aloud*, was among the most coveted accomplishments. The lady must be able not only to spell out the angular black-letter script in her breviary, and the motto dight on the shield of her lord; she must be ready to take her turn in reading from the books, few and curious, but none the less delightful, whence she and her sisters drew all their ideas about far lands, and other times, and the great legends of love and war. Very often while one damsel was reading aloud from the tales of Arthur's knights or of the siege of Troy the others would sit round busily plying their needles, pausing only to smile, or sigh, or exchange quick glances of horror or amusement, as the many-coloured narrative unrolled itself. All women were skilled in needlecraft, and Langland urges his fair and nobly born contemporaries to use their "longė fingres smale" in fashioning vestments and hangings for churches. A knowledge of music was not uncommon. We read in royal household accounts of sums expended on the purchase and repair of various quaintly named instruments destined to be played by the "longė fingres smale" of queens and princesses; and Josyan, the much-suffering heroine of *Bevis*

262

of Hampton, was certainly well versed in music. The pages of illuminated manuscripts are crowded with little feminine figures performing upon rebecks, fiddles, harps, and sackbuts, and portable organs with gaily gilt pipes.

From the early thirteenth-century romance of *Sir Guy of Warwick* we gather that a lady of high degree must have at least seven accomplishments, astronomy, ars-metrick, or prosody, geometry, sophistry, rhetoric, 'clergy,' or clerkly learning, and music, and that her instructors would probably be white-haired scholars from Toulouse.

> Gentil she was, and as demuré
> As ger-fauk or falcon to luré
> That out of mewé were y-drawe,
> So fair was none in soothé sawe !
> She was thereto courteous, free and wise,
> And in the seven arts learnèd withouten miss.
> Her masters were thither come
> Out of Thoulousé, all and some,
> White and hoar all they were,
> Busy they were that maiden to lere,
> And her lered of astronomy,
> Of ars-metrick and of geometry ;
> Of sophistry she was also witty,
> Of rhetorick and of other clergy,
> Lernèd she was in musick,
> Of clergy was her none like.

In earlier times reading was regarded as a more important and useful accomplishment than writing, but by the middle of the fifteenth century the women members of the Paston family in Norfolk could write with fluency and vigour, even if their spelling left much to be desired. Most of the larger nunneries received little girls as boarders, and when Henry VIII had abolished all the convents and monasteries, great and small, one of the grievances set forth by the leaders of the Pilgrimage of Grace was the lack of any place where young girls might be virtuously taught and trained, since the nuns had been scattered and brought to naught. Embroidery, church music, and reading would be the principal studies pursued by the pupils in these convent schools. There is a pretty little story told of two small girls who were fellow-pupils at a nunnery in Friesland. Between these two there was a keen rivalry as to who should acquit herself the better at her lessons. It happened that one of them fell ill, and, in her anxiety lest her friend should outstrip her, she begged that she might have speech with the prioress. When the prioress came the child said, "Good lady! do not let my companion learn any more till I am well again, and I shall pray my mother to give me sixpence, and I shall give it to you, if you will do as I ask; for I am afraid that while I lie sick she may pass me in learning, and I would not that she did so."

The pupils at these schools did not belong to the knightly and noble class only. The daughters of prosperous merchants and worthy citizens walked there two by two with the daughters of famous Anglo-Norman families. The wife of the Miller in Chaucer's Reeve's tale had been

y-fostred in a nonnerye,

and for that reason gave herself airs, and was majestic and disdainful long after she had left the convent to be the bride of simple Symkin of Trumpington mill. In this same century it would appear that children of both sexes were sometimes taught together, for Sir John Froissart tells us that when he first went to school he found little girls there, "whose youth was as tender as his own," and strove to please them with garlands of violets, and gifts of pins, apples, pears, and rings of glass.

In the fifteenth century a very curious and instructive chain of verses was written for the benefit of those mothers who were confronted with the difficult task of bringing up girl-children. It is called *How the Good Wife taught her Daughter*, and it is crammed with excellent advice. Evidently the speaker belongs to the humbler ranks of life, for she warns her daughter that when she has been to the market to sell the 'borel,' or coarse cloth, that she has woven at home she should not afterward go and refresh herself at an alehouse, and also that she must not give way to envious feelings if she sees her neighbour's wife better clad than herself. Most interesting of all is the advice given to the damsel as to how she shall some day teach her *own* boys and girls:

> And if thi children been rebel,[1] and wolè not [t]hem bowe,[2]
> If ony of [t]hem mys-dooth, nouther banne [3] [t]hem ne blowe,[4]
> But take a smert rodde,[5] and bete [t]hem in a rowe,
> Till thei crei mercy, and be of [t]her gilt aknowe.[6]

Ladies of high degree occupied themselves almost as much with spinning as did their humbler sisters, but in their case the

LADY AT HER WHEEL
Luttrell Psalter

cloth was used to make garments for their own households, and not sold in the market. They also cultivated medicinal herbs, and with them made potions, plasters, and ointments for the benefit of the sick. A knight who returned to his castle in a sad plight, owing to a tumble at a tournament or a mishap in the chase, would be promptly 'doctored' by his lady, and dosed and anointed with strange compounds prepared by her own fair hands. It was often unnecessary to send for a professional Doctour of Phisik, and sometimes, when the ladies of the patient's family had done their worst, it must have been hopeless.

More perilous to themselves as well as to others were the

---

[1] rebellious   [2] be obedient.   [3] curse.   [4] slap.
[5] a sharp stick.   [6] and acknowledge their guilt.

activities of Plantagenet ladies who dabbled in sorcery, brewed potions and philtres, and made wax images of their enemies, hoping that as each image melted in a flame or was stabbed with sharp pins the original would "dwindle, peak and pine." Eleanor, Duchess of Gloucester, wife of Duke Humphrey, was accused and convicted in 1441 of having by magical practices endeavoured to bring about the death of the young King, Henry VI, and was forced by way of penance to walk barefoot through London with a taper in her hand. A contemporary poem represents the unfortunate Duchess as making "gret mone," and taking a pitiful farewell of her former splendour, damask, and cloth of gold, and of her minstrels too:

> Ffarewelle, my mynstrels and alle your songe,
> That ofte hath made me for to daunce.
> Ffarewelle; I wott I have done wronge,
> And I wyt my misgovernaunce.
> Now I lyste nother to pryke nor praunce; [1]
> My pryde is put to poverté.
> Thus both in Englond and in France
> All women may be ware by me.

The mysterious but innocent mixtures prepared by medieval gentlewomen were not intended only to cure divers ills and aches. The gift of beauty was prized by foolish folk above the gift of health, and every lady would have her own pet formula for face-lotions and hair-washes. The Middle Ages set up a certain rigid standard of bodily beauty to which all women were anxious to conform. Dark eyes could not be changed to the fashionable 'vair,' or grey-blue; but dark locks *could* be transformed into the desired colour—

> yellow of hue
> As any basin scourèd new

—and very frequently *were*. To be ideally beautiful the lady must possess, as well as eyes of 'vair' and locks of gold, a long, supple, and rounded body, a slim throat unmarred by knobs of bone, white, flexible hands, a graceful walk, a small red mouth,

---

[1] Now I desire neither to ride nor prance.

and a smile that was neither coquettish nor affected, and did not widen too often into a laugh. The golden hair was, perhaps, the most indispensable item in the catalogue of medieval charms. Chaucer's Emelye had her "yelow heer" braided into a plait that hung down "a yerdė long," and few heroines of ballads and romances failed to imitate her example. Despite the seclusion

of her daily life, the medie-val lady was permitted to indulge in certain more or less strenuous pastimes. At home she played ninepins, chess, draughts, and various bat-and-ball games; abroad she hunted, hawked, went rabbiting with ferrets and nets, and shot at deer both with the longbow and the crossbow. But what, be-yond all this unintellectual activity, were her real in-

DRESSING A LADY'S HAIR
Luttrell Psalter

terests, aims, and ideals? As for her destiny, it could follow only one of two well-marked paths, the first of which led to matrimony, and the second to the cloister. This last may not have been the least enviable fate. The nuns of Great St Helen's, Bishopsgate, were sternly rebuked by a fifteenth-century Bishop of London for adding golden borders to their veils, keeping numerous lap-dogs in the cloisters, and receiving visitors of both sexes after dusk. A more amusing life, truly, than that of the married gentlewoman, shut up in some gaunt and gloomy castle while her lord rode forth to hunt the wild boar, or the even wilder Saracen! Whether her fate were set in castle or in cloister, the greater part of her time and thought was devoted to piety. Her husband's chaplain or—if she were a widow—her own recited daily all the offices of the Church, at few of which she and her waiting-women failed to be present. Pious though

267

medieval ladies undoubtedly were, their ruling sin of garrulity was apt to overcome them even in holy places and at solemn moments. We read that on one such occasion St Brice was moved to mirth because he saw a devil writing down all the words whispered to each other by inattentive ladies while St Martin of Tours was celebrating Mass.

LADY WITH HORNED HEADDRESS
Fifteenth century

Almsgiving was one of the virtues most earnestly encouraged by the priest and most diligently practised by the more prosperous of his penitents. There is a charming medieval legend of a certain Countess of Mans "who nourished ever xxx fatherless children, and said that was her sport. Therefore," we are told, "she was loved of God, and had a good life and a good end. At her death there was seen a great cloud of light, full of small children, Innocents, about her." Pilgrimages, as we have seen, were among the relaxations most popular with men and women of all classes. To many a bored and peevish dame such a pious journey must have afforded a welcome and delightful way of escape from the sameness of her life at home. Sometimes it was to pray for the safety of an absent husband or to give thanks for his safe return that she went to some famous shrine. Children were a blessing besought with the greatest degree of hope at Walsingham and at Canterbury. All those kings and queens of Fairy-tale-land who had "everything in the world they wished for *except* a baby" would have done well to burn candles to St Thomas Becket. If one of his suppliants saw the saint in a dream she was assured of a happy answer to her orison. There could be no mistake as to the identity of such a vision; St Thomas made a point of appearing with a diagonal streak of blood across his nose. In his lifetime, however, the same saint did not always find that womankind were particularly obedient and submissive to his will. There exists a letter from him to Ala, Countess of Warrenne, written at the request of the monks of Lewes Priory to whom she refused to pay tithes from her dower-lands after her husband's death. The Archbishop—as he then was—tells his "beloved daughter" that an "amazing complaint" (*stupenda queremonia*) has reached his ears concerning her; he tells her that in withholding their due from the good brothers she is almost committing sacrilege: and for the weal of her soul he admonishes her forthwith to pay these tithes, which in justice she cannot refuse to do. But no deed of gift or transference of tithes from Countess Ala to Lewes Priory has ever come to light; apparently the lady turned a deaf ear to the eloquence of the Archbishop, whom she survived for four years; concerning her the monkish chronicler of the priory recorded rather grumpily in 1174: *Ubi sepulta est nescitur* ("Place of burial not known"). It is curious to realize that had the stubborn Ala lived a hundred years later she would probably have knelt in humble supplication before the shrine of the saint whom in his lifetime she flouted and defied.

Constant wars, brawls, and pestilences tended to swell the ranks of the high-born widows, and as long as they did not remarry these ladies were exceptionally powerful and fortunate. When by reason of their widowhood they became wards of the Crown the decision as to remarriage no longer rested with them, and they were at the mercy of the ruling monarch, who might at any moment impose upon them a second husband of his own choosing. But those who *did* escape this fate were, on the whole, the most enviable of their sex and time. Their piety was practical as well as profound—witness the bequests made to various religious foundations in their wills. Such bequests ranged from a copper bowl or a cow, assigned by a Somersetshire "Squiress" to her parish church, to whole estates set aside to found colleges, priories, or hospitals. It happened occasionally that their pious dispositions were made more emphatic by a bond of kinship with some prelate, priest, or nun. For example, in the fourteenth century Margaret, Countess of Devon, bequeathed to her son William, Archbishop of Canterbury, a gilt chalice and a missal, and Eleanor de Bohun, Duchess of Gloucester, left to her sixteen-year-old daughter, then a nun at the Minoresses' convent in London, a bed, a French Bible in two volumes with gold clasps enamelled with the arms of France, a psalter, and divers books of devotion. Memorable among Plantagenet women whose last thoughts were of the poor and needy was Dame Alice Wyche, widow of Sir Hugh Wyche, Alderman and Merchant of London, who, after assigning certain sums of money and personal belongings to her kinsfolk, set aside the residue of her property for the following purposes: two hundred pounds—a much larger sum then than now—to be divided among poor ploughmen in the country, "such as have wives and children"; two hundred pounds to be expended in giving to each of one hundred poor householders a milch cow and the sum of thirteen shillings and fourpence, and three ewes at eighteenpence apiece; and two hundred pounds for dowries of poor maidens of good character and the repair of roads and highways.

Christine de Pisan, whom we called as a witness with regard

to the conversation of medieval ladies, has left us a charming picture of the interior of a French convent at the dawn of the fifteenth century; but in order to understand how she came to visit this convent, and to have a small daughter among the pupils there, it is necessary to retrace our steps a little, and to follow the course of her very interesting life, which at several points touched Plantagenet England. Christine's father was a Venetian, Tommaso Pisani by name, and she herself was born in the golden city on the Adriatic. At the age of four she was brought to Paris, where Tommaso then lived, and where he performed the double functions of councillor to the Venetian Republic and astrologer to the King of France. If Messer Tommaso cast his

CHRISTINE DE PISAN

daughter's horoscope, and if the prophetic stars spake truly, he must have been decidedly perturbed at the prospect before her—at least, in the first three decades of her existence. At the age of fifteen she was married to one Étienne de Chastel, Notary Royal, and at the age of twenty-five she was left a widow with three young children, two boys and a girl, and with practically no means of supporting either herself or them. Christine then took a decision which, though nowadays it would appear simple and natural enough, required in the fourteenth century an unusual amount of courage and originality. She determined to work for her children with her pen. Valiantly she tackled her task, beginning dutifully with poems in memory of her Étienne, and going on to compose love-songs for happier people than herself. She wrote both in prose and verse, and no female moralist of the late eighteenth century, no Mrs Barbauld or Hannah More, was ever more anxious to improve the minds of her readers. In *Le Dit de la Rose* she describes an imaginary brotherhood whose members bind themselves to defend and uphold the honour of women; in her *Epître au Dieu d'Amour* she herself takes up the cudgels in their defence against the satirist Jean de Meung, whose monumental and interminable *Roman de la Rose* belies its pretty name, and is the reverse of romantic in its view of the feminine character. Christine's courage and devotion soon met with their reward. Her father's old master, Charles V of France, had died in 1380, but she found powerful friends in the new king, Charles VI, and his kinsmen, the Dukes of Berry and Burgundy. Her fame went abroad, and both Henry IV of England and Galeazzo Visconti of Milan were anxious that she should grace their Courts with her presence. She chose to remain faithful to her adopted land of France, but she did not refuse the generous offer of the Earl of Salisbury to adopt her elder son Jean, and bring him up as his own. When the Earl died, four years later, Philippe le Bon, Duke of Burgundy, succeeded him as the patron and adopted parent of young Jean. In the meantime, through the kindness of her royal friends, Christine was able to place her little daughter in the convent founded at Poissy by King Philippe le Bel, and then ruled over by a lady of the blood royal, Princess Marie de Bourbon. On a certain April morning in the year 1400 Christine and a company of knights, esquires, and ladies paid a visit to this convent, a visit which she has described in a rather long but very vivid and charming poem. For six leagues they rode through the gay greenwoods, where the birds were singing merrily. At Poissy they were graciously received by Princess Marie, and then Christine's little daughter came running out and knelt down before her. Hand in hand the two went into the convent chapel, a beautiful building with a soaring vaulted roof and stained-glass windows that shone like webs of precious jewels. They must have been glad to have that moment together there before they rejoined the rest of the party, and, as we should now say, 'went over' the convent. First of all the nuns led their visitors along the cloisters of carved and fretted stone, shaded by the enormous old pine-tree growing in the centre of the green cloister-garth; then they showed them their fair, silver-bubbling fountain, and their garden where beds of sweet lavender alternated with cherry-trees and roses. Farther on there was a pond well stocked with fish, and an enclosure where stags, goats, and rabbits gambolled on the flowery turf. After some very welcome refreshment Christine and her friends went and sat on the grass by the fountain, and talked to the little girls of the convent school, and told them tales of angels and heroes. Christine's own little girl wept so bitterly when the time came to say good-bye that the other ladies had to exert themselves to cheer Christine up when they set off on horseback for home. Their good-natured efforts were probably made easier by the contents of a basket full of cakes, apples, and pears which Princess Marie sent after them so that they might not arrive too hungry in Paris.

Among the books selected by Caxton to be "put in imprint" was a translation of a treatise written nearly a century earlier by a Frenchman, the Knight of La Tour Landry, for the edification of his three motherless daughters. The good Knight is very anxious that the three *demoiselles* should avoid the snares into which so many ladies were wont to stray, and that neither by grave misdemeanours nor by little follies and affectations should they miss the best thing that could possibly befall them—a happy and fortunate marriage. Many improving stories does the Knight relate for their benefit, to warn and illuminate them. Talkativeness was among the failings to be avoided. He relates how a certain unnamed King of England sent an ambassador to choose a queen for him from the family of the King of Denmark. Though the eldest of the King's daughters was the fairest, "she winked oft, and spake before she understood what was said to her, and ever beat her eye-lids together," and was therefore

s   273 rejected by the ambassador, as was the second sister, who had "marvellous much language"; the third sister, whose demeanour was simple, modest, and unaffected, found herself chosen, to her great joy and astonishment, and to the infinite chagrin and dismay of her winking and babbling sisters. Another tale told by the Knight of La Tour Landry marks the

folly of maidens who, for pure vanity and vainglory, insist upon wearing tight and scanty garments when the weather is cold. There was a certain lady who, when a knight came a-wooing to her father's castle, donned such a garment, an unfurred gown fitting closely to the figure, in order to charm his eyes. But her face was so blue and pinched that her beauty was for the moment gone, and the knight offered his heart instead to a younger and far less comely sister who was warmly clad and ruddy of hue!

THE MASTERFUL WIFE
From a manuscript

The position of woman in the Middle Ages was, indeed, a peculiar one. She was the butt of the most vehement and merciless satire, and at the same time the object of the most exaggerated homage and devotion. No young esquire, no bachelor knight, was thought worthy of the name who did not gasp himself green in the face for love of some fair lady; no satirical poet, monk, or layman was accounted a master of his craft unless he made of the image of womankind a sort of Aunt Sally at which to fling his wordy missiles. In Boccaccio, in Chaucer, in all the popular collections of stories in the fourteenth and fifteenth centuries, there is no more familiar or more abject figure than that of the henpecked and hoodwinked husband. Of the Wyf of Bathe's five husbands three, she says, were good, and two were bad; and she makes it clear that it was the good ones who found her most tyrannical and exacting:

They were ful glad whan I spak to [t]hem faire,
For God it wot I chidde [t]hem spitously.[1]

And a nameless versemonger of the same century exclaimed
unkindly:

There were three wily, three wily there were,
A fox and a fryer—and a womán.

If satires and humorous popular tales give us a rather unlovely
impression of married life in Plantagenet England we may
correct the focus by remembering the many women who could
—and did—inspire in the hearts of their husbands the noblest
and most enduring love. The devotion of Edward I to his
Spanish bride, Eleanor of Castile, has become proverbial;
Edward III loved Philippa of Hainault well and long, and not
until old age had clouded his mind and altered his character did
he forget his good Queen in the society of her one-time "damsel
of the chamber," Alice Perrers; no woman was ever more
passionately mourned than was Blaunche the Duchess, first
wife of John of Gaunt, she of whom Chaucer wrote

. . . she was lyk to torchè bright
That every man may take of light [2]
Ynogh, and hit hath never the lesse.

The Wars of the Roses made almost as many real widows as
the Crusades had made temporary ones. Knights and nobles
were exposed to the peril of summary decapitation as well as
of death in battle, and more than one unlucky Yorkist or
Lancastrian was fain to make his last will in haste, with the
executioner's axe poised above his neck. We have already
seen how Earl Rivers did so in the year 1483. Fourteen years
earlier William Herbert, Lord Pembroke, had performed the
same melancholy duty in the guise of a farewell letter to his
wife, Anne, daughter of Sir Walter Devereux. This lady had
apparently promised him that in the event of his predeceasing
her she would not remarry, but would retain undivided control
of her household and of their children. "And, wyfe," he

[1] bitterly, angrily.   [2] may take light from.

writes, . . . "remember your promise to me, to take ordre of wydowhood as ye may be the better mayster of your owne, to performe my wylle, and to help my children, as I love and trust you." After some instructions as to his burial and the singing of Masses for his soul "and for all there soules slayn in the felde for two yere," he ends:

> Wife, pray for me, and take the said ordre that ye promised me as ye had in lyfe my hert and love. God have mercy upon me, and save you and our children, and our Lady and all the Saints in Hevyn help me to salvation.

As no record of Lady Pembroke remarrying has come to light, we may conclude that she kept her promise.

Wars, pestilences, and the hazards of life swelled the number of orphans as well as the number of widows in Plantagenet England. An orphan child who was also heir to a great inheritance became a ward of the Crown, and kings very often recompensed their servants at small cost to themselves by handing over the wardship of some well-dowered little girl. Thus in 1443 Henry VI desired to make some return to William de la Pole, Earl (afterward Duke) of Suffolk, for his services to himself and his father, and therefore instructed his "Right trusty and Right wellbeloved tharchebisshop of Caunterbury" to issue letters patent granting to the Earl the "warde and mariage" of a very important young lady, Margaret Beaufort, only daughter of John Beaufort, Duke of Somerset, and through him great-granddaughter of John of Gaunt. Henry describes her as being "of ful tender age," and she was, in fact, only three years old. Suffolk, an ambitious man whose star was then in the ascendant, probably designed the hand of little Margaret for his eldest son, and may have dreamed of founding a new dynasty in which the blood of the Plantagenets should mingle with the blood of the Poles, one-time merchants and money-lenders. Though Margaret was the wife of another—indeed of three others—that son *did* marry a Plantagenet lady, Elizabeth, daughter of Richard,

LADY MARGARET BEAUFORT
National Portrait Gallery   276

Duke of York, but the last of *their* three sons was killed fighting for Francis I at the battle of Pavia, and with him ended the male line of old William atte Pole, who early in the fourteenth century had laid the foundations of the family fortunes in his counting-house at Hull.

Margaret Beaufort remained only seven years in the wardship of the haughty Suffolk. He fell from power in 1450, was banished, departed for France, but was intercepted by a royal ship, seized, and summarily beheaded with a rusty blade borrowed from an Irish seaman. Meanwhile his young ward was growing up, and the question of finding a suitable husband for her was an urgent one. Henry VI decided that the most suitable person was his half-brother, Edmund Tudor, Earl of Richmond, son of Henry V's widow, Katharine of France, by her second marriage with Owen Tudor. Margaret's heart may have inclined her toward this match, for she announced that a heavenly vision had pointed to the Earl of Richmond as her future lord. They were married when she was fourteen and he about twenty-five, and a year later she was a widow with an infant son, the future Henry VII.

They were perilous times for a solitary and youthful princess connected by blood and marriage with both the warring factions. Very prudently Margaret remained at Pembroke Castle, where her baby had been born, and where she was under the protection of her brother-in-law, Jasper Tudor. Her second marriage linked her again with the Lancastrians, for her husband was the son of Humphrey Stafford, Duke of Buckingham, a doughty champion of the red rose. She remained in Wales during the intermittent fighting which ended in the triumph of the Yorkists in 1461, and it must have been there that news reached her of the execution at Hereford of her father-in-law, Owen Tudor, whose last words were: "The head must now lie on the block that once lay on Queen Katharine's knee." When for a brief season the white rose was in eclipse in 1470 Margaret emerged from her retirement, but the speedy return of Edward IV sent her back to the remoteness and security of the Welsh Marches, and her son, whom the Yorkists distrusted as a possible claimant to the throne, fled to Brittany.

Again a widow, the oft-bereaved lady now contracted a Yorkist alliance and bestowed her hand upon Lord Stanley, who stood high in favour with Richard III and whose influence with his master probably saved her life when the news leaked out that she was lending herself to the scheme of Henry Stafford, Duke of Buckingham, to bring about a marriage between her absentee son and Elizabeth of York, then still in sanctuary with the Queen-Dowager at Westminster Abbey. The luckless Duke was promptly beheaded for his part in the Lancastrian plot, but the marriage which Richard so dreaded duly took place, five months after the battered body of the last of the Plantagenets had been carried from Bosworth Field to Leicester slung across the horse of the poursuivant Blanc Sanglier. Upon that field ended a long and brightly coloured chapter in the chronicles of England. Lord Stanley placed on the head of his Tudor stepson the crown which a simple man-at-arms had found hanging forlornly in a thorn-bush, and a new era began. The Lady Margaret was thenceforth the mother of the King's most excellent Majesty; yet since the greater part of her life had been spent, unquietly and hazardously enough, in the England of Plantagenets it is fitting that she should be ranged among the women of their time. Her piety, her intelligence, her fortitude and patience under affliction, her enlightened patronage of learning and of learned men, would have made hers an illustrious and engaging figure in any age and in any country; but her mind and character were largely formed and coloured by the years she spent at the Court of Henry VI and in the castle of Jasper Tudor, first on the eve of the Wars of the Roses and later while those same rather desultory and spasmodic wars were in progress. There was little in common between Margaret and her namesake, the strenuous, implacable Queen of Henry VI; still less in common between her and the alluring, ambitious

278

Elizabeth Woodville. Yet she was not untypical of the gentle-women who lived and suffered, loved and prayed, in the England over which Margaret and Elizabeth were called to preside as queens-consort.

When she once more enjoyed possession of her estates the Lady Margaret, as she was usually called, took counsel with her chaplain, Dr John Fisher, as to how best she might devote a large part of her wealth to the greater glory of God. At his suggestion she began by founding professorships of divinity at Oxford and Cambridge, Fisher himself being the first to fill the Cambridge chair. Many distinguished scholars both before and since the Reformation have been Lady Margaret Professors, Erasmus and Dr Inge, Dean of St Paul's, among them. It was no doubt because Fisher was a Cambridge man that he used his influence over his patroness so earnestly in the interests of Cambridge, where she enlarged, endowed, and refounded (though she did not actually found) Christ's College and St John's. Happily she could not foresee that her graceless grand-son, Henry VIII, would appropriate to himself the lion's share of these endowments, or that he would imprison and behead the saintly John Fisher [1] whom her son had made Bishop of Rochester and whom she had chosen as her confessor, her chaplain, and her friend.

[1] He was beatified by Pope Leo XIII in 1886.

INDEX

ACCOLADE, the, 13–14

Agriculture, medieval, 76–77, 80–82, 89–90

Ala, Countess of Warrenne, 269

Alabaster, English sculpture in, 104–105

Alisoun, 247, 248–249

Anglo-Saxon language, 239, 248

Anglo-Saxons, 74, 111, 113

Animals, draught, 84–85

Anne of Bohemia, 50, 100, 138, 139

Aquamaniles, 94–95

Architecture, church, 163–167; Early English, 163, 164, 165; Norman, 163, 164, 165; Decorated, 164, 165; Perpendicular, 164, 165–166

Argyropoulos, John, 68

Arms and armour, 33–48, 95, 110; Anglo-Saxon, 33, 34; Norman, 34, 35, 36

Arthur, King, 14, 53, 54–61, 64, 232, 233

Arthurian romances, 24–25, 54–61

Astrology, 152

Augustinian Order, the, 194

BACON, ROGER, 179, 195

Barbour, John, 246

Battleaxes, 43, 44

Beauchamp, Richard, Earl of Warwick, 44, 147, 224

Beaufort, Lady Margaret, 276, 277–279

Becket, St Thomas, 178, 222, 223, 269

Beds and bed-hangings, 156–158

Bell-founders, 98–99

Benedictine Order, the, 186–188, 193

Bernard of Gordon, 153

Billingsgate, 121

Black Canon, Chaucer's, 203

Black Death, the, 74, 86, 88, 182, 241

Blacksmiths, 95, 96

" Blaunche the Duchesse," 241, 275

Boke of Nurture, Russell's, 148, 149

Book of the Order of Chivalry, 64–65

Bore's heed in hand bring I, carol, 256

Bosworth Field, 12, 278

Bristol, 121

Brome Manuscript, the, 214–216

Bruges, William, First Garter King-at-Arms, 28

Brut, Layamon's, 58, 233, 234–235

Brut, Wace's, 57–58, 233, 234

Buckingham, Dukes of—*see under* Stafford

Building materials, 101–102

Burgundy, the Bastard of (Antony, Comte de la Roche), 66, 67

CABOT, JOHN, 121

Cabot, Sebastian, 121

Canterbury Cathedral, 168, 170, 187, 223–224

Canterbury Pilgrims, the, 199–204

Canterbury Tales, The, 61–62, 63, 85, 222, 242

Carmelite Order, the, 195–196

Carols, 253–256

Carpenters, 102–103

Carthusian Order, the, 193–194

Carver, the Lord Mayor's, 141

281

Caxton, William, 54, 60, 61, 64–65, 68, 69, 142, 273
Chapter-houses, monastic, 198–199
Charlemagne, 14, 53, 55, 112
Charles VI of France, 272
Chaucer, Geoffrey, 19, 61–63, 78, 84, 107, 110, 120, 143, 145, 147, 151, 158, 175, 199, 201, 202, 208, 222, 223, 231, 236, 237, 239–244, 245, 274, 275
Chivalry, rise of, 13–16 ; idea of, 53–72
Christine de Pisan, 261–262, 270–273
Chronicon, Geoffrey of Monmouth's, 56–57
Church, the medieval, 162–175
Cinque Ports, the, 121
Cistercian Order, the, 193
Clare, Bogo de, 199
Cobham, Eleanor, Duchess of Gloucester, 266
Cobham, Joan, Lady, 84
Coinage, 111, 125
Colloquies, Ælfric's, 113
Combats, judicial, 31–32
Companies, City, of London, 131–132, 133 ; Barber-surgeons, 135 ; Coachmakers, 135 ; Fanmakers, 135 ; Spectacle-makers, 135 ; Merchant Taylors, 137, 140 ; Girdlers, 138 ; Goldsmiths, 138 ; Grocers, 138 ; Leather-sellers, 138 ; Salters, 140 ; Skinners, 140 ; Brewers, 140–141
Compostella, 221, 225
Confessio Amantis, Gower's, 236, 237, 238–239
Cooks and cooking, 145–147
Corpus Christi, festival of, 217
Costume, 48–52, 82–84
Crafts—*see* Mysteries
Crosby, Sir John, 116–118

De Amicitia, Cicero's, 69
Declaration of Nobleness, Buonaccorsi's, 69
Dictes and Sayings of the Philosophers, The, 65
Dit de la Rose, Le, 272
Doctors, medieval, 149–155, 265
Doctour of Phisik, Chaucer's, 151, 152–153, 155, 158, 223
Domesday Book, 113
Dominican Order, the, 194
Don Quixote, 70
Drama, Greek, 205 ; medieval, 207–219
Dunbar, William, 243
Dyeing, processes of, 107

EDWARD THE CONFESSOR, 131
Edward I, 26, 119, 121, 247, 275
Edward II, 11, 49–50, 100, 154, 226–227
Edward III, 28, 50, 89, 106, 120, 134, 240, 275
Edward IV, 65, 66, 67, 69, 117, 258, 277
Edward VI, 228
Effigies, monumental, 98, 99–100
Eleanor de Bohun, 270
Eleanor of Aquitaine, 49
Eleanor of Castile, 95, 99, 275
Eleanor of Provence, 49, 180
Elizabeth, Queen, 135
Elizabeth of Hainault, 203
Elizabeth of York, 276, 278
Epître au Dieu d'Amour, 272
Erasmus, 224
Esquire, or squire, the, 18–19
Eyre, Sir Simon, 116

Faerie Queene, The, 69–70
Fairs, 118–119, 227
Faringdon, William, 98
Fauconberg, the Bastard of (Thomas Neville), 67, 117

INDEX

Festivals, 227–229
Feudal system, the, 17, 74–75
Fisher, Blessed John, Bishop of Rochester, 279
FitzAlwyn, Henry, 125
Fitz-Otho, family of, 98
Forme of Cury, The, 145, 146
Franciscan Order, the, 195
Frankeleyn, Chaucer's, 106
Friar, Chaucer's, 201–202
Friars, 184, 194–196
Froissart, Sir John, 264
Fulling, 107–108

GADDESDEN, JOHN OF, 151, 153–155
Galen (Claudius Galenus), 150
Geoffrey of Monmouth, 56–57, 232
Ghent, guilds of, 132
Glass, stained, 167, 169
Gloucester Cathedral, 100, 166, 168, 171, 188, 227
Goldsmiths, 98, 135
Gower, John, 231, 236–239, 241
Great St Helen's, Bishopsgate, nunnery of, 267
Grosseteste, Robert, Bishop of Lincoln, 178–181, 195, 227
Guilds, 131–144. *See also* Companies, City

HANSEATIC LEAGUE, the, 115–116, 125
Hawkwood, John, 240
Helmets, 36–37, 41–42, 45–46, 48
Henry I, 133
Henry II, 11, 106
Henry III, 106, 109, 180
Henry IV, 126, 238, 272
Henry V, 28, 29, 100, 122, 126, 127
Henry VI, 29, 52, 276, 277, 278
Henry VII, 277, 278, 279
Henry VIII, 135, 194, 224, 263, 279
Heraldry, 22–24, 27–29, 34–35

Herbs, 154–155, 265
Hippocras, recipe for, 148–149
Hippocrates, 148, 150
Hoccleve, Thomas, 243–244, 247
How the Good Wife taught her Daughter, 264–265
Hugh, Bishop of Lincoln, 100, 101
'Humours,' theory of, 150–151
Humphrey, Duke of Gloucester, 149

Idylls of the King, 59
Iron-workers, 96–98, 135
Isabella of France, 50
Islip, John, Abbot of Westminster, 23
Ivanhoe, 26–27, 29, 31, 70, 200

JERUSALEM, 221, 225
Jews, 116
Joan, Princess of Wales, 158
John, King, 11, 36, 49
John of Gaunt, 157–158, 177, 228, 241
Joiners, 103
Josyan, 262
Jousts, 24–30

KATHERINE OF FRANCE, 277
Knight, the ideal, 19, 61
Knight-errant, the, 16, 20–32
Knighthood, 13–32 ; orders of, 14–15
Knights Hospitallers, 220
Knights Templars, 37, 220

LA TOUR LANDRY, THE KNIGHT OF, 273–274
Lances, 38–39
Land-tenure, 74–75
Langland, William, 78, 79, 176, 231, 236, 241, 244–245, 247, 262
Latymer, Bishop, 228–229
Law and lawyers, 155, 158–161

Law of Apprentices, the, 90
Layamon, 58, 231, 232–235, 251
Leadenhall Market, 116
Leather-workers, 109
Lenten is come with Love to Toune, 249
Lewes Priory, 269
Lincoln Cathedral, 100
Livery Companies—*see* Companies, City
Lollards and Lollardy, 231, 236, 256–257
London, medieval, 125–126, 127–130, 131–132
London Bridge, 119
London Lickpenny, 160–161
Luttrell Psalter, the, 81–83, 84, 90, 91
Lydgate, John, 130, 160–161

MACES, 43–44
Magna Carta, 106–107
Manorial system, the, 16–18, 75–76, 86–87
Mans, Countess of, 268
Margaret, Countess of Devon, 270
Margaret of Anjou, 29, 278, 279
Marie de Bourbon, 272
Marie de France, 59, 78
Mary of Burgundy, 132
Masons and masonry, 100–102
Maypoles, 227, 228
Medicine, the medieval science of, 149–151
Merchant, Chaucer's, 125
Merchant Venturers, 120
Merchants and merchandise, 111–130
Millers, 90
Miracle play cycles, Coventry, 208, 209, 210, 211, 212, 213, 214, 218–219; Chester, 210; London, 210; Norwich, 210, 212; York, 210,

216; Wakefield (Towneley), 210, 217
Miracle plays, 205–219
Mirfield, John, 153
Monk, Chaucer's, 147, 200–201
Monks and monasteries, 184–194, 198–199
Montagu, John, Earl of Salisbury, 272
Montfort, Simon de, 180, 226
Morris-dancers, 228
Morte d'Arthur, Malory's, 54, 55, 61, 64, 65
Mortimer, Edmund, Third Earl of March, 158
Mysteries, 133–137, 141–144
Mystery plays—*see* Miracle plays

NEEDLES and needle-makers, 96
Nevill, Richard, Archbishop of York, 147
Normans, the, 114
Nun's Priest, Chaucer's, 78–79
Nuns and nunneries, 196–198, 263–264, 267

ORIENTAL ideas in Europe, 123–125
Ottoboni, Cardinal, 144

PAINTER-STAINERS, 103–104
Paris, Matthew, 234
Peasants' Revolt, the, 88, 241
Pembroke, Anne, Lady, 275, 276
Pembroke, William Herbert, Lord, 275–276
Perrers, Alice, 275
Petrarch, 240
Philippa of Hainault, 50, 106, 120, 174, 275
Philippe le Bon, Duke of Burgundy, 132, 272
Piers Plowman, 80, 245
Pilgrimage of Grace, the, 263

INDEX

Pilgrims and pilgrimages, 220–227, 268–269
Pins and pin-makers, 96
Pius II, Pope, 69
Poetry, narrative, 230–245 ; lyrical, 246–258
Poissy, royal convent at, 272–273
Pole, John de la, Earl of Suffolk, 276
Pole, William de la, Earl of Suffolk, 84, 276, 277
Potters and pottery, 92–95
Poure Persoun, Chaucer's, 175–176, 223, 257
Prelates, 176–183
Priests, 155, 175–176
Printing, introduction of, 64
Prioress, Chaucer's, 202–203, 204
Purbeck marble, 100–101

RICHARD I, 61
Richard II, 11, 100, 104, 139, 237, 238, 239, 241
Richard III, 12, 28, 67–68, 147, 278
Richard, Abbot of Peterborough, 88
Richmond, Earl of—see Tudor, Edmund
Rivers, Antony Woodville, Earl, 65–68
Robin Hood, 228, 229, 232
Roland, 53–54
Roman de la Rose, Le, 272
Romans, the, 227
Rome, 185, 221, 225
Round Table, the, 58, 61
Russell, John, 149

ST BENEDICT, 185–187
St Brice, 268
St Bridget, Order of, 173, 197–198
St Clare, Order of, 197
St Crispin, 135
St Dunstan, 135
St Eligius, 135

St Erkenwald, 226
St George, 71–72
St Leonard's Convent, Bromley-by-Bow, 203
St Louis, 248
St Martin of Tours, 268
St Michael, 70, 71
St Stephen, carol of, 255–256
Salerno, University of, 150
Salisbury, Earl of—see Montagu, John
Salisbury Cathedral, 164
Science, medieval, 149–151
Sculptors, 104–105
Serfs—see Villeins
Service, commutation of, 76
Shakespeare, William, 208, 235, 250
Shearmen, 108
Shepherds, 90–91, 218–219
Shoemakers, 109
Shoemakers' Holiday, The, 116
Shrines, 170, 221, 223–224, 225, 226
Sidney, Sir Philip, 69
Sigismund, Emperor, 28
Sir Guy of Warwick, 263
Smiths, 95–100
Speculum Meditantis, Gower's, 236
Spenser, Edmund, 69–70, 234, 243
Spinning, 105, 265
Spurriers, 110
Spurs, 40, 43
Squiér, Chaucer's, 19, 62, 124, 223
Stafford, Henry, 277
Stafford, Henry, Duke of Buckingham, 278
Stafford, Hugh, Earl of Stafford, 84
Stafford, Humphrey, Duke of Buckingham, 277
Stanley, Thomas, Lord, 278
Staple, Merchants of the, 119, 120 ; the Ordinance of the, 120
Statute of Labourers, the, 88
Stephen, King, 11

285

Sumer is i-cumen in, 247
Sussex, ironworks in, 95
Swords, 33–34, 38
Syon Convent, Isleworth, 173, 197
Syon cope, the, 173–174

TALLIES, 123
Tanners and tanning, 109
Tenter-grounds, 108
Tewkesbury, battle of, 117
Tiptoft, John, Earl of Worcester, 68–69, 147
Tokens, pilgrims', 225–226
Tonsure, the, 191–192
Torel, William, 99
Tournaments, 24–32
Troilus and Criseyde, 62, 242
Tudor, Edmond, Earl of Richmond, 277
Tudor, Jasper, 277, 278
Tudor, Owen, 277
Tunnoc window, York Minster, 99, 168
Twelfth Night, 209
Tyler, Wat, 88, 238

VESSELS, church, 170–171
Vestments, church, 171–174
Villeins, 16–17, 75–90
Villon, François, 162
Visconti, Galeazzo, 272

Vox Clamantis, Gower's, 236

WACE, ROBERT, 57–58, 233, 235
Wars of the Roses, the, 231, 275, 278
Warwick, Earl of—*see* Beauchamp, Richard
Weavers and weaving, 105–109
Westminster Abbey, 99, 104, 169, 180, 187, 198, 248
Westminster Hall, 140
Whittington, Richard, 18, 125, 126–127, 141
Widows, medieval, 270
William the Conqueror, 14, 74, 113, 131
William of Wykeham, 181–183
Wills, medieval, 155–156
Winchester Cathedral, 164, 181, 187
Wines, medieval, 147–149
Woad, 107
Wolsey, Cardinal, 178
Women, medieval, position of, 259–279
Woodcarvers, 103
Woodville, Elizabeth, 65, 66, 279
Wyche, Dame Alice, 270
Wycliffe, John, 256
Wyf of Bathe, Chaucer's, 110, 120, 223, 274–275

YORK MINSTER, 167, 168, 198